Failed and Failing States

Failed and Failing States: The Challenges to African Reconstruction

Edited by

Muna Ndulo and Margaret Grieco

Cambridge Scholars Publishing

Failed and Failing States: The Challenges to African Reconstruction,
Edited by Muna Ndulo and Margaret Grieco

This book first published 2010 by

Cambridge Scholars Publishing

12 Back Chapman Street, Newcastle upon Tyne, NE6 2XX, UK

British Library Cataloguing in Publication Data
A catalogue record for this book is available from the British Library

ISBN (10): 1-4438-1866-6, ISBN (13): 978-1-4438-1866-7

Contents

List of Figures and Tables

Figures

Tables

Preface

Failed and Failing States: The Challenges to African Reconstruction

A collapsed state, according to William Zartman, is a 'situation where the structure, authority (legitimate power), law and political order have fallen apart and must be reconstituted in some form, old or new'. The former Secretary-General of the United Nations, Boutros Boutros Ghali, described the situation prevailing in a failed state as 'a feature of such conflicts is the collapse of state institutions, especially the police and judiciary, with resulting paralysis of governance, a breakdown of law and order, and general banditry and chaos. Not only are the functions of government suspended, but its assets are destroyed or looted'. In a collapsed state the regime finally wears out its ability to satisfy the demands of the various groups in society, fails to govern and to keep the state together. The collapse is marked by the loss of control over political and economic space. A collapsed state can no longer perform its basic security and development functions and has no effective control over its territory and borders.

State collapse is one of the major threats to peace, stability, and economic development in Sub-Saharan Africa today. As Christopher Clapham observes, while we must not over-generalize, in Sub-Sahara Africa there are a '… distressingly large number of states in which acceptable political formulae have not been developed, and that remain vulnerable to collapse, or have actually collapsed'. The states are not only unable to develop a stable political system but lack administrative capacity to govern effectively and to ignite sustainable economic development. The weakness of the African state was most obvious in the periphery of state systems. Thus, while the core of the state, typically centred on the capital, weakens through mismanagement and political failure, pressure from the periphery forces on the centre causes state collapse. The consequences of failed states include conflicts, war, and refugees. The effects, as is the case with Darfur, often spill over into neighboring states.

Since 1956 Sudan has experienced civil wars with only brief intervals of relative peace. More than two and a half million people have been killed and many more displaced in the continuous war between successive governments of the north and peoples of the south. Darfurians took up arms against the

Sudanese government in 2003 accusing it of decades of discrimination and neglect. The Sudanese government is accused of retaliating by unleashing a militia group, the janjaweed, against the people of Darfur. The United Nations has labeled the situation as the greatest humanitarian crisis of the modern era.

Major challenges confront efforts to avoid collapsed states drawing other countries into a wider conflict and to create structures and favorable conditions to lead to national reconciliation and the reconstruction of a state that has collapsed.

The Cornell Institute for African Development called a symposium entitled 'Failed and Failing States in Africa: Lessons from Darfur and Beyond' to address these critical issues at the Institute for African Development, Cornell University, 18–19 April 2008. Key contributions at the symposium are brought together in this volume. Taken together these essays represent a significant discussion on the challenges presented by the presence of failing states within Africa.

Muna Ndulo and Margaret Grieco
Institute for African Development, Cornell University

CHAPTER ONE

WHAT REALLY WORKS IN PREVENTING AND REBUILDING FAILED STATES: NATION BUILDING, CONFLICT AND CIVIL SOCIETY

Sarah Cohen Wood

Introduction

Investment in the relationship between local government structures and the role of civil society organizations should not be overlooked or minimized in assessing the path to nation building, reconstruction after civil war, or stabilization after regional and systemic conflict. In order to assist the development of state-society relationships, it is important for international agencies and interventions to anticipate and adapt to environments in which both national and local needs are contributing to sustained hostilities. It is imperative to integrate interventions that focus on service delivery at the local level and those that contribute to strengthening governance functions at the national level in order to create stabilization and assist in reconstruction of conflict affected countries. The absence of state-led basic service delivery is not overcome by creating parallel structures through civil society. While service delivery through local non-governmental organizations (NGOs) and civil society organizations is often prioritized for international actors, it is important to note the existing traumatized nature of the environments and the 'fend-for-yourself' mentality that can lead to further competition and violence between social groups. International aid, distributed through various mechanisms, can serve to worsen these pre-existing divisions within the society or create new cleavages. Additionally, regional, ethnic and religious disparities can become politically sensitive, creating greater risks that services are delivered along party or ethnic lines. Similarly, when support for national-level governments is diverted, due to the belief that it takes too long to implement aid through state mechanisms, repressive actions are often taken by the state towards civil society, as evidenced in Nepal, Sudan, Ethiopia, Angola, Burma, the Democratic Republic of Congo (DRC) and Burundi.

A New Nation-building Paradigm

Currently we are using such terms as stabilization, reconstruction and conflict to further describe the conditions and symptom of fragile states. Current efforts to address the diverse range of nation-building needs and priorities in fragile or failed states contexts have in the past and the present been frustrated by a lack of coordination, tensions between short- and long-term priorities and funding mechanisms that place significant restrictions on budget allocation, distribution and reporting mechanisms for development funds. However, the manner in which development agencies implement these projects in these contexts is undergoing a sea change, both within the United States government (USG) and abroad with our partners. A new paradigm that can be termed 'diplomatic development' is emerging. Defined as a broader nation-building strategy, this new paradigm aims to link the various sectors and actors involved in foreign assistance, specifically in fragile and failed state contexts, to more effectively stabilize or contribute to the reconstruction of conflict affected states.

There is also something that is relevant to this discussion which is that the most recent National Security Strategy emphasizes the 3Ds, or the interdependent relationship between *defence*, *development* and *diplomacy*. In the last several years there has been an approach to build the coordination capacity between the State Department, Department of Defence, USAID and other USG partners to build better implementation systems that allow planning to be shared and a common approach to the problem to be developed even across mixed methods. But coordination without implementation is not helpful for nations emerging from decades of protracted conflict or for countries on the brink of war. In Africa a considerable amount of the continent may be considered fragile based on regional needs, nascent peace agreements and warring economies built upon access to key resources.

Conflict prevention is not altruistic, and state conflicts bleed into regional wars and effectively destabilize vast areas of the continent through proxy wars between nations. These proxy wars breed instability on many levels and it is the citizenship of these countries that feed militia groups, rebel movements as well as African Union Peacekeeping forces and UN peacekeepers. These same populations are also the citizens reintegrated back into communities after years of war into ministries, local governments or back into civil society groups. Currently the vision to align development, defence and diplomacy needs capacity building for increased coordination and a shared sense that this approach will lead to less state failure. The National Security Strategy promotes the closer alignment of defence, development and diplomacy and these efforts can be seen in Iraq and Afghanistan where all three Agencies are promoting approaches that are not purely kinetic, but instead seek to find ways to engage civil society in securing stability.

But it is in the implementation of this partnership where coordination and planning fall short. In some settings this shortfall may lead not only to a failure to understand the complexities of fragility, but may even fuel greater regional conflict or more entrenched proxy wars between governments vying for international recognition. One can say that in Africa this combination of the 3Ds has existed for decades and based on funding, capacity and political will one may or may not trump the other. Consider this for a moment:

- In Darfur, South Sudan, northern Uganda, Eastern Chad there is conflict over resources as well as a perception of economic and political neglect for the needs for essential services. Many factional groups or 'rebel groups' often see their conflict with the government as just based on their need. Yet the governments in some of these countries label these groups 'terrorist organizations' or define their actions as terrorism to increase the support for military solutions.
- In these same areas, governments may use militia groups to suppress cross border conflicts as a proxy security force. These same forces prey on citizens when salaries are not paid and these 'security forces' become a further reason for these populations to mistrust their governments. Some of these settings become by virtue of conflict protracted humanitarian environments (Darfur, northern Uganda, eastern Chad, and eastern DRC etc.).
- These humanitarian segments of the country become elements of instability that further disconnect citizens from the perception that their government can provide for them. This disconnect leads to often more extreme isolation between warring factions and the governments that are themselves a part of the same nation.

Civil Society, Fragile States and Fragility: Defining Intervention

A failed or fragile state is a country where citizens have lost faith in their government and the government is *unwilling or unable* to provide for their needs. In these situations civil society is as much at the centre as the government. Many international engagements be them diplomatic or development focus on governance without emphasizing the importance of civil society. The definitions and classification of a state as fragile provides some understanding of the complexities of these settings, but not enough about the character and history of the collapse of this relationship. Ultimately these distinctions and definitions concerning fragility do little to help us identify the appropriate interventions, partnerships and engagements with these nations and countries. They are often just artificial distinctions that mean little in reality on the ground. In some cases this distinction has been detrimental to the US engagement abroad and has only alienated us from the citizens and systems that support nation building and strong and responsive governments. There are some examples of this in the current development of counter-insurgency and counter terrorism strategies that target segments of the population as spoilers, but do not have a strategy for strengthening civil society or building the capacity of the state. When discussing a more unified approach to nation building, it is important to explore and analyse the existing relationships between the government and members of civil society within the community in order to determine the primary actors as well as the spoilers (or in some settings insurgents or extremist in others rebel groups or militias).

Many current definitions of civil society remain amorphous, ambiguous and confusing. However, in this analysis, civil society is defined as citizens, local and international NGOs and social movements that function within the society. In failed states, the government is often incapacitated and civil society may be filling the governance gaps. Civil society in these contexts is often weakened, traumatized and the concept of citizenship non-existent. Understanding the character of these actors and how service provision is implemented within the society is important when undertaking development and capacity-building activities. Civil society is not just NGOs and local associations. Civil society entails a set of interests, often quite disparate, that cut across a society's main identity groups. These interests are expected to be in principle more or less independent of both the state, political parties and other political movements within the society. NGOs and associations are part of civil society only if they act together with citizen, corporate and autonomous institutions to engender the peaceful pursuit of a variety of societal interests, and do so in ways that help to counterbalance any particular partisan force that seeks to dominate.

Focusing on Relationships: Society and the State

When discussing a more unified approach to nation building, it is important to explore and analyse the existing relationships between the government and members of civil society at the national, local and community level in order to determine the primary actors. Many current definitions of civil society remain amorphous and do not define clearly the relationships between warring parties, political groups, and citizenry. In fragile states, reconstruction and stabilization settings, and in post-conflict environments the government is often incapacitated and aspects of civil society may be filling governance gaps. Specific groups may be acting as security forces wither at a local or a regional level, and services that were once the realm of the government are now being bartered within society as a result of a weakened government framework and structure. Civil society in these contexts is often weakened, traumatized and the concept of citizenship almost nonexistent. Instead there may be a clan, party, class, or ethnic group affiliation that trumps a perception of a national identity. Understanding how services are perceived and provided is critical for capacity building activities, governance activities, and for coordination in the field to mitigate conflict.

Within post-conflict environments, four broad types of relationships between the state and civil society exist: 1) tenuous; 2) hopeful; 3) nascent; and 4) evolving. Each when looked at as a typology is useful in coordination and implementation of planning.

Tenuous relationships are often found in protracted post-conflict environments or highly repressive states with regional conflict dimensions. In such contexts, a relationship exists between civil society and the state which is characterized by decentralization, weakness and deep mistrust between national institutions and local government structures. Angola, Burundi, Rwanda, Nepal, Ethiopia and the Philippines are cases that display historically weak institutions and mistrustful citizen interaction with local and national governments. Such pervasive mistrust within the society will inevitably affect interactions with international actors at all levels of society.

Hopeful relationships are characterized by improved dynamics between civil society and the state as evidenced by positive expectations and a population that is willing to place a degree of hope in their leadership. South Sudan is an instructive example of a hopeful relationship in which the Comprehensive Peace Agreement triggered an improved level of expectation and confidence in the national government. However, in many cases where hopeful relationships are present, citizens place unrealistic expectations upon a newly formed or struggling leadership. Consequently, international actors should be cognizant that the existence of a hopeful relationship provides a window of opportunity for the design and implementation of relevant projects to strengthen the government and engage the citizenry.

Nascent relationships are exemplified by authoritarian regimes that are undergoing the transition to a new democracy. Often characterized by citizens with very limited interaction with or experience in governance, advocacy or civil society groups, these relationships can be marked by the lack of recognition of a functioning state. Consequently, international interventions should focus on achieving successful decentralization and the establishment of the basic machinery of a democratic state. In these environments, the program design of donor projects would be vastly different from those in places like South Sudan.

Evolving relationships are exhibited in cases such as Afghanistan, Tajikistan or Sierra Leone where citizens have to negotiate space between the state and other powerful entities such as warlords or alternative power structures that are in contention with state elements. Often these various entities are folded into the state following a peace settlement. Recognition of this reconfiguration of the state to include previously contentious elements is very important as it determines the manner in which local provincial governments, civil society and local institutions are constructed. These reconfigurations impact the manner in which citizens build associations and social networks and determine the amount of social capital available for alignment between different interest groups.

Civil Society, Essential Services, Government and Conflict

The absence of state-led basic service delivery is not simply overcome by creating parallel structures through civil society. While service delivery through local NGOs and civil society organizations is often prioritized by international actors, it is important to note the existing traumatized nature of the environments and the relationships that exist between civil society groups and their weakened government. International aid, distributed through various mechanisms, can serve to worsen these pre-existing divisions within the society or create new cleavages. Additionally, regional, ethnic and religious disparities can become politically sensitive, creating greater risks that services are delivered along party or ethnic lines. Many humanitarian settings turn into this as services poor in and populations become more disenfranchised from the state. In Darfur this is more than evident in the relationship between internally displaced persons (IDP) camp residents and 'rebel groups' who are often embedded in the camps through family members. Similarly, when support for national-level governments is diverted, due to the belief that it takes too long to implement aid through state mechanisms, repressive actions are often taken by the state towards civil society, as evidenced in Nepal, Sudan, Ethiopia, Angola and Burundi. Sometimes it is the state itself that further weakens its own nation building by providing harsh and stringent controls on the delivery of service by local and indigenous groups.

It is imperative to integrate interventions that focus on service delivery at the local level and those that contribute to strengthening governance functions at the national level in order to develop an effective, country-level strategy. These interventions also need to monitor their impact on these societies through regular, in-depth monitoring and polling with local groups and populations to assess the wider implications for civil society development. Support for NGOs has been a main focus among major donors for many years. Besides contracting international NGOs as distributors of humanitarian aid, donors have looked to international and country-based NGOs to carry out an increasing number of roles in pursuit of development, democratization and conflict management. Among others, these tasks have included:

- assisting the government in providing social and other services;
- mobilizing social demands to put public pressure on government to be more responsive to public needs;
- monitoring the state and playing watchdog with regards to human rights and corruption;
- convening issue-specific dialogues between disputing leaders or groups; and
- working at the grassroots level in order to foster inter-group reconciliation through sectoral projects and mediated conflict resolution.

In some countries, local NGOs also have been funded to mount 'people power' campaigns. As in the recent colour revolution, these campaigns are aimed at opening up political regimes to opposition parties and ousting leaders who were holding on to power through irregular methods. In some countries opposition is brutally marginalized through an effective campaign using civil society groups too closely affiliated with the state, as is evidenced in Ethiopia, Zimbabwe and in Rwanda as well. Viewed more broadly, all these programs supporting NGO activities and capacity-building are seen as ways to foster the progressive emergence of a broad civil society, one that both supplements the state in providing for public needs and makes governments more responsive to their populations.

In sum, NGOs form part of the larger policy agenda of the United States, the European Union and the United Nations to promote democratization through a more active citizenry that participates in social and political processes. This aid has been provided in part because it was thought that these many activities would add up to the kind of civil society that is needed to counterbalance the state, as well as to promote greater popular participation in government and social life. Civil society groups provide an entry point for engagement in situations where governments themselves are seen to be untrustworthy partners. Thus, an underlying rationale for boosting NGO capacity is premised on the desire for government accountability achieved through bottom-up, participatory and grassroots processes. But this can also work against the concept of nation building and lead into fragility through popular politics and civil society engagement such as we saw in the West Bank and Gaza with Hamas and in Lebanon with Hezbollah. There are also parts of this emerging in Nepal and on the positive side perhaps the Sudan People's Liberation Movement (SPLM) in South Sudan emerging from the bush as guerilla fighters and leading into positions in the new Sudan in ministries and within the Civil Service.

State-building: The Need for a Comprehensive Approach

The *modus operandi* of intervention in these 'fragile' countries has changed. Recognizing that a different approach is required when working with fragile, weak and failed states, development practitioners and programmes are now focused on very basic state- and nation-building tasks. The developmental objective in such cases is the construction of effective bureaucratic capacity and institutional infrastructures that may in turn effectively channel development assistance. This change in emphasis also necessitates a multi-sectoral, holistic and comprehensive strategy. Agencies from various fields including development, defence, security sector reform, democratization and others, need to develop coherent approaches together and foster interagency coordination. Such interagency coordination is taking root in the US system and in the UK, which are both emphasizing intergovernmental coordination including deeper multilateral cooperation.

To do the comprehensive, integrated, cross-sectoral work that is called for in fragile or failed states, efforts are now being made in Washington to coordinate the several kinds of agencies that are engaged in development, diplomacy, security sector reform, institution-building and peacekeeping. Ironically, within the Washington community, it is often NGOs and private think tanks that are taking the lead in sponsoring and facilitating discussion forums to foster intergovernmental as well as NGO coordination.

In the conversation about failed states and policy, NGOs no longer seem to have a place at the table. The question that arises, therefore, is the particular place that NGO support and civil society promotion occupy, given the current preoccupation with how to prevent and rebuild failed states.

So let us ask ourselves where people fit into the concept of a nation being built from fragments.

1) Does civil society promotion have any compelling use in settings of state failure and post-conflict recovery? How do we work more effectively with local organizations and indigenous groups already fractured from a weakened or predatory state?
2) What are the different roles to be fulfilled by civil society and NGOs in different stages of conflict and under differing regimes? What goals and priorities need to be set for the differing environments across a spectrum of societies?
3) Finally, how do we actually implement the appropriate roles for NGOs and civil society through a comprehensive and strategic country approach? With whom does one engage? Should aid be provided directly to the concerned state; to auxiliary NGO service implementers; to peace alliances, international or domestic; to for-profits; or to partnerships between non-governmental organizations, civil society and state institutions?
4) What is the best balance between local and international inputs to ensure local ownership? How does one organize the requisite intergovernmental and multilateral cooperation?

Country-level Strategies

Taking into consideration the differing relationships and roles of civil society and the state within the various fragile and failed state environments, it is important to determine the most appropriate mechanisms for implementing development and nation-building interventions at the local as well as the national level. The most daunting questions facing international development organizations in these contexts are often where to start, and how to effectively begin to build institutional capacity. International actors, therefore, need to understand the enabling factors that allow a society to function and then examine how they might facilitate a healthy society-state relationship. In line with the emerging paradigm of diplomatic development, there is a recognized need for international development interventions to be implemented through more effective mechanisms at both the local and the national level. It is crucial for international actors to analyse and understand the country context and move beyond what might be done at a project level to focus on a country-level impact.

Specifically, international interventions need to identify and build upon the pre-existing relationships and supportive networks within the local environments in the country of interest. In the absence of effective state governments, local actors, institutions and governing structures often develop and can be nurtured through international support to strengthen civil society initiatives at the community level. However, these efforts alone are insufficient to ensure the level of investment and the integrated approach that is necessary to achieve a cohesive and coordinated civil society. A country-level strategy necessitates collaboration amongst donors in the implementation of a harmonized, national implementation strategy to harness effectively the development potential among the broad range of civil society actors. The current development paradigm is not designed to support this type of comprehensive country-level strategy. Consequently, current mechanisms for aid coordination needs to be reviewed to develop and strengthen efforts to create an integrated, cohesive, nation-building strategy for countries identified as '*failed or fragile states*'

Conclusion

As members of a nation that is striving for a comprehensive vision and approach to working collectively to build security within as well as abroad there are several things that the National Security Strategy as well as the myriad of interagency strategies designed to counter insurgencies and movements within borders that we need to consider. They have less to do with terrorism and more to do with the citizenship of these nations and their access both to government services as well as relationship with their government that allows civil society to strengthen its own support for nation building. These suggestions are not prescriptive, but rather can provide better guidance for more integrated interventions between concerned international engagement and a responsiveness to host country need:

1) *Conflict analysis and mitigation*: understanding better the root causes of conflict, mechanisms for targeted conflict mitigation with key groups/spoilers as well as a process for the implementation of peace and reconciliation that leads to a sense of justice (local justice or a

strengthening of rule of law and human security needs in the country). Militia movements are used as strategies within many nations (Sudan, Uganda, Yemen, Kenya, DRC, Rwanda, etc.)

2) *Citizenship and civil society strengthening*: there is a direct relationship between the concept of citizenship and the role of civil society. You cannot build a nation without understanding that citizens recognize when political, development or humanitarian and military strategies are in direct contrast and conflict with one another. Need for access to services, rights to land and also a sense of security and will always trump political involvement in these settings further entrenching a character of a war and a place for conflict in the political landscape. (Northern Uganda – humanitarian and political/military setting).
3) *Citizens access to government*: there is a direct relationship between strengthening local groups and citizen involvement in service delivery, advocacy and in civic participation. In countries where access to government is limited either by geography or political, social and economic neglect there is a lot of work in increasing access to government. It is not only about decentralization of government services and presence, but also about strengthening citizens' abilities to work directly with government on jointly rebuilding areas that have long been neglected. This process in and of itself is a part of reintegration and reconciliation of fragmented societies long at war.
4) *Community-driven approaches to reconstruction*: providing interventions and projects that support the direct involvement of government with its citizens. More implementation as well as planning, management and monitoring of infrastructure projects and interventions that put a face on government and develop distinct relationships across groups. These efforts can also be used as tangible ways to show implementation of peace agreements and protocols by showing engagement between parties and responsive government involvement with citizens aligned between former rebel/extremist groups and decentralized and responsive government entities. This is an important approach to peace implementation and, in disarmament, demobilization, reintegration and reconciliation, critical (Liberia, DRC, Uganda, Angola, Mozambique, Burundi etc.).

Chapter Two

The Effectiveness of the International Community's Response to the Humanitarian Crisis in Darfur: A Legal Assessment

Dunia P. Zongwe

Introduction

It is blood, adrenaline and tears that water the drought-stricken semi-desert land of Sudan's western region of Darfur. Since July 2000, when attacks on villages surged (Keibida 2006, 43), reports have poured in of raids, bombings, rapes, lootings, the burning of villages and the killing of civilians. Although both government soldiers and Darfur rebels are responsible for the bloodbaths, most observers point accusing fingers at the much dreaded Arab militias, also known as Janjaweed (UNHCR n.d.; Prosecutor's Application).[1] Today, the Darfur conflict has claimed more than 200,000 innocent lives (CIA 2009), displaced at least two million Sudanese,[2] and forced approximately 235,000 people from Darfur to flood 17 refugee camps in neighbouring Chad. In 2006, 1.7 million Sudanese cried out for food assistance after the conflict destroyed the local economy, markets and trade in Darfur (Human Rights Watch 2006).

Global civil society, human rights activists in Sudan and elsewhere, reacted with an outpouring of outrage and indignation, complaining that the international community is not doing enough to alleviate the suffering of people in Darfur. The present chapter attempts to answer the concerns about the effectiveness of the international community's response to the humanitarian crisis. First, it describes the measures taken by various international actors; it then discusses the effectiveness of the measures; it concludes the discussion on the effectiveness of the international response and makes some recommendations for the resolution of the humanitarian crisis in Darfur. Ultimately, the broader contextual issue to which this chapter speaks is: how can the international community effectively intervene in a 'failed' state?

The chapter finds that measures by the International Criminal Court (ICC), the European Union (EU) and United Nations (UN), serve the principle of the state's responsibility to protect people from genocide, crimes against humanity and war crimes. Nevertheless, it finds that the measures, realistic though they may be in the prevailing political circumstances, have not been very effective in alleviating the suffering of the peoples of Darfur. The basic argument is that the international community has been framing the Darfur crisis more in humanitarian and legal terms,[3] without confronting the internal politics that emasculates the efficacy of the international community's response.

It is against this backdrop that the chapter proposes that, alongside the intermediation of the ICC, the EU, and the UN, the international community should adopt multilateral diplomacy, involve non-state actors and mobilize the global civil society, as measures to help solve the humanitarian crisis in Darfur. Multilateral diplomacy is necessary and imperative because the lack of foreign political will to address the political economy of the Darfur conflict is likely to undermine the measures already taken. The participation of non-state actors and the global civil society can circumvent the lack of political will and its consequences for the situation on the ground (see Claude 2006; Santos 2001).

Methodology

This chapter assumes that politics, whether domestic or international, prevails not only in the formulation of rules and theory but also in the actual practice of states. The chapter is therefore premised on the broad theoretical assumptions of the critical legal studies school of jurisprudence. These assumptions have implications for the methodology of the chapter in that they insist on the role of politics in finding a lasting solution to the humanitarian crisis in Darfur.[4]

Now considered a defunct intellectual movement (see Freeman 2001, 1055), the critical legal studies school of jurisprudence lives on through other legal movements and disciplines that it influenced. Scholars like Martti Koskenniemi, Philip Allott and David Kennedy have investigated and highlighted the part that politics play in traditional public international law (Koskenniemi 2005; Allott 1990; Kennedy 2002). In a nutshell, critical legal scholars submit that law is politics. For these scholars, law does not have an existence independent of the national interests shaping and colouring international law and international relations. This continuity between politics and law is most apparent in the recent debates on the characterization of the Darfur humanitarian crisis as genocide and in the prosecution of the Sudanese President for this crime.[5]

The role played by national interests and political considerations in the international community's response to the humanitarian crisis in Darfur brings in sharp focus the pertinence of insights from the critical legal studies school of thought. Legal philosophers were too quick to bury critical legal studies jurisprudence. They buried it alive while the ambiguous response of UN members called for its exhumation. The UN is so inexorably replete with internal contradictions, divergent interests and a bureaucratic culture that it has failed to show decisive leadership in several humanitarian crises (see Coicaud 2007), notably in Darfur.

The methodology in this chapter is a triptych – states (politics), international law, and society (the humanitarian crisis in Darfur) – that can be graphically presented as follows:

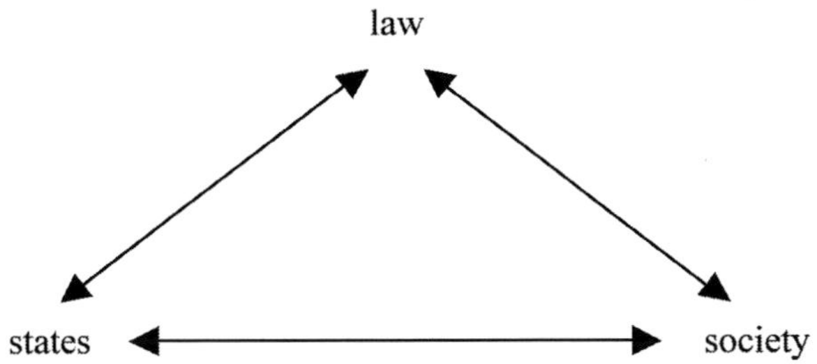

Accordingly, the methodological point of this chapter is that, in order to be effective, international measures must also define the Darfur crisis in political terms, and not mainly in humanitarian assistance and legal terms as they so often have done (Prunier 2005). All told, however, the assessment carried out in this chapter is largely legal and normative in nature. In this regard, the assessment concentrates on international politics, history, and sociology only insofar as they directly have legal ramifications.

Failed States and International Human Rights

Sudan, the largest state in Africa, exhibits all the characteristics of what political scientists describe as a 'failed' state. According to the Failed States Index of the Fund for Peace, Sudan is the world's most failed state (Fund for Peace 2009). The Index reveals that demographic pressures, chronic human flight, uneven economic development among group lines, progressive deterioration of public services, and factionalized elites, have rendered Sudan a 'failed' state (ibid.). It also reveals that massive refugees and internally displaced persons (IDPs) movements, group grievances, state criminalization and deligitimization, widespread human rights violations, security apparatus operating as a state within a state and intervention of external political actors, are singularly acute (ibid.). In addition, Sudan ranks 173rd out of list of 180 countries in terms of transparency (Transparency International 2008). Human development in Sudan is, however, relatively high for similarly situated failed states. Sudan ranks 147th on the UN Development Programme's list of 177 countries by human development (UNDP 2008).

The oft-used concept of 'failed state' is contested and controversial. The concept fails to accurately account for huge disparities within and between regions in a country, painting, as it does, entire countries with the same brush as either weak or strong along graduated scales of institutional efficiency. Most importantly, it fails to provide a reliable paradigm for action or intervention in countries confronted with daunting humanitarian emergencies like Sudan.

Moreover, the concept of 'failed state' does not readily lend itself to legal analyses, nor can it fully integrate existing legal frameworks. In international law, a state, before it can be recognized as such, only needs a permanent population, a defined territory, an effective government, and the capacity to enter into relations with other states.[6] Even where one of the above four requirements is not present, once recognized as an independent state, a political entity remains a state. The withdrawal of recognition, for example because a state has descended into anarchy and lawlessness, is a politically unacceptable theoretical possibility without precedent (Dugard 2005, 110).

International human rights law has a less diffuse, more localized, approach when a state is incapable of performing one or more of its core constitutional obligations. Whereas the concept of 'failed state' concentrates on a state's institutional capacity in general, human rights law stresses on a state's capacity to prosecute and ensure accountability for violations as determining factors for intervention. Thus, the basic logical structure of the case for humanitarian intervention is as follows. State sovereignty implies the primary responsibility to protect people from genocide, war crimes and crimes against humanity. If a population is suffering serious harm as a result of internal war, insurgency, repression or state failure, and the state is *unwilling or unable* to avert it, the principle of non-intervention yields to the international responsibility to protect.[7]

In sum, international legal practice is functionalist and acknowledges that the creation of a state is essentially and eminently political. It confirms that a *state may fail* to fulfil one or more, if not all, of its constitutional functions, but a *state may never be failed*, unless and until the international community makes a decision to that effect.

Darfur: The Humanitarian Crisis

Darfur in western Sudan, Mogadishu in southern Somalia and North Kivu in eastern Democratic Republic of Congo (DRC) form a trilogy of the most tragic, most ignored (BBC 2008) and deadliest (International Rescue Committee 2007) humanitarian situations on the continent, respectively. Allegations that Sudan's President Al Bashir committed genocide by causing serious mental harm to the people of Darfur and by deliberate infliction on them of conditions of life calculated to bring about their physical destruction seal the gravity of the Darfur crisis (Prosecutor's Application).

Although the root causes of the Darfur conflict are complex and multi-layered (Nantulya 2004), two factors have played a prominent role in causing and sustaining the conflict, namely struggles around land and resources, and the marginalization of the peoples of Darfur by the central government (UN High-Level Mission in Darfur 2007).[8] The rebels – mostly from the African tribes of Darfur like the Fur, the Masalit and Zaghawa[9] – pleaded for equality and justice for all Sudanese and not just redress of more narrow tribal interests (ibid., ¶ 25–7). The rebels started to attack the Sudanese government in late 2002, and those attacks accelerated in 2003 (ibid.). Given that the army was being consistently defeated, the Sudanese government military based its response on three elements: military intelligence, the air force and the Janjaweed. The ruling National Congress Party's (NCP) three-pronged counter-insurgency strategy systematically and primarily targeted the civilian populations of Darfur, especially the tribal groups from which the rebels are drawn (ibid.), with disastrous humanitarian consequences. The crisis took on an international dimension when over 100,000 refugees poured into neighbouring Chad, pursued by Janjaweed militiamen, who clashed with Chadian government forces along the border.

Grave and massive violations of human rights and international criminal law occurred in Darfur as well as in other parts of Sudan. On 14 July 2008, the ICC Prosecutor Luis Moreno-Ocampo applied for an arrest warrant for Sudanese President Al Bashir, accusing him on ten criminal charges of genocide, crimes against humanity and war crimes. Prosecutor Moreno-Ocampo accuses President Al Bashir of genocide under the Rome Statute establishing the ICC[10] for killing members of the Fur, Masalit and Zaghawa ethnic groups (Rome Statute art. 6(a)). It also accuses Al Bashir of crimes against humanity for committing, as part of a widespread and systematic attack against the Darfur population with knowledge of the attack, acts of murder (Rome Statute art. 7(1)(a)), extermination (Rome Statute art. 7(1)(b)), forcible transfer of the population (Rome Statute art. 7(1)(d)), torture

(Rome Statute art. 7(1)(f)) and a massive number of rapes (Rome Statute art. 7(1)(g); Prosecutor's Application). The accusatory instrument recalls that the government-backed Janjaweed raped women in front of their mothers and fathers, and that rape is an integral part of the government's destructive pattern to 'kill the will, the spirit and life itself' (Rome Statute art. 7(1)(g)). Finally, Prosecutor Moreno-Ocampo accuses Al Bashir of war crimes for intentionally directing attacks against the civilian population (Rome Statute art. 8(2)(e)(i)) and pillaging towns (Rome Statute art. 8(2)(e)(v); Prosecutor's Application).

The humanitarian situation in Darfur is alarmingly precarious. The situation is marked by high levels of insecurity, poor harvests, difficulties in bringing supplies into Darfur, attacks on humanitarian workers, reduction in the quality of humanitarian services, reduced food rations and overcrowded IDP camps (Darfur Humanitarian Profile 2008). By 1 July 2008, there were over 2 million residents in need of humanitarian assistance in addition to nearly 2.5 million IDPs in Darfur (ibid.), making Sudan the country with the world's largest population of IDPs (Institute for Security Studies n.d.). Unfortunately, the actual scale of those affected by the Darfur conflict is not known because persistent insecurity in Darfur still impedes accurate monitoring.

Darfur: The International Community's Response

For the purposes of this chapter, 'international community' refers to individual national governments and treaty-based intergovernmental institutions.[11] Best epitomized by the UN system in general, the 'international community' encompasses such intergovernmental institutions as the African Union (AU) and the Inter-Governmental Authority on Development (IGAD), but it excludes the ICC.

Very often, the international community responds to humanitarian crises by deploying peacekeeping troops, under a UN Charter Chapter VII mandate, in countries and areas facing major security threats and humanitarian emergencies. The deployment of peacekeeping troops to protect human rights and put an end to human suffering is an expression of an international democratic culture, developed out of a sense of international solidarity (Coicaud 2007, 6ff). Surely, the UN's endorsement of a peacekeeping operation in Darfur under a Chapter VII mandate – which provides for the use of force when the UN Security Council (SC) determines that a certain situation constitutes a threat to international peace and security[12] – is a projection of such solidarity. As Jean-Marc Coicaud put it (2007, 7), failing to respond to the 'plight of the other, failing to show solidarity, diminishes the humanity of all'.

The international community responded to the humanitarian crisis in Darfur on three levels: national, continental and global.[13]

National Measures

National measures are those adopted by individual states to address the humanitarian crisis in Darfur. Both Chad and the US were major players in attempts to resolve the humanitarian crisis in Darfur. However, the measures taken by the US were more robust than those taken by Chad. In 2004, Chad brokered negotiations in N'djamena. The negotiations led up to the signature of a Humanitarian Ceasefire Agreement (Cease Fire Agreement) between the Sudanese Government, the Sudan Liberation Movement/Army (SLM/A), and the Justice and Equality Movement (JEM) on 8 April 2004. The Cease Fire Agreement established a Cease Fire Commission (CFC)[14] that it entrusted with the effective monitoring of the rules and provisions of the cease fire (Cease Fire Agreement art. 4).

The US, on the other hand, issued on 19 August 2006 a threat to Sudan over the 'potential consequences' of the Sudanese government's opposition to the replacement of the 7, 000 AU force with a 17,000 UN force. Moreover, on 13 October 2006, President Bush imposed further sanctions against those deemed complicit in the Darfur atrocities under the 2006 Darfur Peace and Accountability Act.[15] The measures were said to strengthen existing sanctions by prohibiting US citizens from engaging in oil-related transactions with Sudan, freezing the assets of complicit parties and denying them entry to the US. The Darfur Peace Act calls on the US to take a more active role in stopping the genocide that the US alleged took place in Darfur and encourages North Atlantic Treaty Organization (NATO) participation (Darfur Peace Act sec. 6(c)).

It was the sense of the US Congress that the AU should ensure an orderly transition to a UN peacekeeping operation, with a mandate to protect civilians and humanitarian activities (Darfur Peace Act sec. 4(3)). The Congress also understood the role of the UN peacekeeping operation to consist in assisting in the implementation of the 2005 Darfur Peace Agreement (DPA), and deter violence in Darfur (ibid.). Later, the US Congress enacted the 2007 Darfur Accountability and Divestment Act,[16] which requires the identification of corporations that conduct business in Sudan and prohibits government contracts with such corporations.

Continental Measures

The African Union (AU) took several measures to resolve the humanitarian crisis in Darfur. However, it is important to note that the AU, like the UN yet unlike the US, never defined the crisis as amounting to genocide. Rather, the AU stated that the core of the conflict in Darfur is political and socio-economic in nature (African Union Peace and Security Council 2005). Likewise, neither the EU nor Human Rights Watch backed the Bush administration's conclusion that the atrocities in Darfur constitute genocide (see Hagan and Rymond-Richmond 2009, 31).

On 12 February 2007, the Peace and Security Council (PSC) of the AU decided to dispatch as soon as possible a mission to Chad, the Central African Republic (CAR) and Sudan to undertake a comprehensive assessment of the situation on the ground and identify the obstacles to the implementation of the peace agreements (African Union Peace and Security Council 2007). On 5 May 2005, the AU and the US State Department orchestrated the DPA by the government of Sudan with the faction of the SLA led by Minni Minnawi in Abuja, Nigeria. The accord called for the disarmament of the Janjaweed militia, and for the rebel forces to disband and be incorporated into the army. The AU deployed a 7,000 force, the AU mission in Sudan (AMIS).

In January 2005, under the auspices of the IGAD, the Comprehensive Peace Agreement (CPA) was signed in Nairobi between the Sudanese government and the Sudan People's Liberation Movement (SPLM). The civil war in Southern Sudan, Africa's longest civil war, ended through the CPA. The CPA grants Southern Sudan autonomy for six years followed by a referendum on independence from the rest of Sudan (CPA 2005).

Lately, the EU has also undertaken measures to contribute to the resolution of the humanitarian crisis in Darfur. On 25 September 2007, the SC, acting under Chapter VII, authorized the EU to deploy for a one-year period an operation aimed at supporting the UN in the CAR and Chad (MINURCAT) (SC Res. 1778). The Council of the EU decided to deploy the EU Force (EUFOR) in eastern Chad and in northeastern CAR on 28 January 2008 (2008 J.O. (L 34) 39). In March 2008, the EUFOR troops arrived in Abeche, eastern Chad, to facilitate humanitarian aid and protect refugees and IDPs in camps in a vast volatile region bordering Darfur until 15 March 2009 (*France 24* 2008) (SC Res. 1834), when a UN operation replaced it (*Euronews* 2009).

Global Measures

The significance of the measures taken at the global level lies in the fact that this is the first time that the international community responded collectively on an African crisis.[17] To be sure, there was no resolution passed by the UN Security Council (SC) before the 1994 genocide in Rwanda. Unlike its inertia during the 1994 Rwanda genocide, the SC has taken many historic resolutions and measures in respect of the crisis in Darfur.

The SC passed a number of important resolutions to address the humanitarian crisis in Darfur. At least four of these resolutions are fundamental. First, on 18 September 2004, the SC passed a resolution which called for a Commission of Inquiry on Darfur (Cassese Commission) to assess the Sudanese conflict (SC Res. 1564).[21] Subsequently, the Commission of Inquiry reported on 31 January 2005 that, while inhuman acts may have been committed with genocidal intent, the government authorities pursued no genocidal policy in Darfur, directly or through the militias under their control.[18] One scholar criticized the Cassese Report that its conclusion rests on 'dubious logic' (Abass 2008). Nevertheless, the ICC appears to have sided with the Cassese Report in that it found no reasonable ground to believe that Sudanese President Al Bashir was directly or indirectly responsible for genocide.

Second, on 24 March 2005, while not exclusively directed to Darfur, the UN established the United Nations Mission in Sudan (UNMIS) (SC Res. 1590). The UN authorized deployment of up to 10,000 military personnel, a civilian component, and a UN structure to support and oversee the implementation of the CPA (ibid.). On 29 March 2005, the SC imposed an arms embargo on all parties in Darfur, provided for travel bans, and froze the assets of individuals who continue to violate commitments to end the conflict (to be designated by the SC Panel of Experts) (SC Res. 1591). Unlike AMIS, UNMIS was empowered to use force to protect civilians under threat of physical attack (SC Res. 1706).

Moreover, on 31 March 2005, the SC, acting under Chapter VII, resolved to refer the Darfur situation to the ICC (SC Res. 1593) and required Sudan and all other parties to the Darfur conflict to cooperate with the ICC (ibid., ¶ 2). This referral is an historic decision as this is the first time that the SC refers a situation to the ICC in terms of Article 13(b) of the ICC Rome Statute. The referral is all the more historic as this means that the US, China, and Russia – all permanent members of the SC that do not accept the ICC's jurisdiction – did not veto the referral. The referral allowed the ICC to examine and act on alleged perpetrators of crimes in Darfur, including those identified by the Cassese Commission.

Finally, on 31 August 2006, the SC approved a resolution to extend to Darfur the mandate of the UNMIS, which currently has 10,000 in-country personnel monitoring the North-South CPA, and to send a new peacekeeping force of 17,300 to the region (SC Res. 1706, ¶ 1, 3, 8, 9). The UN did not deploy such force until July 2007 because the Sudanese President Omar Al Bashir had expressed strong opposition to the resolution (Mail and Guardian 2007; Bommenel 2007). It is on 31 July 2007 that the SC authorized, with the consent of Sudan, the deployment of a AU/UN hybrid force in Darfur (UNAMID) (SC Res. 1769). UNAMID's mandate is much broader than that of UNMIS (Yihdego 2009). The SC mandated UNAMID to prevent the disruption of the DPA and armed attacks and, without prejudice to the responsibility of the Sudanese government, to protect the civilians (SC Res. 1769, ¶ 15(a)(ii)). UNAMID began its formal operations on 31 December 2007 and has deployed in about 55 locations throughout the three Darfur states (UNAMID 2008). Yet again, the lack of cooperation on the Sudanese government's part is slowing down UNAMID operations (ibid.).

International Criminal Court Investigations and Prosecution

The ICC, seen by some as part of the problem and by others as part of the solution, is in any event an essential piece of the Darfur puzzle. In this chapter, the ICC is not regarded as part and parcel of the international community, but it nonetheless plays a subsidiary role in the multilateral management of the Darfur crisis.

On 27 February 2007, the ICC summoned the Sudanese interior minister (Ahmad Muhammad Harun) and the Janjaweed militia commander (Ali Muhammad Ali Abd-Al-Rahman 'Ali Kushayb') in relation to war crimes and crimes against humanity.[19] Article 13(b) of the ICC Rome Statute confers jurisdiction on the ICC over a national even though the national's state has not ratified the ICC Rome Statute. Sudan has not ratified the ICC Rome Statute and claims that it is able to prosecute the people accused of war crimes and crimes against humanity. On 6 March 2007, Sudan attempted to frustrate the ICC's work by trying three suspects[20] itself in a special criminal court in Geneina on charges relating to attacks in Darfur (Human Rights Watch 2007).

More recently, ICC Prosecutor Moreno-Ocampo applied for an arrest warrant for Sudanese President Al Bashir for genocide, crimes against humanity and war crimes. On 4 March 2009, the Pre-Trial Chamber I of the ICC issued an arrest warrant for President Al Bashir.[21] It is the first time that an international court has issued an arrest warrant for an incumbent president. After it had examined evidence, supporting material and other information submitted by the ICC Prosecutor, the Pre-Trial Chamber held that there are reasonable grounds to believe that President Al Bashir is criminally responsible under the Rome Statute as an indirect perpetrator, or as an indirect co-perpetrator, for war crimes and crimes against humanity (ibid.). For the Chamber, Al Bashir has legally and effectively been President of Sudan and Commander-in-Chief of the Sudanese army from March 2003 to 14 July 2008 and, as such, he played an essential role in coordinating the design and implementation of the government counter-insurgency campaign that caused the alleged war crimes and crimes against humanity (ibid., 6–7).

The accusation of genocide in particular, the most heinous international crime (Cassese Report, 128), for Al Bashir elicited an immediate and aggressive response from the Sudanese government. The AU, the Arab League, some humanitarian organizations and legal experts, have raised concerns that the ICC Prosecutor's application might reverse the peace process. There was also strong opposition to a genocide charge both at the UN and within the ICC Prosecutor's own office (Hagan and Rymond-Richmond 2009, xxi). Since the indictment, President Al Bashir has been heavily lobbying the international community to drum up support for his move to have the ICC Prosecutor's arrest warrant suspended, if not withdrawn altogether. As a consequence, the AU, the Arab League, Russia and China, have indicated that they will support President Al Bashir's move for the suspension of the ICC prosecution (*International Herald Tribune* 2008).

In contrast, states (like the US (Corder 2009) and the United Kingdom (UK) (UK Mission to the UN 2009)), human rights groups (like Human Rights Watch (2009)), and Darfur rebel movements (SLM and JEM) (*BBC News* 2009a and b), greeted Al Bashir's arrest warrant with praise for justice and the ICC. Meanwhile the AU formally requested the SC to defer the proceedings initiated against President Al Bashir in accordance with article 16 of the Rome Statute.[22] Several human rights scholars and activists the world over have decried what they perceive as the politicization of international criminal justice. Ironically, each side of the argument accuses the other of politicizing the principles of international criminal law. It is the submission of this chapter that international justice and politics cannot be completely disassociated and that activists will have to engage politics if the measures undertaken by the international community are to be effective.

The Effectiveness of International Measures

The Test for the Effectiveness of International Measures

How does one determine the effectiveness of international measures? Are there any manageable and measurable criteria by which to define 'effectiveness'? To some, this question may seem trivial, but it is actually of central importance. If not defined, the question as to whether international measures in Darfur are effective would be highly subjective and open to all sorts of abuses. 'Effectiveness' can be defined in so many ways. However, following the methodological position of this chapter, the test for effectiveness uses three criteria, drawn from critical legal studies jurisprudence, namely:

1) the practical effect of international measures on the humanitarian situation;
2) the extent to which the measures promote the principle of state responsibility to protect citizens from genocide, crimes against humanity, and war crimes; and
3) the realism of the measures in the prevailing political circumstances.

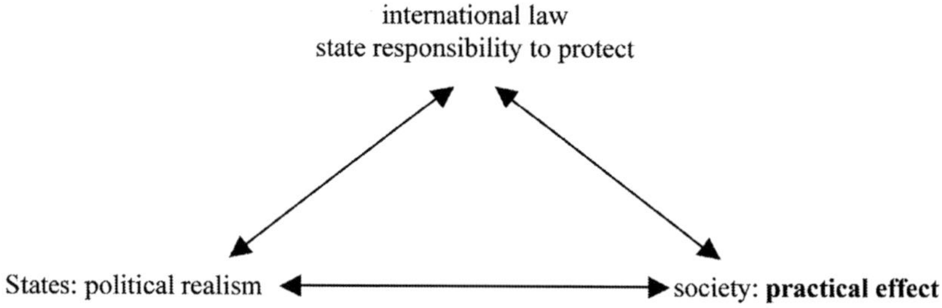

The Practical Effect of Measures on the People in Darfur

The practical effect of international measures on the people in Darfur is the central criterion for the effectiveness of these measures. At its most basic, the concept of effectiveness links a certain action or group of actions to their consequences in practice.[23] Effectiveness means the capability of producing an effect. Thus, effectiveness means the capability of reducing or alleviating the suffering of the people in Darfur.

The Principle of State Responsibility to Protect Citizens

To be effective, the measures taken by the international community must have the effect of limiting the Sudanese state sovereignty over its citizens if the state fails to protect them. The principle of states' responsibility to protect populations from genocide, crimes against humanity and war crimes lays down that, first of all, national governments should exercise their sovereignty in a responsible way and that providing safety for its citizens is a prime duty and that, secondly, there is a secondary responsibility incumbent upon the international community to act should a national government be unable or unwilling to discharge its duties in this respect (RTP Report, 17; Schrijver 2006). Thus, the state responsibility to protect the citizens, which is related to but distinct from humanitarian intervention, qualifies the principle of state sovereignty, as provided for in articles 2(7) of the UN Charter and 4(g) of the AU Constitutive Act (see Kindiki 2003). However, the SC, acting under Chapter VII of the UN Charter, must authorize humanitarian intervention for such intervention to be legal (Dugard 2005, 515). The measures taken by the international community must therefore circumscribe the Sudanese government's sovereign powers over the people in Darfur and its citizens in general.

Since the SC has started using it in 2005 (SC Res. 1674), the responsibility to protect is emerging as a principle of international law. There have been disagreements as to the legal status of the principle. However, most scholars today would agree that it is more accurate to say that the principle is a declaratory and not yet a binding principle of international law (see Matthews 2008). The responsibility to protect comprises humanitarian intervention, but the two concepts are not synonymous. The International Commission on Intervention and State Sovereignty re-conceptualizes the issue and prefers the language of responsibility over that of humanitarian intervention (RTP Report, 9).

Humanitarian intervention is very controversial and applies only in exceptional circumstances (Franck 2002, 125ff). Prevention is the most crucial dimension of the responsibility to protect in that, provided that it devotes resources, the international community should always exhaust prevention options before humanitarian or military intervention (RTP Report, 19–20). History and legal practice support a more nuanced reconciling of the pursuit of peace (as evidenced by article 2(4) of the UN Charter) and of justice through the protection of human and humanitarian rights (as evidenced by universal agreements) (Franck 2002, 138–9). More specifically, article 4(h) of the AU Constitutive Act provides for the right of AU intervention in a member state following a decision of the AU Assembly in respect of 'grave circumstances', namely war crimes, crimes against humanity and genocide.[24] Since the UN and the AU found that war crimes and crimes against humanity were committed in Darfur and that the Darfur situation constitutes a threat to regional and international peace and security, it is therefore easier to justify humanitarian intervention in Darfur.

The Realism of Measures in the Prevailing Political Circumstances

The effectiveness of the international measures will also depend on the prevalent political realities, which will in turn dictate the outcomes of these measures. The international political configuration of the Darfur conflict shows that it is practically difficult to make a decision and marshal regional, continental and international support needed for an effective humanitarian intervention into Darfur (Moni 2005; Louis 2001). Internationally, the intervention will need the support of the permanent five veto-wielding members, but three of these five members are 'friends' of the Sudanese government. Sudan is a key ally of the US in the latter's fight against global terrorism;[25] Russia is the main supplier of arms to the Khartoum government; and both Russia and China have significant oil interests in Sudan (Motsi 2006). Uganda and Burkina Faso, which currently sit on the SC, are not likely to deviate from the AU position.

National Measures

Virtually all the measures taken by Chad and US were not effective. Although Chadian and American measures were realistic in the existing political circumstances, they did not produce the desired results for the people of Darfur and in promoting the principle of states' responsibility to protect their citizens.

The Chad-brokered 2004 Humanitarian Cease Fire Agreement failed. However, the US threat to the Sudanese government, although not effective, has the real potential of producing the desired results over time. It would therefore not be right to discard it as useless and inherently ineffective. The same applies to the two Darfur acts and the economic sanctions imposed under them by the US on the Sudanese. The measures taken by the US were more robust than Chad's (even if some analysts believe that US geopolitical interests, rather than respect for human rights, motivates the US involvement in Sudan) (Motsi 2006).

Continental Measures

The measures of the AU have also been ineffective. The CFC and DPA failed dismally. In particular, disunity among some rebel groups, especially the SLA/M, contributed to the failure of the DPA (see Pounds 2008). The measures by the AU did not have any significant impact on the lives of the people of Darfur; they have not served the principle of states' responsibility to protect their citizens in any meaningful way. The AU and African regional bodies are under-resourced and lack the institutional capacity to protect or otherwise make a positive impact on the peoples of Darfur (International Crisis Group 2006, 10; International Peace Academy 2002). For example, AMIS was incapable of protecting both its own personnel and the people in Darfur from violent attacks because it was 'terribly under-resourced in both human and logistical terms' (Yihdego 2009, 64). UNAMID is facing similar resource constraints.[28]

But it seems to be all the AU could do in the circumstances. This is because the AU does not have the political will to intervene in terms of article 4(h) of the AU Constitutive Act into one of its most important member states.[29] In July 2009, the majority of a divided[30] AU declared in Libya that AU member states shall not cooperate with the ICC for the arrest and surrender of Sudan President Al Bashir (AU's Bashir Declaration, ¶ 10). The AU regretted that the SC had neither heard nor acted upon the AU's request to have the criminal proceedings against Al Bashir deferred (ibid., ¶ 9).

Robert Barnidge claims that the behaviour of the AU vis-à-vis the Darfur crisis reflects a determination by that regional body to have more control over conflict mediation and resolution on the continent (Barnidge 2009, 101). On the other hand, Waranya Moni suggests that African leaders are not interested in ordering actions that would set precedents for the half a dozen African states (such as Zimbabwe, Nigeria, Côte d'Ivoire and Uganda) that are facing serious political crisis that could lead to civil wars (Moni 2005). As regard the EUFOR troops deployed in eastern Chad in 2008, it is still uncertain whether such deployment was practically effective in managing the crisis, though admittedly the force might have helped avoid a larger humanitarian catastrophe in the sub region.

Global Measures

Notwithstanding important decisions made by the UN and the ICC, the international response, especially that of the UN, to the humanitarian crisis in Darfur has not been successful in improving the situation on the ground. In fact, the humanitarian crisis in Darfur worsened (International Crisis Group 2006, 1), but Mahmood Mamdani says that the opposite approach – that is, an Iraq-style intervention into Darfur – is doomed to fail (Mamdani 2007). The ICC Prosecutor's application for an arrest warrant for President Al Bashir and the summonses against the interior minister and the militia leader went a long way towards enforcing the principle of states' responsibility to protect their citizens against genocide, war crimes and crimes against humanity. Yet given the interests in Sudan of some members of the SC, including such veto-wielding permanent members as the US,[31] Russia and China,[32] it is unrealistic to expect the SC to take more drastic measures. With reference to the arrest warrant for President Al Bashir, the SC permanent members will be deadlocked as to whether the SC should support or suspend the ICC prosecution against him. At any rate, the SC decision to refer the Darfur situation to the ICC under Chapter VII of the UN Charter has considerable symbolic value, sending as it does a signal that the humanitarian situation in Darfur is and continues to be a threat to regional and international peace and security (SC Res. 1593; SC Res. 1679; Michelo Hansungule). Ironically, the real prospects of ICC prosecution radicalize the opposition of the Sudanese government to the UN deployment in Darfur.[33]

A graphic summary of the qualitative evaluation of the international community's response to the Darfur crisis is shown in Table 2-1.

A Complementary Approach to the Implementation of Measures: Multilateral Diplomacy

The conflicting interests in international relations have to a great extent paralyzed states involved in the humanitarian crisis in Darfur, thereby hampering the national, continental and global measures undertaken by the states. The author suggests that multilateral diplomacy – the political equivalent of joint ventures – and the participation of non-state actors, the global civil society and social movements, constitute a most efficient way of addressing the lack of political will (Yolanda Spies). The non-state actors (global civil *society*) are very much less subject to political influence and they can exert the necessary political pressures on *states* like the US, Russia, and China (ibid.), which in turn will reinforce the diplomatic pressure on Khartoum to comply with international *law* and measures. The Arab League, especially Egypt and Libya,[34] are very influential and may exert a great deal of pressure on the Sudanese government because it is an Arab government (ibid.).

Table 2-1 The international community's response to the Darfur crisis – qualitative evaluation

National measures	2004 Cease Fire Agreement	US sanctions and corporate divestment
Practical effect	Failed	May succeed with time
Responsibility to protect	Failed	Failed
Political realism	Realistic	Realistic

Continental measures	Cease Fire Commission	2005 Darfur Peace Agreement	UNAMID
Practical effect	Failed	Failed	May succeed with time
Responsibility to protect	Failed	Failed	Succeeded
Political realism	Realistic	Realistic	Realistic

Global measures	UN/AU peacekeeping operations	ICC prosecution	EUFOR operations
Practical effect	Failed	Failed	May succeed with time
Responsibility to protect	Succeeded	Succeeded	succeeded
Political realism	Realistic	Realistic	realistic

Thomas-Jensen and Spiegel noticed that most of the pro-Darfur measures taken by the Bush administration and the US Congress were a direct result of mounting pressure from American student movements, religious leaders, and elected officials (Thomas-Jensen and Spiegel 2008). The Bush administration even voiced objections over what it perceived as an unconstitutional intrusion by states and grassroots movements into foreign policy, which it sees as the preserve of the federal government.[35] Furthermore, citizens around the world have galvanized key players like China, France and Great Britain into assuming a more assertive role in finding a solution to the Darfur crisis (Thomas-Jensen and Spiegel 2008). Therefore, multilateral diplomacy and the engagement of non-state actors can productively complement and strengthen the effectiveness of the measures the international community took.

Conclusion and Recommendations

Several specialized agencies and organizations have generally concluded that the response of the international community to the humanitarian crisis is not effective (UN High-Level Mission in Darfur 2007, ¶ 67; International Crisis Group 2006, 18). However, one wonders if it is perhaps too early for analysts to conclude that the measures taken by the international community are ineffective. A considerable number of measures have been taken at the national, continental and global level to resolve the intractable humanitarian crisis and conflict in Darfur. Of all the measures, the sanctions of the US on the Sudanese government, UNAMID, and the involvement of the ICC (Michelo Hansungule), are most likely to produce the desired results, to serve the principle of states' responsibility to protect their citizens from genocide, war crimes and crimes against humanity. Such measures are the best outcomes given the existing institutional structures and political realities. However, as the lack of political will on the states' part may thwart the effective implementation of these measures (Prunier 2005, 124–48), it is imperative to adopt multilateral diplomacy and take non-state actors on board.

Accordingly, the US, Chad, Libya, Egypt, the AU, the Arab League, the European Union and the UN, acting together and/or even unilaterally, should now (International Crisis Group 2006):

1) apply sanctions on:
    a) NCP leaders found responsible for atrocities in Darfur. These sanctions may include asset freezes and travel bans;
    b) The economic interests on the Khartoum regime's commercial entities and affiliated businesses, the main conduit for financing NCP-allied militias in Darfur. The possibility of sanctions on Sudan's petroleum sector should also be explored, difficult though it may be; and
2) fully cooperate with and support the work of the ICC in its efforts to entrench the principle of states' responsibility to protect their citizens from genocide, war crimes and crimes against humanity.

Apart from these more commonly accepted recommendations, the international community should also adopt a multilateral diplomacy involving non-state actors like non-governmental organizations and broad-based social movements in order to mobilize energy in the global civil society and thereby circumvent the lack of foreign political will to address the political and economic structures that underlie the Darfur conflict.

Notes

1 It literally means 'the devils on horseback'.

2 Prosecutor's Application for Warrant of Arrest under Article 58 Against Omar Hassan Ahmad Al Bashir (Summary of the Case), International Criminal Court (14 July 2008), available at http://www.icc-cpi.int/library/cases/ICC-02-05-152-ENG.pdf (hereafter Prosecutor's Application).

3 For instance, Yihdego (2009) examines the applicability and compliance with international humanitarian law rules in Darfur. Yihdego's recommendations are legalistic and largely confined themselves to urging the international community and parties to the Darfur conflict to observe international humanitarian law rules. The political dimensions of the conflict are not addressed, raising questions as to the realism of Yidhego's recommendations.

4 Reuters (2007) (reporting that the UN Under-Secretary for Humanitarian Affairs said that only a political solution could end the suffering in Darfur).

5 See Hong (2008) (stating that the failure to call the crisis in Darfur genocide, because of political sensitivities, is a violation of the moral obligation to act); Trahan (2008) (attempting to demonstrate that all the legal requirements regarding the genocide has been met in Darfur). In contradistinction, see Mamdani (2009) (arguing that the atrocities in Darfur result from a violent counterinsurgency and do not amount to genocide).

6 Montevideo Convention on the Rights and Duties of States, 26 December 1933, 165 L.N.T.S. 19, art. 1.

7 The Responsibility to Protect, Report of the International Commission on Intervention and State Sovereignty 17 (International Development Research Centre 2001) (hereafter RTP Report).

8 The Arab ethnic groups armed by the Sudanese government to attack black African communities of the Fur tribe also fought among themselves (IRIN 2007).

9 President Al Bashir reportedly refers to the members of these African tribes derogatorily as 'Zourga', which means 'Blacks'. See Hagan and Rymond-Richmond (2009).

10 Rome Statute of the International Criminal Court, UN Doc. A/CONF.183/9. art. 6 (hereafter Rome Statute).

11 This definition follows the norm in international law that the primary subjects of international law are states. That is why the 'international community' of states refers in this chapter to individual states and intergovernmental institutions. Despite the fact that states have created the ICC, the ICC is, as a normative matter, independent from states.

12 The SC declared that the situation in Darfur was a threat to international peace and security and to stability in the region in SC Res. 1556, UN, preamble, Doc. S/Res/1556 (30 July 2004).

13 However, the present chapter cites only the major measures taken by the international community.

14 Humanitarian Cease Fire Agreement on the Conflict in Darfur, Sudan-SLM/A-JEM, 8 April 2004. art. 3 (hereafter Cease Fire Agreement).
15 Darfur Peace and Accountability Act of 2006, H.R., 3127, 109th Cong. (2nd Sess. 2006) (hereafter Darfur Peace Act).
16 Darfur Accountability and Divestment Act of 2007, H.R. 3127, 110th Cong. (1st Sess. 2007) (hereafter (Darfur Divestment Act).
17 Interview with Michelo Hansungule, Professor, Centre for Human Rights, University of Pretoria (20 March 2007) (hereafter Michelo Hansungule).
18 International Commission of Inquiry on Darfur, Report of the International Commission of Inquiry on Darfur to the United Nations Secretary-General 131ff (2005) (hereafter Cassese Report).
19 Warrant of Arrest for Ali Kushayb, International Criminal Court (27 April 2007), available at http://www.icc-cpi.int/library/cases/ICC-02-05-01-07-3_English.pdf; Warrant of Arrest for Ahmad Harun, International Criminal Court (27 April 2007), available at http://www.icc-cpi.int/library/cases/ICC-02-05-01-07-2_English.pdf. The ICC issued the summonses in terms of rule 58(7) of the Rules of Procedure of the ICC.
20 Including the Janjaweed leader.
21 Pre-Trial Chamber I, Warrant of Arrest for Homar Hassan Ahmad Al Bashir, International Criminal Court (4 March 2009), available at http://www.icc-cpi.int/iccdocs/doc/doc639078.pdf (hereafter Al Bashir Arrest Warrant).
22 African Union, Decisions and Declarations of the 13th Ordinary Session of the Assembly of the African Union (1–3 July 2009) ¶ 9 (hereafter AU's Bashir Declaration).
23 *Oxford Dictionary of Current English* (2006), sv. 'effectiveness'.
24 See Rome Statute arts 6, 7, 8, for the definition of genocide, crimes against humanity and war crimes.
25 Interview with Iqbal Jhazbhay, Professor, University of South Africa (22 March 2007).
26 Interview with Yolanda Spies, Senior Lecturer, Department of Political Sciences, University of Pretoria (19 March 2007) (hereafter Yolanda Spies).
27 See Barnidge (2009) (stating that, after signature, the Humanitarian Cease Fire Agreement proved to be a paper tiger).
28 See UN 2009 (stating that, despite the arrival of additional troops and enabling units, the UNAMID mission's actual operational impact has been limited by logistical constraints, inadequate supply of critical equipment and the continued absence of key military enabling units); UNAMID 2008; Yihdego 2009, 66.
29 With a gross domestic product estimated at US$48 billion, Sudan is the eighth largest economy in Africa, after Libya, Angola and Morocco.
30 Greenberg (2009) (explaining that AU Chairman Muammar Gaddafi, President of Libya, and President Al Bashir himself bullied and manipulated African countries into making the decision to refuse to cooperate with the ICC). Apparently, only Sudan, Senegal, Djibouti and the Comoros backed the AU declaration on the ICC prosecution of President Al Bashir. Botswana is the only AU member state

that has openly declared its continued commitment to cooperate with the ICC arrest warrant for President Al Bashir.

31 Even the US, the only country that has so far characterized the armed hostilities in Darfur as genocide, has not been consistent in its stance. See Hagan and Rymond-Richmond (2009, 32ff) (saying that, although the US has responded more strongly than other nations to what it called genocide in Darfur, it also flip-flopped on the issue).

32 Huang (2008, 829) (reminding that oil companies from India, Malaysia, and the United Arab Emirates have also oil interests in Sudan).

33 Interview with Immaculate Motsi, Department of Political Sciences, University of Pretoria (22 March 2007) (hereafter Immaculate Motsi, interview).

34 Libya trains the Janjaweed militia (Immaculate Motsi, interview).

35 Bechky (2009) (recalling that the President George W. Bush raised 'grave constitutional questions' about the Darfur Divestment Act by challenging Congress to answer the question why should Congress enable state participation in US foreign policy.) President Bush nevertheless signed the Darfur Divestment bill into law.

References

Abass, Ademola (2008), 'Proving State Responsibility for Genocide: The ICJ in Bosnia v. Serbia and the International Commission of Inquiry for Darfur', *Fordham International Law Journal* 31(4), 882–85.

African Union Peace and Security Council (2005), Communiqué on the Situation in the Darfur Region of the Sudan, 3 July, ¶ 6.

African Union Peace and Security Council (2007), Communiqué of the 70th Meeting of the Peace and Security Council, 12 February, ¶14.

Allott, Philip (1990), *Eunomia: New Order for a New World* (Oxford: Oxford University Press).

Barnidge, Robert P. (2009), 'The United Nations and the African Union: Assessing a Partnership for Peace in Darfur', *Journal of Conflict and Security Law* 14(1), 93–113.

BBC (England) (2008), 'Somalia is "Most Ignored Tragedy"', 6 October, http://news.bbc.co.uk/2/hi/africa/7653928.stm.

BBC News (UK) (2009a), 'Warrant Issued for Sudan's Leader', 5 March.

BBC News (UK) (2009b), 'SLM-Minnawi Backs ICC Move Against Sudan President', Sudan Tribune, 7 March.

Bechky, Perry S. (2009), 'Darfur, Divestment, and Dialogue', *University of Pennsylvania Journal of International Law* 30(3), 823–904.

Bommenel, Alain (2007), 'No to UN Force in Darfur', *Africa and World News*, 17 February.

Central Intelligence Agency (CIA) (2009), *The World Factbook: Sudan*, https://www.cia.gov/library/publications/the-world-factbook/geos/su.html (last visited 27 September 2009).

Coicaud, Jean-Marc (2007), *Beyond the National Interest: The Future of UN Peacekeeping and Multilateralism in an Era of US Primacy* (Washington, DC: United States Institute of Peace Press).

Comprehensive Peace Agreement (CPA) (2005), Sudan-SLM/A, 9 January.

Corder, Mike (2009), 'Wanted for War Crimes in Darfur: Sudan's President', Associated Press, 5 March.

Darfur Humanitarian Profile, United Nations Office for the Coordination of Humanitarian Affairs (2008), *Darfur Humanitarian Profile No. 32* (as at 1 July), http://www.unsudanig.org/docs/DHP%2032_narrative_1%20July%202008.pdf.

Dugard, John (2005), *International Law: A South African Perspective* (Cape Town: Juta and Co. Ltd).

Euronews (2009), 'Eufor: European Troops at the Heart of an African Conflict', 29 April, http://www.euronews.net/2009/04/30/eufor-european-troops-at-the-heart-of-an-african-conflict/.

France 24 (2008), 'The Challenges of Eufor's Chad Mission', http://www.france24.com/en/20080928-eufor-chad-mission-darfur-european-force-mandate-special-report&navi=DOSSIERS (last visited 14 October 2008).

Franck,Thomas M. (2002), *Recourse to Force: State Action against Threats and Armed Attacks* (Cambridge: Cambridge University Press).

Freeman, Michael D.A. (ed.) (2001), *Lloyd's Introduction to Jurisprudence* (London: Sweet and Maxwell).

The Fund for Peace (2009), *Failed States Index*, http://www.fundforpeace.org/web/index.php?option=com_content&task=view&id=99&Itemid=140 (last visited 27 September 2009).

Greenberg, David (2009), 'African Union Declaration Against the ICC Not What it Seems', *Foreign Policy In Focus*, 6 August, http://www.fpif.org/fpiftxt/6333.

Hagan, John and Rymond-Richmond, Wenona (2009), *Darfur and the Crime of Genocide* (Cambridge: Cambridge University Press).

Hong, Mai-Linh K. (2008), 'A Genocide by Any Other Name: Language, Law and the Response to Darfur', *Virginia Journal of International Law* 49(1), 235–72.

Huang, Chin-Hao (2008), 'US-China Relations and Darfur', *Fordham International Law Journal* 31(4), 827–42.

Human Rights Watch (2006), 'Q & A: Crisis in Darfur', December, http://www.hrw.org/english/docs/2004/05/05/darfur8536.htm.

Human Rights Watch (2007), 'Sudan: Allow International Monitoring of Darfur Trials', 7 March, http://www.hrw.org/english/docs/2007/03/07/sudan15456.htm (last visited 14 October 2008).

Human Rights Watch (2009), 'ICC: Bashir Warrant is Warning to Abusive Leaders', 4 March, http://www.hrw.org/en/news/2009/03/04/icc-bashir-warrant-warning-abusiveleaders.

Institute for Security Studies (n.d.), 'Security Situation: Sudan', http://www.issafrica.org/index.php?link_id=14&slink_id=5254&link_type=12&slink_type=12&tmpl_id=3 (last visited 13 October 2008).

International Crisis Group (ICG) (2006), *Getting the UN into Darfur* (Brussels: International Crisis Group).

International Herald Tribune (2008), 'Holocaust Scholars want Al Bashir Prosecuted', 15 October, http://www.iht.com/articles/ap/2008/09/15/europe/EU-War-Crimes-Sudan-Holocaust.php.

International Peace Academy (IPA) (2002), *The Infrastructure of Peace in Africa: Assessing Peacebuilding Capacity of African Institutions* (New York: International Peace Institute).

International Rescue Committee (IRC) (2007), *Mortality in the Democratic Republic of Congo: An Ongoing Crisis* (New York: International Rescue Committee).

IRIN (2007), 'Sudan: Inter-Communal Violence Causing More Suffering in Darfur', 13 March, http://www.irinnews.org/report.aspx?ReportID=70665.

Keibida, Gafar (2006) 'Background to the Conflict', in I. Ali Hayder (ed.) *Darfur Report 2006* (Khartoum: Sudanese Study Center).

Kennedy, David (2002), 'The International Human Rights Movement: Part of the Problem?', *Harvard Human Rights Journal* 15(Spring), 245–67.

Kindiki, Kithure (2003), 'The Normative and Institutional Framework of the African Union Relating to the Protection of Human Rights and the Maintenance of International Peace and Security: A Critical Appraisal', *African Human Rights Law Journal* 3(1), 97–117.

Koskenniemi, Martti (2005), *From Apology to Utopia: The Structure of International Legal Argument* (Cambridge: Cambridge University Press).

Louis, Pierre A. (2001), 'Inconsistency and the Tragedy of Africa's Neglect', *Carnegie Council on Ethics and International Affairs Human Rights Dialogue* Series 2(5), 6 January, http://www.cceia.org/resources/publications/dialogue/2_05/articles/886.html.

Mamdani, Mahmood (2007), 'The Politics of Naming: Genocide, Civil War, Insurgency', *London Review of Books*, 8 March, http://www.lrb.co.uk/v29/n05/mamd01_.html.

Mamdani, Mahmood (2009), *Saviors and Survivors: Darfur, Politics and the War on Terror* (New York: Pantheon).

Mail and Guardian (South Africa) (2007), 'Sudan Rejects UN Peace Mission', 17 February.

Matthews, Max W. (2008), 'Tracking the Emergence of a New International Norm: The Responsibility to Protect and the Crisis in Darfur', *Boston College International and Comparative Law Review* 31(1), 137–52.

Moni, Waranya (2005), 'The UN Report on Darfur: What Role for the AU?', *Pambazuka News*, 10 February, http://www.pambazuka.org/en/category/features/26831/print (last visited October 15, 2008).

Motsi, Immaculate (2006), 'The Motives and Interests of International Presence in Sudan', Centre for International Political Studies E-briefing paper 46.

Nantulya, Paul (2004), 'Sudan: Causes of Conflict, and the Peace Process', Centre for International Political Studies, E-briefing paper 55.

Oxford Dictionary of Current English (2006) 4th edn (Oxford: Oxford University Press).

Prunier, Gerard (2005), *Darfur: The Ambiguous Genocide* (Ithaca, NY: Cornell University Press).

Reuters (2007), 'Sudan Suspends Darfur NGOs as UN Official Visits', 22 March, http://www.reuters.com/article/homepageCrisis/idUSGEO243302._CH_.2400.

Santos, Boaventura de Sousa (2001), 'The Postmodern Transition : Law and Politics', in Michael D.A. Freeman (ed.), *Lloyd's Introduction to Jurisprudence* (London: Sweet and Maxwell), 1308.

Schrijver, Nico J. (2006), 'The Future of the Charter of the United Nations', *Max Planck Yearbook of United Nations Law* 10, http://www.mpil.de/shared/data/pdf/pdfmpunyb/schrijver_10.pdf.

Taber, Katherine Pounds (2008), Bringing Peace to Darfur: Lessons of the Darfur Peace Agreement, *Houston Journal of International Law* 31(1), 171–212.

Thomas-Jensen, Colin and Spiegel, Julia (2008), 'Activism and Darfur: Slowly Driving Policy Change', *Fordham International Law Journal* 31(4), 843–58.

Trahan, Jennifer (2008), 'Why the Killing in Darfur is Genocide', *Fordham International Law Journal* 31(4), 990–1057.

Transparency International (2008), *Corruption Perception Index*, http://www.transparency.org/policy_research/surveys_indices/cpi/2008 (last visited 12 October).

UK Mission to the UN (2009), 'Sudan: International Criminal Court Issue Arrest Warrant for President Bashir', 4 March, http://ukun.fco.gov.uk/en/newsroom/?view=News&id=14683152.

UNAMID (2008), 'African Union/United Nations Hybrid Operation in Darfur', *Background*, http://www.un.org/Depts/dpko/missions/unamid/background.html (last visited 5 October 2009).

UN High Commissioner for Refugees (UNHCR) (n.d.), 'Chad: Country Operations Profile', http://www.unhcr.org/pages/49e45c226.html (last visited 3 October 2009).

UN High-Level Mission in Darfur (2007), 'Report of the High-level Mission on the Situation of Human Rights in Darfur' (advance unedited version) ¶ 27, http://www.issafrica.org/dynamic/administration/file_manager/file_links/UN_SUDAN.PDF?link_id=&slink_id=4195&link_type=&slink_type=13&tmpl_id=3.

United Nations Development Programme (2008), '2007/2008 Human Development Index Rankings', http://hdr.undp.org/en/statistics/(last visited 12 October 2008).

United Nations Secretary-General (2009), 'Report of the Secretary-General on the Deployment of the African Union-United Nations Hybrid Operation in Darfur', ¶ 9, delivered to the Security Council, UN Doc. S/2009/83.

Welch, Claude E. Jr (2006), *Protecting Human Rights in Africa: Roles and Strategies of Non-Governmental Organisations* (Philadelphia: University of Pennsylvania Press).

Yihdego, Zeray (2009), 'Darfur and Humanitarian Law: The Protection of Civilians and Civilian Objects', *Journal of Conflict and Security Law* 14(1), 35–6.

Security Council Resolutions

SC Res. 1564, ¶ 12, UN Doc. S/Res/1564 (18 September 2004).
SC Res. 1590, ¶ 1, UN Doc. S/Res/1590 (24 March 2005).
SC Res. 1591, ¶ 3(c), UN Doc. S/Res/1591 (29 March 2005).
SC Res. 1593, ¶ 1, UN Doc. S/Res/1593 (31 March 2005).
SC Res. 1674, ¶ 4, UN Doc. S/RES/1674 (28 April 2006).
SC Res. 1679, UN Doc S/Res/1679 (16 May 2006).
SC Res. 1706, ¶ 12(a), UN Doc. S/Res/1706 (31 August 2006).
SC Res. 1769, ¶ 1, UN Doc. S/Res/1769 (31 July 2007).
SC Res. 1778, ¶ 6, UN, Doc. S/Res/1778 (25 September 2007).
SC Res. 1834, ¶ 1, UN, Doc. S/Res/1834 (24 September 2008).

CHAPTER THREE

ETHICS IN FOREIGN POLICY-MAKING: US AND CHINA'S APPROACHES TO THE CRISIS IN DARFUR, SUDAN

Marcel Kitissou, John McGarrah and Pierre G. Kablan

Introduction

The irony of history is that current events portray the people of Nubia as poor and deprived of history. Actually, they have a very rich history dating back to the splendour of Ancient Egypt. They are not only victims of modern politics but are also robbed by policies that leave them by the side of the road of development and by projects that obliterate their contribution to humanity. For example, construction of dams threatens sites that represent the legacy of the history of people in the region and, therefore, constitutes a loss for world civilization as a whole.

In addition, the conflicts in Sudan in general, and the crisis in Darfur in particular, should be placed in the broader context of the Sahel region. The Sahel has been one of the oldest killing fields in the world. The Sahel can be defined as an area situated on the west coast of Africa, between Nouakchott in Mauritania and below Dakar in Senegal; it passed through Darfur and reaches the Horn on the east coast, roughly along the 13th parallel. Since the 1970s, the Sahel has moved further south and became drier. It is projected that global warming will make precipitation even less reliable in the region, thus making ecology-based conflict more likely.

It is often said that Africa looks like a gun. And the Democratic Republic of Congo (DRC) is the trigger. The Sahel has also been described as a bullet traversing the body of Africa from west to east, or *vice versa*. It is a line that both unites and divides Arabs and Blacks, Muslims and Christians (and Animists), nomads and farmers: 50 million people, poor, fighting for life, and against each other, separated by lines in the sand that are invisible and governed by traditions that are difficult for outsiders to comprehend.

Darfur is one of many – albeit smaller – conflicts in this killing field which, since the development of modern means of transportation, no longer serves as a road for long-distance trade. These conflicts, on a smaller scale, can be observed in Chad, Mali, Mauritania, Niger, Nigeria and Senegal. It is a perpetual struggle between nomads and farmers over access to grass, water and soil.

The crisis in Darfur falls into that tradition of communal strife. However, it has taken on a different dimension because of the exploitation of this endemic difficulty by the government in Khartoum and the involvement (or lack of it) by major powers.

Darfur in an Evolving World

The end of the Cold War era, with the collapse of the Soviet Union in 1991 and the emergence of a new trend of globalization, has at least 12 major implications:

1) the world is no longer separated by ideologies and the East-West competition has been replaced by a North-South struggle in which religious discourse dominates;
2) during the 10-year period between 1991 and 2001 (when terrorist attacks were perpetrated against the World Trade Center in New York City and the Pentagon in Washington, DC) arguments were made to link peace and development;
3) afterwards, thanks to the Administration of US President George W. Bush, democracy and human rights, coupled with the war against terrorism, have become global norms;
4) methods of governance, and of repression, that existed before the collapse of the Berlin Wall in 1989 lost their legitimacy, but new ones emerged after 9/11 accompanying the war on terrorism;
5) the dissolution of empires (and of Cold War-related zones of influence) created the space for new types of conflicts to emerge, from Eastern Europe to Africa;
6) the massification of poverty, particularly in many Third World countries, and the availability of light weapons make communal strife more deadly as such conflicts are, in their majority, intra-state;
7) resource-based conflicts have replaced ideology-based conflicts in the competition for access, control and retention of power;
8) the nature of warfare has been transformed by the emergence of violent non-state actors;

9) while the power base of Christianity remains in the northern hemisphere and its population base is located in the South, one witnesses an increased use of religion as an instrument of politics, power and war;
10) China has emerged as major global actor, creating international structures outside US control; this has made globalization a bifurcated phenomenon and its governance uncertain;
11) as during the Cold War era, it is not uncommon to see local political entrepreneurs exploit local divisions and international competition to their own advantage, hence making communal strife intractable;
12) African countries, for the most part, have adapted to the new global environment and coped with pressures for democratic reforms by practicing what Nicolas van de Walle of Cornell University called a partial reform syndrome, and what Marina Ottaway of the Carnegie Endowment for International Peace described as semi-authoritarian regimes (Ottaway 2003).

It is in this general international context that the conflict in Darfur, Sudan, broke out.

Darfur and the Issue of Ethics

In light of the endemic weakness of African countries in designing conflict resolution mechanisms and implementing a sustainable peace, one should examine the role of the international community in conflicts and conflict resolution on the continent. The crisis in Darfur is a typical case. If outside entities see the Darfur conflict only as an opportunity to advance their national interests by exploiting the local situation, then ethical behaviour in foreign policy is a major issue. How real is *real politik* in Darfur? This chapter will examine the issue of ethics in foreign policy-making and discuss the roles of two major players in the region, the United States and China.

Darfur and the United States

If democracy – and the ideals associated with it, such as freedom, justice and equality – is the best form of government as professed by the US for many of its foreign policy decisions, those decisions must reflect democratic principles as aims and values worthy of protection beyond the official borders of the US. Thus, ethics becomes a balancing act caused by the necessity of prioritizing a hierarchy of values or solutions over others. Many of the norms that dictate behaviour between states rely on the structures created by the Allied Powers at the end of World War II. For instance, in order to adequately describe, name and ultimately prosecute the events of the Holocaust, the term genocide was defined by a United Nations General Assembly (UNGA) Resolution in 1948. Genocide was defined as:

> Any of the following acts committed with intent to destroy, in whole or in part, a national, ethnical, racial or religious group, as such: (a) Killing members of the group; (b) Causing serious bodily or mental harm to members of the group; (c) Deliberately inflicting on the group conditions of life calculated to bring about its physical destruction in whole or in part; (d) Imposing measures intended to prevent births within the group; (e) Forcibly transferring children of the group to another group.

When considering the events in Darfur, the term to rely on is 'intent'. It seems paradoxical to even debate an idea such as 'intent' as part of an ethical component of foreign policy. On the one hand, democracies such as the US must be cautious in order to not present policy that appears militaristic, tyrannical, or oppressive towards citizens of another country. On the other hand, if democracies value life and freedom, it seems necessary to aid in the end of violence that costs lives and in the end of violation of human rights that causes suffering. The idea of genocide existing in Darfur was expressed by former Secretary of State Colin Powell in 2004 (CNN.com 2004), when he indicated that the violence in Darfur was 'coordinated', and in fact was genocide. This designation only created another ethical dilemma. Based on the Genocide Convention, when it is determined that genocide is being committed, it is the responsibility of that state/institution to end the genocide. Yet, some assume that this responsibility also requires coordinated action more than direct intervention. Thus, even when labelled genocide, there was no immediate response from the US and its allies in the form of intervention. The response by the international community came in the form of an inquiry, which concluded in 2005 that, although violence which included rape, kidnapping and murder was occurring, it lacked intent:

> Generally speaking, the policy of attacking, killing and forcibly displacing members of some tribes does not evince a specific intent to annihilate, in whole or in part, a group distinguished on racial, ethnic, national or religious grounds. Rather, it would seem that those who planned and organized attacks on villages pursued the intent to drive the victims from their homes, primarily

for purposes of counter-insurgency warfare. (United Nations Department of Public Information 2005)

While some in the US Congress agreed with the findings of the Commission of Inquiry, the Congress had already passed policy to indirectly act in Darfur. In 2004, the US Congress passed and the President signed into law the 2004 Comprehensive Peace in Sudan Act. This policy was aimed specifically at imposing sanctions on the monetary interests of those responsible for the violence, as well as providing non-military assistance to the civilians in the Sudan and neighbouring Chad and to the African Union mission to Sudan. During the course of 2005, the United Nations (UN) provided additional direction through the passage of three resolutions in the Security Council. On 24 March 2005 the UN Security Council (UNSC) unanimously passed Resolution 1590, sponsored by the US. Resolution 1590 called for the deployment of more than 10,000 military personnel to the region.

On 29 March 2005 the UNSC passed Resolution 1591, with abstentions by three countries, including China. Resolution 1591 encouraged member states to freeze assets held by Sudan within their countries and demanded an immediate cease-fire. On 31 March 2005, the UNSC passed Resolution 1593, which called for reconciliation and recommended that those responsible for the violence be held accountable by the International Criminal Court (ICC). Four countries, including both the US and the People's Republic of China abstained. The fact that the US and China are not parties to the ICC would suggest why they abstained from this resolution. Nevertheless, the US has been involved in ad hoc tribunals to prosecute individuals in several instances since Nuremberg. Even if the US and China do not recognize the jurisdiction of the ICC, the intention of the UNSC Resolution 1593 was to dictate concrete policy as a means of ending the violence in Darfur.

These policies, coupled with 'boots on the ground' provided by both the UN and the Africa Union (AU), did not resolve the conflict. In fact, as discussed when defining the problem, the UN Commission responsible for investigating the violence indicated that the situation in Darfur was not genocide. However, in January of 2005, the Sudanese government and the Sudanese People's Liberation Army (SPLA) signed a Comprehensive Peace Agreement (CPA) aimed at reallocating legitimate political authority between the South and the North and curtailing the continuing violence in the Darfur, the Western region of Sudan. While the CPA may not have had the desired effect, it was at least a starting point for further negotiations. Even though the US was involved in the creation of the CPA, the US Congress simultaneously began to discuss the effectiveness of its 2004 Bill meant to silence the conflict and aid the civilians already displaced. In 2005, two hearings held in the Congress dealt directly with the CPA and the aforementioned 2004 Act.

On 22 June 2005 the House International Relations Committee held a hearing entitled 'Sudan: Consolidating Peace While Confronting Genocide'. A member of the Committee, recent presidential candidate Ron Paul (R-TX), indicated that 'the time for name-calling is over'. Both the US and the European Union (EU) have labelled the events in Darfur as genocide. However, no intervention has taken place by these nations. The legal use of the term genocide in the international community requires countries to act, even if unilaterally, to end the genocide. At this, the House took up discussion of HR 3127, the Darfur Peace and Accountability Act. This act was, among other things, a restatement of the original Comprehensive Peace in Sudan Act of 2004. Later in 2005, during floor discussions on this bill, there was another hearing held to discuss in detail the situation in Sudan. Jendayi Frazer, the Assistant Secretary for African Affairs at the US Department of State, provided testimony that labelled the reoccurring violence in Sudan as 'intolerable'. Part of HR 3127 was the continuing monetary assistance provided to the AU and the humanitarian efforts in Sudan. This must also include accountability, provided through the AU and the resolutions proffered by the UNSC. These hearings, the 2004 Peace Act, the statements of Colin Powell which were later refuted by the IC Inquiry, and the 2005 Peace Agreement may have caused the violence to temporarily lessen, but the wax and the wane of violence required a more explicit statement.

The Darfur Peace and Accountability Act of 2006 was created and originally sponsored by Henry Hyde (R-IL) in June of 2005, although later cosponsored by 136 other representatives, most of which were Democrats. The purpose of the bill, as specifically stated, was 'to impose sanctions against individuals responsible for genocide, war crimes, and crimes against humanity, to support measures for the protection of civilians and humanitarian operations, and to support peace efforts in the Darfur region of Sudan, and for other purposes' (HR 3127). In general terms, the bill continued the sanctions against Sudan, demanded compliance with the multiple peace agreements, offered assistance to the AU and the United Nations Mission in Sudan (UNMIS) through the North Atlantic Treaty Organization (NATO) as well humanitarian assistance to the people of Sudan, and called for the promotion of peace throughout the different regions of Sudan. What made this bill different from the original 2004 Act are the specifics, which include the denunciation of the violence as genocide, thus demanding action. The bill also asked for the immediate suspension of rights of Sudan as a voting member of the UN General Assembly, the denial of visas to those complicit in the genocide and a student loan forgiveness programme for those from Sudan who would be willing to return to help with the reconstruction process.

HR 3127 was eventually passed in the House on 5 April 2006. Before it was discussed and passed in the Senate by unanimous consent in September of 2006, President George W. Bush issued an Executive Order on 1 May to isolate, freeze and annex resources held by those travelling to/from the US as well as business done by Sudan within the US. Both HR 3127 and the President's Order expanded on existing legal documentation as a means of pursuing a more aggressive foreign policy to stop the violence in Darfur. The bill was presented to the President in October of 2006 and was signed as PL 109–344 on 13 October. Even though each action of both the legislative and executive branches seems to be only continuations of existing policy, they at least name the events in Darfur for what they are and specifically list all parties responsible, i.e. those who should be held accountable.

Since that time, other hearings and debates on bills have taken place in the US Congress, but both the 2007 Sudan Accountability and Divestment Act and continuing testimony on the US response to what it labels as 'alleged' genocide deal specifically with steps the federal government has taken to deal with violence in Sudan in a domestic sense. This specifically means forbidding US companies to engage in business with Sudanese interests, and the extradition of those who are complicit in the violence that may be here in the US. In fact, in multiple 2007 hearings before Congress, Andrew Natsios, the US appointed Special Envoy to Sudan, indicated that the Bush Administration has labelled the violence as genocide, but would not directly answer whether or not he believed it to be. He also noted that negotiation was still the best way, but if it failed then the US would take 'drastic measures'. He noted that the situation required a political solution and the US could not ignore what other countries were doing (Congressional Research Service 2007).

Among the other countries present in Sudan, China plays a prominent role. The following section will discuss China's policy in Sudan and its role in regard to the crisis in Darfur.

China and the Crisis in Darfur

'Business is business. We try to separate politics from business. Secondly I think the internal situation in the Sudan is an internal affair, and we are not in a position to impose upon them', said the Chinese Deputy Foreign Minister Zhou Wenzhong in an interview with the *New York Times* on 22 August 2005.

In the era of Chairman Mao Zedong, since the 1950s, China dealt with Africa as part of a show of solidarity with countries that shared some of China's experience of Western oppression. As part of the Cold War politics, the presence of China in Africa was also to counter the West while balancing the influence of the former Union of Soviet Socialist Republics (USSR). However, these links were fostered in an ideologically charged time, when China sought to display affinity with other socialist countries and to demonstrate an almost nihilistic aversion to the institutions and norms of international relations. Although it joined the UN in 1971, any real alteration of China's foreign policy did not come until the reforms initiated by Deng Xiaoping post-1979. African countries were practically prioritized in Beijing's foreign policy after the incidents of Tiananmen Square led to blame and ostracism by Western powers. Then military adventures were by replaced by business ventures on the African continent.

Even under Deng Xiaoping, reform was piecemeal and cautious, predicated on careful changes to China's domestic political economy, which allowed for marketization of the economy while retaining a totalitarian state under the rule of the Communist Party. According to Christopher Alden, senior lecturer in International Relations at the London School of Economics, in an article for *Yale Global* magazine, China's foreign policy changed in 1993 when it shifted from being an oil exporter to being an oil importer.

Africa has been an underdeveloped but rich source of supply. The eastern giant has been willing to buy stakes in corners of the continent deemed less profitable or too difficult by the West.

Although China has always depended heavily on the Middle East for oil, it is diversifying its sources to secure its supply. As a consequence, it now imports energy from countries in Africa such as Angola, Nigeria and Sudan. In these countries, China is working hard to make sure that energy cooperation is 'win-win and mutually beneficial' enterprise.

It first established a presence in Sudan's Muglad oil fields a decade ago. By 2005, it was buying between 50 and 60 per cent of Sudan's oil exports – about 7 per cent of China's consumption needs. China has invested more than US$8 billion in joint exploration contracts in Sudan, including the construction of a pipeline from the southern oilfields to the Red Sea with a tanker terminal at Port Sudan. An estimated 10,000 Chinese are working in the country.

Ambassador Guijin stated: 'We follow five basic guidelines of peaceful coexistence in our relations: mutual respect for sovereignty and territorial integrity; mutual non-aggression; non-interference in each other's internal affairs; equality and mutual benefit; and peaceful coexistence – and these also apply to Africa.'

Perhaps most telling are the cases of Sudan and Zimbabwe, two countries that have been engaged in long-standing human rights abuses of their own citizens. China is actively and unconditionally engaged with both.

More important for Sudan, perhaps, is Beijing's political support, given the international spotlight on Darfur and on the implementation of the north-south Comprehensive Peace Agreement. When the UN Security Council wanted to take a resolution in September 2007 to punish Sudan for failing to stop atrocities in the troubled western region of Darfur, it was forced to water down the proposal to avoid a Chinese veto. China, Russia, Pakistan, and Algeria all abstained in the vote for the weaker resolution that passed by eleven to zero.

Beijing has also been accused of protecting President al-Bashir – and Chinese oil interests in Sudan – by 'repeatedly using its UN Security Council veto power to block further sanctions on the regime' (AFP, 2 February 2007). A Council on Foreign Relations January 2006 report said that China has additionally been a major supplier of weapons to Sudan, a claim elaborated upon by the June 2006 Amnesty International report, entitled 'China: Sustaining Conflict and Human Right Abuses – The Flow of Arms Accelerates'. The report revealed that an unknown number of Chinese aircraft and helicopters were supplied to Sudan in the 1990s and at least 222 military trucks were sighted in 2005. To characterize Beijing's reluctance in taking more aggressive measures to intervene in the Darfur region as solely based on petro-politics, however, would be a gross simplification of China's interests and motivations.

To be certain, China has significant energy interests in the country. Sudan's oil reserve estimates of 1.6 trillion barrels are considerable and China has invested heavily in the country's oil infrastructure. In addition to constructing numerous pipelines and refineries, the state-owned China National Petroleum Corporation is the majority owner (40 per cent) of the Greater Nile Petroleum Oil Company, the largest oil company operating in Sudan. China has also invested some $2 billion into the country's Merowe hydropower dam, which is expected to provide for all of Sudan's energy needs when it opens in 2008. According to Western sources, in January 2008, Sudan ranked as China's fifth largest oil supplier with a share of 6.5 per cent of China's oil imports (Dow Jones Newswire, 28 February 2008). Yet, Sudan's reserves, ranked 33rd in the world, are hardly as impressive as Saudi Arabia's 262.7 trillion barrels, ranked first, or Angola's 25 trillion barrels, ranked 13th. Moreover, Sudan's oil production has been slower than expected, reaching only 365,000 barrels per day (bpd) in 2006, well below the 500,000 bpd target (*Sudan Tribune*, 7

March 2008). It seems unlikely, therefore, that China's oil interests in Sudan are the sole consideration behind its actions or lack thereof.

While China's economic relations with Sudan are substantial, Sudan's share in China's overall foreign economic relations should not be overstated. In 2005, China's trade with Sudan increased by 55 per cent year-on-year (imports by 53 per cent and exports by 58.5 per cent). Yet Khartoum's share in China's total foreign trade remained between 0.2 and 0.3 per cent. China's trade with Angola and South Africa, in comparison, were more substantial. In 2004, Sudan ranked 4th on China's FDI destinations list with $146.7 million (or 2.7 percent of the total). However, in 2005, Sudan's ranking declined to eighth with $91.13 million (or 0.7 per cent of the total). Of the Chinese accumulated FDI at the end of 2005, Sudan's share was 0.6 per cent.

This by no means is an attempt to minimize China's economic involvement in Sudan. The value of China's contracted projects in Sudan in 2005 ($1.33 billion) was 83 per cent more than in 2004 ($725.65 million). It does mean that, in relative terms, Sudan is far from being a critical trading partner of China and, therefore, economic concerns are at best only a partial explanation of why Beijing protects Sudan.

On the military front, China has maintained stable relations with Sudan over the years, and as Chinese Defence Minister Cao Guangchuan asserted in his public statements, China's military, the People's Liberation Army (PLA), attaches great importance to developing relations with the Sudanese army and is ready to promote cooperation between the two sides in various fields (*Xinhua*, 31 March 2006). Nevertheless, following the implementation of the UN Security Council arms embargo in December 2005, Chinese arms sales to Sudan are likely to have been halted altogether. What should also be noted is that Sino-Sudanese military relations are far less extensive than Khartoum's relations with other governments, notably Russia. In fact, Chinese analysts, attempting to deflect recent international criticism away from China, argue that the cause behind the escalation of the Darfur conflict to what is now almost a civil war, is due in large part to the influx of modern weapons from other countries during previous regimes.

Beijing's Response to Potential Intervention

Beijing is undoubtedly interested in encouraging peace and stability in Sudan in order to create a more receptive environment for its burgeoning economic activities, but its approach differs from its Western counterparts. Following its long-standing policy of non-interference, Beijing prefers that internal conflicts be settled by the parties directly concerned (the government and its adversaries). As Beijing stated, 'Resolving the Darfur issue should be realized through dialogue and peace talks' (*Zhongguo Tongxun She*, 3 February 2007). If such a domestic attempt were to fail (or if an agreement was reached but still needed to be implemented), Beijing would then prefer that a regional organization take charge of the process. Only if the regional approach were to fail would Beijing reluctantly agree to an intervention by the United Nations, at which point it would have no choice but to become involved as well.

Reflecting its preferences, China's active involvement in Sudan's peace settlement began only after the Sudanese government and the former rebel Sudan People's Liberation Movement (SPLM) signed the Comprehensive Peace Agreement (CPA) on 9 January 2005, thereby ending 21 years of civil war in southern Sudan. On 24 March 2005 a unanimously adopted UN Security Council resolution authorized the dispatch of peacekeeping forces to the region. The Chinese were quick to comply and in May 2005, they sent their first group of peacekeepers to Sudan. A more organized Chinese detachment was deployed in May 2006 and, in January 2007, it was replaced by 435 People's Liberation Army (PLA) transportation engineers and medical troops (*Xinhua*, 18 January 2008). Stationed in southern Sudan, however, these contingents are isolated from Darfur, where the conflict continues.

The stalemate in Darfur has in fact resulted in China's support for the intervention of African Union peacekeeping forces, as well as the efforts of the Arab League. When visiting Sudan in early February 2007, Chinese President Hu Jintao said that 'the African Union and the United Nations should play constructive roles in a peacekeeping mission in Darfur' (*Xinhua*, 2 February 2008). Yet for Beijing, the situation in Darfur is fundamentally different from the one in southern Sudan. Whereas the CPA was accepted by the government as well as by the rebels – thereby paving the ground for UN peacekeeping operations – the Darfur Peace Agreement that Khartoum signed on 5 May 2006 with a main rebel faction has been rejected by other rebel groups and, consequently, has been turned down by Khartoum as well. This has been a critical factor influencing China's voting behaviour at the UN Security Council.

Beijing welcomed the 16 May 2006 agreement to hand over the Darfur peacekeeping mission from the African Union (the African Union Mission in Sudan, whose 7,000 troops had been unable to stop the Darfur atrocities and whose mandate was due to expire on 30 September 2006) to the UN Security Council by January 2007. While the Chinese delegate voted for this resolution – adopted unanimously – the delegate still expressed his country's reservations, stating: 'If the United Nations is to deploy a peacekeeping operation in Darfur, the agreement and cooperation of the Sudanese Government must be obtained. That is a basic principle and precondition for the deployment of all peacekeeping operations' (Resolution 1679).

Based on this agreement, on 31 August 2006 the UN Security Council approved the deployment of up to 17,300 troops (and up to 3,300 civilian policemen) to Darfur and 'invited the consent of the Sudanese Government … for that deployment'. Although Wang Guangya, the China's representative, supported the deployment, he insisted that the 'consent of the Sudanese Government' should have been obtained before the vote and should have been clearly included in the resolution. Since both amendments were rejected, China abstained during the vote (Resolution 1706; *Xinhua*, 31 August 2006). Sudan categorically opposed the UN peacekeeping force deployment in Darfur as 'entirely unacceptable'. As it stands, the resolution may be interpreted as allowing UN troops to move into Darfur even without Sudan's consent if it is needed to halt the atrocities in the area (AFP, 1 September 2006). Fully aware of this humanitarian crisis, Beijing offered assistance valued at 40 million yuan ($5.1 million) to improve the living conditions and the overall situation in Darfur as well as a 100 million yuan interest-free loan ($12.8 million) to the Sudanese government (AFP, 2 February 2008).

Beijing's response toward the situation in Darfur reflects not only its pragmatic approach but also its fundamental concerns and ideological principles. Beijing is certainly worried that the US-led efforts to stop human rights abuses in Sudan (and elsewhere) could at some point be directed at China itself. In addition, China is likely to be troubled by the implications that an intervention would present for its own sovereignty, national unity and territorial integrity – ideals that are highly valued by Beijing. During his most recent trip to Sudan in February 2008, President Hu Jintao introduced four principles for handling the Darfur issue. As evidence of Beijing's concerns, the first principle that Hu underlined stated: 'Respect Sudan's sovereignty and territorial integrity. Resolution of the Darfur issue will definitely benefit the process of reconciliation among ethnic groups throughout Sudan, benefit safeguarding of national unity in Sudan, and benefit regional peace and stability' (*Xinhua*, 2 February 2008). Wen Xian, a senior *People's Daily* editor, elaborated that 'any program or schemes for the settlement of the Darfur issue, if not favorable to the maintenance of Sudan's national unity, is bound to complicate the problem' (*People's Daily*, 7 February 2008). To be sure, precedents that erode the territorial integrity of sovereign states by the United Nations are unacceptable to Beijing. For instance, in a hypothetical case of a conflict in Tibet or Xinjiang, China would never permit UN peacekeeping forces onto its territory. Instead, Beijing would quickly and forcefully resolve the situation. Implicitly, this is precisely what they had expected from Khartoum: the restoration of stability at all costs.

It is Sudan's evident inability to do so, combined with the international pressure and the threats to China's economic interests, that have forced Beijing to convince Khartoum to accept the UN peacekeeping contingent in Darfur. From the very beginning, Beijing has cautioned that external intervention would only complicate the Darfur issue. As an editorial in the *People's Daily* warned, 'The situation has worsened since some Western countries are eager to "internationalize" what had been a pure internal affair of Sudan. The Darfur issue wouldn't have escalated so fast, we should say, without intervention from external powers driven by their own interests' (*People's Daily*, 12 May 2006). Denying that any US pressure has been exerted on Beijing to persuade Sudan to accept the UN peacekeeping force in Darfur, Beijing itself, though not terribly enthusiastic about the situation, ultimately favors an early settlement along these lines. Already, Chinese energy interests have been threatened, and in late November 2007, two rebel groups attacked a Chinese oil facility located between south Darfur and west Kordofan (*Sudan Tribune*, 4 March 2007).

China's special envoy to Sudan attempted to hint cautiously and delicately just before Hu Jintao's visit: 'We hope that the Sudanese side could pay attention to the international community's concern' (*Zhongguo Tongxun She*, 17 January 2008). In its reports about Hu's meeting with al-Bashir, Xinhua mentioned that the talks had been 'frank', 'candid' and 'sincere', Chinese euphemisms that reflect disagreements. Reportedly, President Hu Jintao 'has advised' al-Bashir that an efficient peacekeeping force is required to restore peace in Darfur (*The Star*, South Africa, 13 February 2008). Still, Beijing will by no means use threats, let alone approve of sanctions, to force Sudan to accept UN peacekeeping forces in Darfur and has stated that 'exerting pressure or imposing sanctions will only further complicate the issue' (*Xinhua*, 24 January 2008).

Sudan has been subject to US sanctions since the 1990s. It has been condemned in numerous United Nations resolutions, and Western firms that do business there risk alienating customers and investors. And yet a $4 billion complex of offices, parks and hotels is rising at the confluence of the White and Blue Niles, complete with the new sail-shaped headquarters of Petrodar, a Chinese-Malaysian-United Arab Emirates oil partnership. Thanks to these investors, along with Kuwaitis, Saudis, Indians and Pakistanis, Sudan's petro-economy is flourishing. In 2008, at the time of writing, the economy was expected to grow 13 per cent thanks to oil exports, most of which to China.

Thus, Sudan's government feels that it can ignore Western accusation of genocide because it has no need for Western money. But the bigger question is why China, along with Sudan's other Arab and Asian partners, feels free to trample on basic standards of governance and international norms of human rights. In spite of its records of human abuses, China's economic model rests on access to Western markets and that access cannot be assured amidst popular resentment against China's growing trade surpluses or in a world plagued by instability. Equally, China seeks acceptance at the world's diplomatic top table and, for that reason, Beijing's cause is unlikely to be advanced if China is perceived to be complicit in genocide. Newspaper advertisements leading up to the 2008 Beijing Games launched by human rights campaigners calling on the world to boycott the Genocide Olympics are a point in case.

China recently demonstrated its leverage over the Sudan, prevailing upon the regime to allow the embattled African Union force in Darfur to be supplied with better equipment. But China should join with the United States and others to broker a cease-fire in Darfur, without which even a beefed-up peace monitoring force cannot protect civilians. In recent past, fighting has intensified in the region and spread into neighbouring Chad. Refugees fled to the Central African Republic, which is embroiled in its own internal conflict. A regional catastrophe is brewing that could be worse even than the past three years of killing.

This crisis in Darfur can only be fixed by a concerted effort involving internal and international players. President al-Bashir has been able to get away with his repressive regime largely because China, a permanent member of the UN Security Council, continues to protect him with the threat of using its veto power. One major reason Beijing stands behind Bashir is oil. China is trying to diversify its oil sources beyond the crisis-prone Middle East, and Africa is one obvious alternative. Already, an estimated 7 per cent of China's imported oil comes from Sudan.

Another factor is Beijing's extreme sensitivity to any UN encroachments on national sovereignty. China fears that by assenting to UN intervention in Darfur over the protests of the Sudanese government, it might open the door to unwanted meddling in its own affairs, with regard to Tibet for example. No such precedent would be established, however, if China uses its influence with al-Bashir to win his agreement to a UN force.

China is generally thick-skinned about human rights criticisms. Its practices at home leave much to be desired, and it has never been reluctant to do business with unsavoury regimes, those particularly shunned by the West. However, genocide is a delicate matter. One indication that supports the assumption that China is now embarrassed by its association with President al-Bashir is that, when Prime Minister Wen Jiabao visited Africa in 2008, he pointedly avoided visiting the Sudan.

Surely Beijing does not want the world to see it as the main obstacle to sending a UN forces to end the killings in Darfur. Notwithstanding, right now, that seems to be the case. Other countries' roles, including that of Russia, are less visible. Given China's history of cooperation with Khartoum, if it dropped its objections, it would probably play a leadership role in helping find a peaceful resolution to the crisis in Darfur.

After four years of tireless efforts, Darfur advocacy groups have had little success in pressuring the Bush administration or any other Western government to move decisively against the Sudanese government for its atrocities in Darfur. These groups are right to dismiss the Bush administration's latest sanctions initiative as mere posturing. Like all of the President's efforts to date, it is too limited in scope and lacks a wider, more holistic diplomatic strategy. These groups are focusing instead on the two 'Cs' of humanitarian advocacy – China and celebrities – as a remedy for a crisis that has killed between 200,000 and 400,000 people and displaced more than 2.5 million. But in pointing the finger at China, proponents of stronger actions are merely helping the White House evade moral responsibility for a humanitarian disaster that it has labelled 'genocide'.

With its oil ties to the Sudanese regime and its resistance to UN Security Council resolutions condemning Khartoum, China is, in a way, a convenient scapegoat for human rights advocacy groups. Some celebrities, such as Hollywood heavyweights Steven Spielberg and Mia Farrow, have added their voices to the criticism of China. The campaign has had some results. Beijing's usual foreign policy approach – 'non-interference' in Sudan's domestic affairs – has been evolving under the pressure. China has become more active in trying to persuade the Khartoum regime to cooperate with the international community. It is willing to pursue a peace settlement and, indeed, President Hu Jintao pressured Sudanese President Omar Hassan al-Bashir on this issue and duly urged him to cooperate with the United Nations on his visit to Khartoum in February 2008. Beijing has also appointed a full-time envoy tasked with assisting in resolving the Darfur crisis.

Threatening a 'Genocide Olympics' alone would not bring peace (or peacekeepers) to that troubled region. No amount of criticism will convince Beijing to pursue a coercive strategy and a non-consensual deployment of UN peacekeepers that Khartoum rejects. China has the economic leverage to gain the ear of President Bashir, but that hardly means it has the ability – or, more to the point, the will – to bully him into accepting a large UN peacekeeping contingent in Darfur. China's multibillion dollar investments in Sudan's petroleum industry are a much-needed source of energy for its mushrooming economy. Beijing may make tactical moves to pressure Sudan, but it will not choose human rights over oil, a matter of national security.

And, even if China were capable of convincing Bashir, the Sudanese government is not the only impediment to an effective peace process. Nowadays, more people may well be dying from tribal clashes than from marauding Janjaweed or government forces. The infighting of fractured rebel groups and the sheer number of displaced people with no homes to return to are also immediate and significant obstacles to peace. China has little influence over the rebel movements and is ill-positioned to act as a neutral mediator between them because of its ties to Khartoum.

A Multilateral Approach

Ending the Darfur conflict requires much more than what China alone can offer. Positions taken by world leaders, limited Western unilateral sanctions, and promises of firmer action at some indeterminate time in the future have proven insufficient. Only a top-level, sustained, and aggressive multilateral mediation effort backed by the United States, the European Union, and African, Arab, and Chinese governments can stop the violence and reverse the massive displacement of people.

Chinese Foreign Ministry spokesman Liu Jianchao said it was understandable if some people did not understand China's policy on Darfur, though 'some people may have ulterior motives, and this we cannot accept'. He did not elaborate on what the ulterior motives might be. China has made significant changes to its policies in Sudan within the last year, appointing a special envoy to the region and sending 140 engineers to help prepare for the arrival of a planned hybrid peacekeeping force. The efforts have earned appreciation from the United States.

Realizing that its almost unqualified support for Sudan was hurting its image as peaceful and responsible global power, China balanced its thirst for oil against its international obligations and, in the process, convinced Sudan to accept UN peacekeepers on its soil.

China has quietly changed its Darfur policy from a laid-back approach to a behind-the-scene diplomacy. Before the passing of UN Security Council Resolution 1769 authorizing the $2 billion (Sh130 billion) a year 26,000-strong United Nations-African Union Mission in Darfur (UNAMID), China arranged low-key meetings with Sudan to discuss the deployment.

For a country that has been Sudan's staunchest diplomatic protector, largest trading partner and a leading investor, the shift is significant.

Beijing has asserted its role and position as a world power by mediating the Darfur crisis. Significantly, this is China's first time in its 37 years at the UN Security Council to convince a sovereign country to accept a UN peacekeeping force on its territory. Khartoum cannot afford to lose Beijing's friendship.

The 2007 United Nations Commodity Trade Statistics Database (UNCOMTRADE) records that China represents as much as 64 per cent of Khartoum's trade volume. Between 1999 and 2006, oil exports to China increased from 266,126 tons to more than 6.5 million tons. A report to European Parliament on China's energy policy in sub-Saharan Africa notes that in 2005 and 2006, China imported 47 percent of Sudan's total oil production. China National Petroleum Corporation (CNPC), the largest foreign investor so far in Sudan, channelled more than \$4 billion (Sh264 billion) into the country. It is also the main shareholder in the Greater Nile Petroleum Company (GNPC), Sudan's national oil company. Accordingly, CNPC has acquired several oil exploitation concessions with a near monopoly over a vast oil block in Darfur.

Apart from oil, Chinese companies are involved in other areas. The Petroleum and Natural Gas Exploration and Development Corporation has implemented a polypropylene exploitation project in Khartoum. Half of the shares in the Khartoum Chemical Industry Company are owned by Beijing which wholly owns the Sudanese Petrochemical Trade Project.

To its credit, China has balanced its economic interests, international pressure and security to protect its interests in Darfur and the entire region. Thus, its role in Darfur and willingness to respect the sovereignty of a partner enhance mutual business interests in the region.

China is walking a tightrope on its policy toward Sudan. On the one hand, the conflict affects China's ability to expand its economic and energy interests in the country, while it also damages China's reputation as a 'responsible stakeholder', an image that it is labouring to establish. On the other hand, China is equally supportive of Sudan's sovereign right to settle its internal affairs or agree to international intervention. China is hardly likely to surrender its foreign policy pillar of non-intervention and surely does not want to become associated with the West, least of all with the United States. Consequently, Beijing has opted for the middle road, juggling its relations with all parties according to a 'doctrine of the mean'.

Conclusion

The Iraq war, by damaging the US's image in the world and diminishing its ability to project global leadership is a demonstration that, in the current era, ethics is an instrument of foreign policy no longer left to moralists alone. Might, it seems, no longer makes right. And *real politik* has shown its limits.

On the contrary, China has been more skilful than the US in using soft power. Chinese support to Sudan in the Darfur crisis has evolved. But does it mean that China has become more ethical? It is hard to say. Had Khartoum won a quick and decisive victory, there would not have been a need for Beijing to improve its attitude. It is tempting to say that the military stalemate in Darfur is a compelling reason for China to encourage peace settlement so that business can continue as usual.

The larger international community also bears responsibility for the continued atrocities in Darfur. At one time, 'Genocide Olympics' movement was in the process of becoming overwhelmed by the situation in Tibet at the expense the 'genocide' in Darfur. There were, reportedly, fewer than 20 people killed in Tibet. There are between 200,000 and 400,000 people killed and more than 2.5 million displaced from their homes in Darfur. Still, concerns about Tibet, in the days preceding the 2008 Beijing Olympics, were louder than about Darfur. Can ethical standards be selective?

References

Amnesty International (2006), 'People's Republic of China: Sustaining Conflict and Human Rights Abuses. The Flow of Arms Accelerates', http://www.amnesty.org/en/library/info/ASA17/030/2006, accessed 30 January 2007.

Congressional Research Service (2007), *Genocide and the Rule of Law*, Hearing of the Senate Judiciary Subcommittee on Human Rights (Washington DC: Government Printing Office).

CNN.com (2004), 'Powell Calls Sudan Killings Genocide', September, http://edition.cnn.com/2004/WORLD/africa/09/09/sudan.powell/, accessed 30 January 2007.

Ottaway, M. (2003), *Democracy Challenged: The Rise of Semi-Authoritarianism* (Washington, DC: Carnegie Endowment for International Peace).

United Nations Department of Public Information (2005), *Report of the International Commission of Inquiry on Darfur (ICID) to the United*

Nations Secretary-General (Geneva: UNDPI), http://en.wikipedia.org/wiki/Commission_of_Inquiry_on_Darfur.

United Nations General Assembly (1948), *Convention on the Prevention and Punishment of the Crime of Genocide*, 9 December, http://www.hrweb.org/legal/genocide.html, accessed 30 January 2007.

Further Reading

Copson, W.R. (2007), *The United States in Africa: Bush Policy and Beyond* (London: Zed Books).

Kitissou, M. (ed.) (2007), *Africa in China's Global Strategy* (London: Adonis and Abbey).

Klare, M. (2004), *Blood and Oil: the Dangers and Consequences of America's Growing Dependence on Imported Petroleum* (New York: Metropolitan Books).

Rotberg, R.I. (ed.) (2004), *When States Fail: Causes and Consequences* (Princeton, NJ: Princeton University Press).

Salopek, P. (2008), 'Lost in the Sahel', *National Geographic*, April, 34–67.

Chapter Four

Lessons from the Failure to Rescue Darfur

John H. Weiss

Introduction: An Activist-Historian Confronts the 'Failed State' Frame

I start with a disclaimer and a clarification. Although I studied African affairs as an undergraduate, at a time when most of the states whose failure we are discussing had just emerged from colonial status, and spent a quarter of my time on African history in graduate school after my years as an Army officer, until four years ago my teaching and research at Cornell have been almost exclusively confined to the fields of modern European political and social history and the history of international relations. When this conference was first proposed, its theme was 'The Crisis in Darfur: Conflict, War, Refugees, War Crimes, the Peace Process and Reconstruction'. I thus felt that I might be able to contribute something by drawing upon the high-speed learning and relearning I have been doing while teaching a course on Sudan each semester as well as sponsoring conferences on related subjects.

Now the organizing theme has shifted to the matter of failed states in Africa and elsewhere. I welcome the introduction of cross-national comparisons. At the same time, I must specify that my contribution to this conference is given not so much from the point of view of a professional historian as it is from the point of view of an anti-genocide activist. As a scholar, however, I am engaged in writing a full-length study comparing the response to state-committed atrocity crimes in Darfur and elsewhere in Sudan with the response to similar events in Bosnia from 1992 to the present, the latter a case where I combine more extensive documentary research with a good measure of personal knowledge.

The category of 'failed state' has been a research topic examined more by political scientists and economists than by historians. Nevertheless, political figures trained in history such as Michael Ignatieff have cultivated that terrain. Ignatieff has pointed out how until the end of the Cold War both academic analysts and human rights activists focused upon strong states, especially Communist ones, as the source of threats to national security and world peace. Once the Berlin Wall fell, the emphasis shifted to weak states who could not protect their citizens and who even carried out extensive human rights violations in their attempts to avoid getting an 'F' in state-building. In a short concluding essay to a collective volume entitled *The New Killing Fields: Massacre and the Politics of Intervention*, Ignatieff (2002, 230) writes that '[n]othing enfeebled American policy more in the 1990s than the refusal to notice that untended human rights and humanitarian crises have a way of becoming national security threats'. He observes that 'Where state order disintegrates, basic economic infrastructure also begins to collapse and a new economic order begins to take root. Armed ethnic groups, bandits, and guerrilla forces take over, using violence to secure the forced allegiance of the local population and to extract the remaining surplus. As the weakening government struggles to regain control, it engages in more and more egregious attempts to terrorize the population into obedience, and rebel groups use more and more drastic forms of counter-terror to demoralize government forces' (ibid., 236). Ignatieff thus implies that such weakening governments produce unstable and criminal states which are in turn a threat to the national security of those larger, stable, and well-organized (if not democratic) states with major interests in the maintenance of international order.

Applying the 'failed state' notion to Sudan, however, produces some puzzles. Select one of the standard definitions of a state, such as that offered by political scientist Eric Nordlinger (1981, 3 and 9), that is, a collection of offices (and, as a historical phenomenon, those occupying the offices) exercising functions over a defined territory and in which the office-holders control a dominant share (if not a monopoly) of the means of violence.[1] If we take as an important measure of success the length of time those offices have exercised their functions and provided a living for their office-holders, the state of Sudan has been not a failure but a remarkable success. It certainly does not deserve to be grouped with Sierra Leone or Somalia, perhaps not even with unrecognized but independent, quite functional, and even semi-prosperous Somaliland.

Sudan: Failed State or Successful Empire?

Consider the achievements of the Sudanese state, the Republic of Sudan. It has provided continuity and functionality to an elite of office-holders since the military coup of 1989. This elite, the overwhelming majority of its top levels drawn from three towns north of Khartoum, has successfully co-opted and subordinated a small but useful number of capable operatives from almost all the political parties and ethnic groups in the country.[2] It has successfully concluded contracts with several large oil firms and kept control of the lion's share (and most of the hyenas' share) of the revenue from those firms by gaining control of both the Ministry of Energy and the Ministry of Finance in the so-called Unity Government of 2005. The economy of the provinces where its control is strongest, especially the Khartoum-Omdurman area, has been growing during the last decade at a rate between 10 and 12 per cent per annum. It has used the revenue from its oil wells, its gold mines, its overseas remittances, and its borrowings to assemble a substantial collection of weapons of war accompanied by foreign experts trained in their use

In international affairs the Sudanese state has proved triumphant. In actions referred to as genocide by scholars such as Alex de Waal, by human rights organizations, or by important governments, it has radically diminished peoples and cultures in the Nuba Mountains, the Shilluk Kingdom, Dinka territory, and Darfur.[3] Since the *jihad* that destroyed the lives and cracked the cultures of Nuba mountain people began soon after the NIF seized control of the Sudanese state in 1989, it can be pointed out that Omar Bashir and his associates, who will enter their third decade of rule next summer, lead the most enduring genocidal regime in history, eight years longer than the Nazis, ten years longer than Milošević, 16 years longer than the Khmer Rouge, and about 20 years longer than the *génocidaires* of Rwanda.

In the matters of media policy and international relations, the Sudanese state has set a standard of success that must be the envy of other authoritarian powers normally placed in the strong, stable state category, such as Egypt, Burma, or Uzbekistan. Sometimes the tactics are heavy-handed, as when journalists from Al-Jazeera were briefly imprisoned after they made what Gérard Prunier considered a fairly straightforward, unsensational documentary about Darfur in November 2004.[4] In most cases, however, the Government of Sudan (GoS) makes effective use of the tactic of permit manipulation, imposing, then denying or delaying entry permits, import permits, travel permits, photography restrictions, publication permits, or visa restrictions. After observing the Sudanese regime's masterful deployment of a broad range of techniques of bureaucratic warfare, a deployment with deadly consequences for Darfuris just as for others in the South, it would seem difficult to support a diagnosis of state failure.[5]

In its conduct of diplomacy, Sudan has outplayed its rivals while securing its position with patrons and allies such as China, Russia, and various Arab countries. Whatever may be personal antipathy for Omar Bashir on the part of some African Union officials, he has established his regime's dominance over the AU, very nearly capturing the Presidency of that organization himself in January 2007. The Government of Sudan (GoS) gained the support of

Nigerian President Obasanjo soon after the UN became publicly seized of the Darfur crisis. Obasanjo became the most prominent user of the meretricious slogan 'African solutions for African problems' and later provided Khartoum valuable service in his lamentable attempts to pressure rebel leaders at Abuja to accept the patently flawed Darfur Peace Agreement. Never losing its awareness of the essential elements of its international position, the Bashir regime has demanded, and in various forms received, deference to its claims to sovereignty from every official diplomatic visitor, from secretaries-general of the United Nations to the head of the UN Security Council to European and North American Secretaries of State, Deputy Secretaries of State, Assistant Secretaries of State for African Affairs, Special Envoys, Congressmen, Canadian senators and MPs, assemblages of prestigious former holders of high office such as the Elders, and delegations of many NGOs.[6]

Such officials were all too often swayed by some, if not all, of the key points in Khartoum's line:

1) the conflicts were merely continuations of endemic 'tribal struggles';
2) the sole consideration relevant to assessing the causes of these 'tribal conflicts' was the decades-long desiccation of the Sahel that kept decreasing the amount of land available for grazing or raising crops;
3) the government had no connection to the depradations of the janjawiid militias who did much of the destruction;
4) even if the government had given some help to the janjawiid early in the conflict, it had no control over them now;[7]
5) the rebels had killed civilians themselves, so there was 'wrong on both sides'.

This latter argument, the suggestion of moral equivalence between the government/militia destruction, where, for example, current estimates of civilian deaths run between 200, 000 and 400, 000, and opposition attacks, in which by the end of 2006 less than one thousand civilians had died, proved disappointingly influential among both commentators and international officials.[8]

Genocide Unpunished: The Consequences

Whether caused by calculated naivety, organized hypocrisy, political poltroonery, or Khartoum's successful manipulation of information and limitation of access, the failure of outsiders to respond effectively to events in Darfur has had wounding consequences that reach well beyond Sudan. As leading human rights advocates have noted, Darfur became the graveyard of 'The Responsibility to Protect'. Posited as a fundamental principle of international action in a Canadian-sponsored report of the same name in December 2001 and adopted unanimously by the UN General Assembly in 2005, the Responsibility to Protect appeared to many as the first blow against the Westphalian world order that allowed sovereign states to treat their own populations any way they wished. It died in Darfur, where the disinclination of officials from all governments to take the slightest political risk to enforce it became as clear as did their casuistic skill in arguing that it did not apply. One wonders how many of the diplomats voting to adopt it at the UN World Summit took it seriously in the first place.

More serious was the blow struck to the attempt to use an international convention to prevent the crime of genocide. On 9 September 2004 Secretary of State Colin Powell, testifying before the Senate Foreign Relations Committee, announced that the Bush Administration had concluded that the Bashir regime had committed genocide. Because the UN Convention on the Prevention and Punishment of the Crime of Genocide, to which the United States had become a state party in 1988, was taken by many to require that states take action to punish perpetrators, the Senators then asked Powell if he thought current policy commitments of the Bush Administration were sufficient to deal with the matter. Powell answered that that such actions as were currently being taken were sufficient (US Senate Foreign Relations Committee 2004).

What was actually being done in Darfur at the time was the slow deployment of 300 underequipped African Union troops. The mandate the UN granted these troops, however, did not allow them to take actions that would stop the genocide, but merely to monitor a long-shattered ceasefire and to protect a group of about 80 unarmed observers.[9] The African Union, moreover, never showed any inclination to report that for the purpose of protecting civilians their mission was all but useless. Only in July 2005, at a meeting in Dakar, did the Foreign Minister of Senegal, Cheikh Tidiane Gadio, blow the whistle on the African Union's deadly charade. He directly confronted Secretary of State Condoleezza Rice, who had just claimed that the African Union had averted 'the humanitarian disaster that was forecast'. Pointing out that 'the militias are still very active ... killing people, burning villages, raping women', he tried to explode the myth that the African Union troops alone could stop the killing (Rice 2005).[10]

The four-year-long American failure to take any effective action after a finding of genocide establishes, then, a most disheartening precedent. Turning the 1948 Convention into a compelling call to action on the part of its signatory states is goal for which human rights activists have striven for more than half a century. The Bush Administration and the Congress chose, however, to place their hopes for the end of the genocide in an untested, two-year-old organization of dubiously governed states, a grouping that succeeded the Organization of African Unity, which itself had previously been unwilling to stop genocides in several of its members.[11]

The consequences of the failure for the victims, the members of the several peoples and cultures of Darfur that have been radically diminished, can be outlined briefly: lives of enduring deprivation and boredom in a desolate archipelago of camps for displaced peoples stretched across Darfur and eastern Chad. Those not in the camps have not escaped entirely the subordination and surveillance of the officials of the aid agencies or the Khartoum regime who run the camps in Darfur, however, for the populations of the adjacent towns or the hiding places in woods and wadis have also become dependent on the resources brought to the camps from abroad.[12] In the more fortunate camps the warehouses will continue to improve: America-based corporations receiving the contracts to build more permanent structures have expressed their satisfaction with the competence of the Khartoum-based companies to which they have subcontracted the work.[13] What flourishes not at all in any kind of warehouse, however, is hope, the expectation that someday the inhabitants will have an opportunity to express their humanity by reasserting a measure of control over their own destiny, nourishing their capacity for the creation of culture, and seeking to acquire justice and recompense.[14]

The preference of American government authorities for rhetorical tokens over really effective action suggests that even arguments from a realist perspective, those which consider only a narrowly defined national interest, have little weight in moving policy.

1) For instance, the Gaza Strip is just one example of the widely accepted proposition that confining an aggrieved population of refugees to a prison-like space for a long period of time has as its most dependable result the creation of a toxic political culture. In general, moreover, refugee concentrations destabilize the environs, if not the entire region. Echoing Ignatieff, prominent analysts such as the *New York Times*' Nicholas Kristof (2005) have argued that such instability in Sudan is a threat to the American national interest, but statements about Darfur from the American Administration have seldom mentioned the problem.
2) The Sudan's close relationship with Iran has produced Iranian confidence that in the former country it can find an ally and an eager customer for its

'nuclear technology', which President Ahmadinejad has already offered the Sudanese even though the Iranian program does not yet have a fully developed nuclear capacity. This prospective nuclear tryst between the two nations, both treated as pariahs by many of the world's most powerful countries, has certain features in common with the cooperation between Germany and the Soviet Union after World War I. Both also treated as pariahs by the Allies, they agreed at Rapallo in 1922 to cooperate for each other's mutual economic benefit. Secretly, the Soviets helped Germany evade the Treaty of Versailles by allowing German pilots and other specialists to train on its soil.

3) Sudan is almost certainly playing a double game in the matter of terrorism. On the one hand, it acts as a partner in the so-called 'war on terror', feeding to the CIA tidbits of information gained from its surveillance of followers of Osama Bin Laden who stayed behind after he left Sudan in 1996. On the other, it trains, in camps outside Sudan, selected janjawiid leaders to become themselves potential enforcers of Khartoum's will by terrorist tactics directed not only against Darfuris but against perceived opponents of the regime in Europe and America. Judging from the reaction of officials within the American national security establishment to information about this training conveyed from janjawiid defectors, the regime's ventures to this particular dark side are no secret to Washington. Yet the double game is allowed to continue, and no one has called out Sudan on the matter.

Rhetorical Failures

Many actors in the Darfur drama make their calculations on the basis of considerations other than those of the national interest as defined by the realist school, however. Herein lies one important explanation for the weakness of the attempts to remedy and rescue. These latter groups articulate their goals within several discourses that differ substantially in their specificity, their susceptibility to measurement, and their ability to mobilize those with the power to take actions that might dissolve the archipelago of displaced-person camps and renew Darfuris' ability to control significant aspects of their political and cultural life, two indicators this chapter has chosen to represent ending the genocide.

Even those who speak of 'ending' or 'stopping' the genocide move in differing locations on the linguistic terrain. Some assert that they place highest value on the maintenance of the variety of the human fabric, the brightness and integrity of the tiles in the world's mosaic of cultures. To those holding these convictions, the Darfur disaster appears as the latest in a series of episodes that have placed whole peoples on the endangered species list.[15] Such expressions of high and serious rhetoric can have considerable impact upon the general public, as they should. They are certainly improvements over appeals that never get beyond requests that high officials 'do something', 'hold a summit' (as if an assembly of high officials would in itself prompt Khartoum to call off its enduring, multifaceted warfare against the Darfuri people), or 'save Darfur'. Their effectiveness diminishes, however, if the officials empowered to accomplish such goals find themselves unable to introduce such sharply imaged declarations of value into a discourse of national interest calculations or operational decisions in such a way as to have an influence upon the setting of policy priorities.[16]

The drafters of the Convention on the Prevention and Punishment of the Crime of Genocide avoided metaphorical language in favour of legal phrasing. They define the crime as any of a set of acts 'committed with intent to destroy, in whole or in part, a national, ethnic, racial, or religious group as such' including 'deliberately inflicting on the group conditions of life calculated to bring about its physical destruction in whole or in part'. This language, when adopted by courts such as the International Criminal Tribunal for the Former Yugoslavia and the International Criminal Tribunal for Rwanda, has been sufficient to convict men such as Radislav Krstic and Jean Kambanda of the crime of genocide.

In the case of Darfur an approach based on the Convention's legal language has been less successful. The UN Commission of Inquiry appointed to investigate the situation in Darfur, perhaps wishing to avoid a repeat of the dangerous American precedent in which a finding of genocide was followed by inaction, concluded that it could not make a finding of genocide because not enough evidence of intent 'at least on the part of the central government', had been educed (Commission of Inquiry on Darfur 2005, 2–3). The Government of Sudan initially welcomed the report in a triumphant tone, until they had a chance to reflect on the full text, which found ample evidence in Darfur of genocide's companions in the category of atrocity crimes: crimes against humanity and war crimes.

If the Commission's grounds for declining to find evidence of genocide were based upon its lawyerly reading of the terms of the Convention, the reasons that certain aid organizations and human rights groups did not adopt the term are not yet fully known. Sources close to Médecins Sans Frontières have nevertheless claimed that when MSF President Jean-Hervé Bradol rejected the notion that genocide was occurring in Darfur, the resulting uproar within the top ranks of the organization nearly produced a lasting split.

Amnesty International's London headquarters also faced numerous attacks for its refusal to assert genocide despite the fact that its reluctance to criticize regimes was a well known part of its standard policies.

An examination of blogs, websites, written statements put out by various organizations, and presentations made at various conferences suggests that certain activists and analysts who claimed that genocide was not taking place in Darfur held an exclusive and limited notion of genocide. They often made it explicit that not the Convention's definition but mental images of previous genocides served as templates to which the events in Darfur did not seem to fit: no gas chambers; no Nazi *Einsatzgruppen* or Serb commandos machine-gunning lines of victims; no mounds of machete-sliced bodies piled up in churches or along roads.[18] Rapid and extensive massacres certainly occurred, but Darfur's remote location assisted skilled and strenuous efforts by the GoS to limit access to the region while claiming that no significant killing was taking place. Thus even the evidence provided by satellite images of burned-out, deserted villages may not have had a convincing impact on those who sought to determine if mass slaughter had occurred. The images did not show killing. Do photographs showing that targeted populations have been uprooted because their village has been burned to the ground, emptied completely of instruments of living, their wells poisoned to insure that they do not return, present direct, visual evidence of the 'deliberately inflicting on the group conditions of life calculated to bring about its physical destruction in whole or in part?' (Convention on the Prevention and Punishment of the Crime of Genocide, Article 2 (c)). It takes a modicum, if only a modicum, of imagination to realize that many individual expellees will die from starvation, disease, later conflict, or despair as a result of these actions and that, as a distinct people, the Fur, Zaghawa, Massalit, Dajo, or other groups will be partly destroyed. Novelty in methods and timing seems to have blinded would-be rescuers to what John Prendergast (Prendergast and Cheadle 2007), one of the leading activists, has termed 'genocide in slow motion'.

A full explanation for the avoidance of the genocide designation on the part of some of those who addressed the Darfur disaster lies beyond the scope of this paper. The importance of the variation in the discourses used by these groups must be pointed out, however, because it had a damaging effect on the attempt to specify a common set of objectives for rescuers. When Darfur first gained the attention of the international media, it was framed not in the legal/political language of the Convention on Genocide, which for most readers entailed specific contractual obligations, [19] but in two more open-ended languages, that of humanitarianism and that of human rights. Mukesh Kapila, the UN official who first went public about the events, stated to the press that this was 'the world's greatest humanitarian crisis' and that it was 'a human rights catastrophe on a par with Rwanda' (LeBor 2006, 162).

One can argue about whether or not these two languages, through their historical patterns of use by technical professionals or by journalists, skirt the edge of euphemism. The Indian Ocean tsunami of December 2004, also called a humanitarian crisis, could be evoked to place the Darfur disaster in a comparative framework with completely different moral and political reference points. Calling politically or ethnically motivated murder a human rights violation, moreover, inserts the act into the broader set of actions that have come to occupy the agenda of the human rights movement, but it also may move the act to a higher level of abstraction and therefore to increase the emotional distance between describer and victim.[20] One must ask, moreover, if it benefits the victims of genocidal murder and rape to have such acts inserted into a continuum of violations that includes the violation of the right to education or health care. What is more certain is that ending a humanitarian crisis and ending human rights violations are goals which are both dangerously general and open to widely varying interpretations. If the victim populations, within or dependent upon camps, suddenly were able to receive WFP-approved allocations of food or water and UNHCR-approved supplies of tents or bricks, and the 10,000 aidworkers (but not the Darfuris) could travel about freely, the press, or perhaps the humanitarian organizations, might even stop speaking of a humanitarian crisis. But the radical diminishing of peoples and cultures would not have ended.

Double Roots: the Nature of the Genocidal in Sudan

If the failure of some to see that the events in Darfur constitute a genocide has helped to weaken and dilute the campaign to help the victims of violence, an analysis which sees a single dominant motive behind the actions of Bashir's regime risks the defeat of any consequent policy recommendations. The racism of Arab supremacist ideology has rightfully commanded attention as an originating and mobilizing element. The US State Department's analysis of the report of the Darfur Atrocities Documentation Team, the principal basis for the Bush Administration's finding of genocide, stated that 'numerous credible reports corroborate the use of racial and ethnic epithets by both the janjaweed and GoS military personnel: "Kill the slaves! Kill the Slaves!" and "We have orders to kill all the blacks" are common' (Totten 2006, 200).[21] The Arab Gathering (Tajamu al Arabi), formed by the Libyans in the 1980s and taken over by the Bashir regime soon after the 1989 coup that put it in power, became a principal instrument in elaborating the ideological basis for the genocide, promising to 'change the demography' of Darfur in order to establish the domination of the racially pure Arabs.[22] Violent destruction of the lives and property of non-Arabs, and their violent uprooting, coincides, moreover, with non-violent GoS Arabization policies. Arabs from Egypt, Niger, Burkina Faso, Chad, Mali, and elsewhere receive instant citizenship, financial aid, privileged job placement, and land allocations. At least forty thousand have now been settled at the sites of villages from which the non-Arab Darfuris have been expelled. The tribal makeup of the IDP and EDP populations provides final proof of the racial basis of the Government targeting: the only Arabs to be found in the camps are those, like members of the Targam, who have lost out in battles over land with other Arab tribes (International Crisis Group 2007, 3).

An explanation for the campaign of killing and uprooting based solely upon the targeting of non-Arabs as non-Arabs contains important weaknesses, however. It tends to suggest a dangerously oversimplified view of the nature of intergroup relations and personal hierarchies of identities in Sudan. Especially in North Sudan and the Khartoum region, intermarriage between Arabs and non-Arabs is not uncommon.[23] Within the numerous Khartoum-area universities, tribal identities were often less important than other distinctions in patterning friendships. Members of the targeted tribes, such as the Fur, could be found holding government offices even before the Darfur Peace Agreement of May 2006 incorporated Minni Minawi's Zaghawa-dominated rebel faction . Although a large number of non-Arabs serving in the Sudanese Army, finding themselves discriminated against in matters of promotion and assignment, joined the Darfur rebels, the regular Sudanese army (SAF) remains about 40 per cent Darfuri, both Arab and non-Arab, and as such has engaged the South in the long civil war.

Relations between Arabs and non-Arabs in Darfur have in fact always been characterized by conflict *and* cooperation. In the recent Government-rebel conflict discussed in this chapter the majority of the Arabs in Darfur have distanced themselves from both rebels and government.[24] The notorious janjawiid militias were recruited largely from the Abbala (camel-herding) Northern Rizeigat, especially the Mahamid branch led by Musa Hilal, some of the smaller Arab tribes (Taalba, Hotiya, Al Rawas, Bahadi, Saada), and Arab convicts released from prison on the condition that they would join the militias. The region's largest tribal grouping, the Southern Rizeigat, consistently refused to join in the fight against Darfuri rebels (ICG 2007, 9).

Reducing the Darfur conflict to a clash between Arab *génocidaire* and non-Arab victim risks stereotyping *all* Sudanese Arabs as perpetrators, freezing a dynamic situation into a dichotomous frame, and exacerbating the divisions between groups in Darfur. ICC prosecutor Moreno-Ocampo's request for the indictment of Bashir attempted to avoid such stereotyping by individualizing the responsibility, accusing only Omar al-Bashir, the President of Sudan, but the language of his report conformed to the language of the convention: 'Al Bashir intends to destroy in substantial part the Fur, Masalit and Zaghawa ethnic groups as such'. The society that constituted the Darfur region, an independent sultanate for three centuries before 1916, a distinct pattern of economic and cultural interactions between many groups and many groupings of individual identities, discrete sets of loyalties and affinities, the core of the West of the East-West division posited by those anthropologists who challenged historical interpretations organized only around the North-South division, did not seem to fit the International Criminal Court's Convention-based definition of a 'national, ethnical, racial, or religious group'. If Moreno-Ocampo had included 'Darfur as a whole' in his list of victims, along with the Fur, Massaleit, and Zaghawa, he would have presented a more complete picture of what was lost when Khartoum unleashed its armies, its aircraft, and its militias. A punctilious reading of the ICC's charter might not have made such a locution as 'Darfur as a whole' seem acceptable as a targeted group, but the listing of non-Arab tribes as the only victims risks unintentionally promoting in the popular mind the equation of 'Arab' with 'perpetrator'. Such a conflation could then block the recognition of any changes in attitude and loyalty offering opportunities for Arab-non-Arab alliances and reconciliation, as will be discussed further below.

Attacking Darfur's non-Arab inhabitants achieved an objective paramount for *many* of Sudan's leaders: the maintenance of Arab domination. For *all* of Sudan's ruling elite (and for many in the capital who were members of the coalition of erstwhile regime opponents who joined the government bloc in the Unity government), a broader, more general goal has driven its action: the monopolization of power and resources at the center. Khartoum has always behaved not as the capital of a nation-state but as the central city of an unusually predatory empire. The peoples of its internal colonies, whether in the South, the Nuba Mountains, the East, or Darfur, have been regularly attacked, raided for slaves, press-ganged for cannon fodder, sucked into its industrialized agricultural schemes to become Africa's most regimented rural proletariat, seduced by Khartoum-Omdurman's hoard of cultural capital (i.e., all of Sudan's important schools and universities) into becoming encapsulated future servants of the regime, or abandoned to foreign aid organizations.

For Sudan's internal colonies, then, the choices have been to submit, to accept the suffering of marginalization, or to fight. Only the force of arms can provide autonomy or independence. When in mid-1989 the elected government of Sadiq al-Mahdi was about to make a peace granting a measure of self-rule to the South, Bashir and his National Islamic Front staged their coup.

To maintain its monopoly, the Sudanese empire has demonstrated considerable resourcefulness and flexibility in technique. When the Nuba mountains threatened Khartoum's supremacy, Bashir played the Islamist card, proclaiming himself 'imam of the jihad', promoting the attacks on the peoples of those mountains in central Sudan as a holy war.[25] For several years his government was able to conceal from the world that a substantial proportion of the victims of its attacks were in fact practicing Muslims (de Waal 1995, 286–95). In the case of Darfur, assuring the centre's continued monopolization of power and resources faced obstacles: the people were almost all Muslim; transporting first-line ground troops and their weapons to distant Darfur was especially costly; the loyalty of the available SAF troops, more than a third of which were Darfuri, could not be guaranteed; and the war against the SPLA in the South and the Nuba mountains was not concluded, only suspended. The solution was to pay and equip local Arab militias, promise them loot and land, assure them that the zurga were not real Muslims, and back them up with government aircraft (flown often by Eastern European mercenaries) and, when needed, the armoured vehicles of the Popular Defense Forces.

In this manner Bashir and his associates successfully launched the genocide. If someone had interviewed the directors of the campaign at the time, they would have probably have agreed with the characterization of their actions by Darfur expert Alex de Waal as 'counterinsurgency on the cheap'.[26] A counterinsurgency that targets civilians, however, in particular those who are members of a particular ethnic group, becomes an atrocity crime.[27]

On 19 May 2004, after 14 months of deadly rampage, Bashir went to Nyala to review the janjawiid, 'equipped with their racist ideology and warrior culture', as they 'paraded past him astride their fierce horses, shouting and brandishing their automatic weapons' (Collins, 2004, 10). As the following years made clear, however, Khartoum never reestablished effective rule in the region. Rebel groups retained control of most of the countryside, inflicted upon the GoS forces defeats bad enough to cause major mutinies, and were able to use Darfur as a staging area for a 400-vehicle attack on Sudan's capital on 10 May 2008. Since 2004 Darfur has remained in chaos, destructive violence, and deprivation.

The Political Uses of Chaos

Khartoum has found a way to make this kind of outcome, spawned by both its neglect of Darfur and its genocidal attacks on the region, serve well its overall goal of the monopolization of power and resources and its corollary, the marginalization of the periphery. Khartoum's contribution to the collective primer on how to prosper as rulers of a murderous state would fit well in a chapter entitled 'the instrumentalization of turbulence'. The cost of bringing order and security (not to mention development) to its western provinces, with an area larger than that of France, has always seemed too high to a regime accountable only to itself, its ideology, and, secondarily, to the Lumpenproletariat element within the riverain population, the *awlad-al-bahar*, ready to pack its rallies and demonstrations. Not development but 'counterinsurgency on the cheap' recommended itself all the more highly when it could be joined with polished techniques in the fields of bureaucratic warfare, media manipulation, diplomatic deception, and world-class skill at destruction by delay. Those within the elite who might have been indifferent to their Arabizer colleagues' racist project to diminish the Fur, Zaghawa, or Massaleit were nevertheless attracted to the low price tag of the janjawiid-plus-bombs approach when it was supplemented by a knowledge of how to use negotiations to increase the disorder. In the case of Sudan the two motivations, Arab supremacy and the maximum engorgement of the center, have combined to produce a single result: radical diminishing of the peoples and cultures of Darfur, a.k.a. genocide.

As long as Darfur remains in chaos, the political and economic security of the Bashir regime seems likely to endure. The beneficiaries of the capital district's economic boom, unrivalled in Africa, will survey their blossoming skyscrapers from the comfort of their air-conditioned malls, replying to those outsiders who would call them to the task of redressing Darfur's grievances: 'Let us enjoy our oil'.[28]

Insecurity, disorder, and division among opponents offer other advantages. Diplomats sent to advise and reporters sent to observe remain all the more befuddled and bereft of a sense of how things might move forward. Chaos sets conditions whereby the responsibility for its creation can easily seem to have many authors. The fragmentation of the opposition to Khartoum, especially that within the armed rebel groups, has provided a major obstacle to those in search of a negotiated peace. Some analysts have argued, however, that it also serves an excuse: the degree of fragmentation of Khartoum's opponents is regularly exaggerated.[29]

The United Nations' plan to deploy peacekeeping troops to Darfur has, in addition, offered the GoS a way to calibrate its management of the disorder. The 'hybrid' force is made up of units that served in the African Union mission in Darfur, supplemented by additional units from African countries.[30] Authorized to reach a final total of 26,000, it has currently deployed some 9,700 soldiers and police during its first nine months of operation. Although it has a mandate to use force to protect civilians, few cases have emerged where it has done so: the pattern of passivity followed by the African Union has continued.[31] Prospective donor countries, asked to supply attack helicopters – although most of the hybrid force units are not even supplied with flashlights – have been understandably hesitant to give equipment to a force whose prospects for even minimal progress toward fulfilling its peacekeeping and security missions seem so dim.

On the other hand, the UNAMID hybrid force provides valuable service to the Government of Sudan. The GoS never did devote many resources to the repression of banditry, but now UNAMID must get involved in it to assure the delivery of humanitarian aid. More importantly, UNAMID supplies Khartoum with intelligence about the activities and deployment of rebel forces by way of its supervision of the joint rebel-GoS committees that are set up to investigate incidents and mediate local disputes.

Moreover, the GoS can regulate easily the activities of the international force. UNAMID cannot travel to many destinations without the permission of the GoS; the GoS controls its communications; and it cannot make arrests of militia members without GoS agreement. Its interpretation of its protection mission apparently includes guarding, escorting, and monitoring, but it has not yet taken action in accordance with a more proactive definition of protection, one regularly used in military operations by NATO members, which gives primacy to the location of proximate threats and their isolation and neutralization. Finally, the inferiority of UNAMID's weaponry renders it vulnerable to attack by almost any armed group present in Darfur. In short, dominated by the GoS and deprived of the ability to conduct military operations of any size, it has become Khartoum's tame auxiliary police force. The regime was undoubtedly well aware of the limitations of UNAMID, as well as its potential usefulness, but it gained considerable political capital with its domestic constituency by its displays of nationalistic anger at the UN resolutions authorizing the force and during the noisy negotiations with the UN over the arrangements for the execution of its mandate.

Once the UN members signed on to resolutions such as 1706 and 1769, which envisioned a United Nations takeover of the peacekeeping mission in Darfur, the countries sponsoring the resolutions rapidly diminished the attention they gave to other possible courses of action. The positions of the engaged governments are now reasonably clear. The UN's Department of Peacekeeping Operations struggles to deliver some benefit to victim populations despite the inherent political constraints that confine its efforts to tokenism. UN officials ritualistically complain that the DPKO is not getting support from the UN's more powerful sovereign members while fully aware that its missions have always served as an excuse for the big powers to avoid having to take any serious political or military risks themselves. The Bush Administration has made it clear several times in several ways that preserving its counterterrorist intelligence feed from Khartoum trumps any attempts to save Darfur. It will study all kinds of policies, but in the end it will do nothing to which the GoS might seriously object. The Harper Government interprets Canada's longstanding commitment to conducting international interventions only within a multilateral framework to mean that in the case of Darfur the United Nations is the only True Path to salvation.[32]

Activist organizations signal their frustration by redefining their missions from rescuing Darfur to understanding and stopping atrocity crimes everywhere. The multiplicity of objectives – and the failure to discuss boundary problems, priorities, or overlapping points between them – hinders the accomplishment of any of them. Do those trying to aid Darfuris wish to stop the genocide, bring total peace and security to Darfur, change the regime in Khartoum, create democracy, federalism, and the rule of law in all of Sudan, put the ranking perpetrators on trial, or just put enough medical buildings, suitable homes, and food supplies in the camps so that the humanitarian crisis can be declared ended? No two of these goals are identical and several could be seen as conflicting. Very rarely have groups engaged each other in discussions of the relationship of one to the other.

Some Steps to a Better Outcome

Meanwhile, the radical diminishing of the peoples and cultures of Darfur – a way to describe events there that is more inclusive, but perhaps also less controversial, than 'genocide' – enters the mid-point of its sixth year. Proposals about how to begin to reverse this diminishing that take into account the political and intellectual obstacles described above are surprisingly rare and in need of considerable examination and evaluation. Nevertheless, having responded to Ignatieff's observation that weak states, not the strong states of the Cold War, have generated the worst recent human rights violations by depicting Sudan as not a weak state but as a successful, exploitative empire-state that has made the cultivation of chaos in its internal colonies a vital instrument of its repressive rule, I am obliged to propose some steps to a solution.

1) *Listen to the Darfuris themselves*. After five years of reporting about events in Darfur, we still have information about the political attitudes, knowledge, and goals of only a tiny sample of its inhabitants or of the Darfuris outside the region. Some of the leaders of the larger rebel movements and armed groups have presented demands and articulated political visions during negotiations with the GoS, and one can find entire constitutions on some of the groups' websites.[33] One can gain only the faintest idea, however, about how much support these proposals of the leadership command in the remainder of the population. Selected groups of leaders of some of Darfur's civil society organizations have been consulted on a few occasions, but there has been nothing systematic about these meetings, no rapporteur was assigned, and no effective use has ever been made of the outcomes. The entire process of surveying and consulting will need to be conducted on a scale and with a fund of resources much larger than any previous attempt.[34]

   Of the many sectors of Darfuri society who have not been surveyed or consulted, probably the most important is the constellation of tribes, clans, and sections, constituting approximately one-half the population of the region, who identify themselves as Arabs. Since the summer of 2006 evidence has emerged that failure to connect with Arab opinion risks missing a major opportunity for an alliance of Arab and non-Arab in opposition to the Bashir regime. In the words of one of the best-informed analysts of Darfur society, relations between Darfuri Arabs and the Government, and between Arab armed groups who fought for the Government and their previous non-Arab opponents, have undergone a 'seismic political shift' (Flint 2007; see also Flint and de Waal 2008, 252–62).[35] Alienated from the GoS for various reasons, certain Arab groups were already beginning to form alliances with rebel groups who had originally been their opponents. Two social analysts who had visited Darfur in the violent summer of 2004 returned two years later to conduct followup interviews with the same Arab and non-Arab notables. On the side of the non-Arabs, the language of the victims had shifted. Early in the conflict, the focus of anger was on the janjawiid militias and 'Arabs' in general. By the summer of 2006, feelings had changed. Those who organized the violence were now the villains. Darfuris, both tribal leaders and ordinary citizens, stressed that the Government in Khartoum was their enemy, not the 'Arabs'(Fadul and Tanner 2007, 294).

2) *Empower Darfuri leaders.* Any attempt to take advantage of this opening for a realignment of forces will need to do more than analyze the results of opinion surveys. Persons with skills that could make them effective leaders will need to be identified and trained. The cadres of important rebel groups, realizing their need for training in negotiating skills, visited the leadership of the SPLA in Juba in the months after the end of the failed peace negotiations in Abuja. As the history of the maturation of the Sudan Peoples Liberation Movement indicates, the development of an empowered political class in Darfur may be a slow process. To those who entered political activity before 2002 will have to be added those who demonstrated initiative and organizing capacity not only on the battlefield but in the IDP and EDP camps, the universities in Khartoum, the worker communities around Port Sudan, and the Diaspora.
3) *Provide protection and security assistance* to the identified leaders, bringing about meetings of the leaders and possible leaders of Darfur, probably in the presence of representatives of the South, but without the subversive presence of Khartoum's representatives, will require both external force that poses a credible threat – something the UN has never provided in its entire history – in order to impose an unacceptable cost upon the GoS for any attempt to prevent the meetings by threatening, arresting, or killing prospective participants. Whenever it could learn of assemblies of rebel leaders occurring without its own agents being there, the GoS has bombed them. The text of the Darfur Peace Agreement incorporated so-called Darfur-Darfur Dialogue and Consultations, but they have been regarded by most as harmless but pointless airings of opinions. In any case, they have had no power to enforce any decisions or provide any security to vulnerable populations.

Since it is virtually certain that an assembly of Darfuris would end up demanding some form of autonomy within a federal Sudan, at least as much self-government as was granted (on paper) to the South,[36] the objective of the meetings would probably be to enact that autonomy by creating an interim regional administration. Actually to implement the installation of a regional administration, however, might require the assistance of serious external military force. Neither hapless, virtually unarmed UNAMID forces nor, of course, units from Khartoum can be expected to be much help in providing the security civilians will need to begin returning to the sites of their homes or otherwise rebuilding lives interrupted by the genocide.

It is not easy to locate precedents for the type of joint action between troops employing advanced weaponry and a readiness to use it and diplomats or expert advisors equipped with advanced local knowledge and sufficient resources to apply it in the creation of post-genocidal institutions. The military unit will have to demonstrate its capability to impose an unacceptable cost on Khartoum if it attempts to undermine the constitution of the interim regional administration and at the same time be ready to act later as a robust policing force taking guidance from that administration as it works out ways to establish sufficient security on the ground. Recent history suggests that the usual practice has been to conceive of a universe of possible cases containing only two very different combinations: standard limited-scale UN peacekeeping/monitoring directed entirely from UN headquarters and something like Iraq, where full-scale, large-unit intervention was controlled entirely by the intervening countries and the nation-building activities were radically subordinate, underplanned and under-resourced.

However, Operation ARTEMIS in 2003, where 1,800 European Union troops, supported by French aircraft, stabilized a much-deteriorated situation in Bunia (eastern DRC) in three months, may offer useful lessons. Even more applicable ideas can be found in the case of the first months after the American intervention in Afghanistan began in October 2001. While the joint American-Northern Alliance operation kept Taliban forces from interfering, experts with deep local knowledge selected important Afghan leaders, took them to Bonn, and produced an Interim Administration and a draft constitution in less than a week. Afghan's nascent army, NATO, and US forces then provided security during the grand council (*loya jerga*), that provided Afghanistan with a constitution and a far more representative government than it had ever had before. Finally, the Kosovo intervention of 1999 provides a case in which military action and diplomacy were both heavily resourced and pursued in tandem. The operation's outcome did not fit a peace-and-development idealist's model. It did not make Kosovo a Canada, a Switzerland, or a Costa Rica. Nor did it bring about immediate regime change in Serbia. But it shut down Milošević's genocidal project. In contrast, the Sudanese empire-state, never confronted with a combination of serious political and military resources dedicated to saving Darfur, can contemplate a promising future not as a failure but as a model for would-be *génocidaires* of the twenty-first century.

Notes

1 To insist on the full Weberian definition of a state, which includes a *monopoly* of the means of force, would risk having to list states without control of substantial parts of their peripheries such as Pakistan or Moldova, or states with large internal areas where their writ does not run, such as gang-controlled central Honduras or rebel-dominated southern Colombia, as non-states, a move that mapmakers and UN officials might find disturbing. Adding 'legitimate' before 'force', moreover, seems to beg the question.

2 The fact that the Sudanese state is dominated by a narrowly recruited northern elite was pointed out by associates of Sudan's dominant political mentor and *eminence grise*, Hassan al-Turabi, after his 1999 expulsion from power by the officials he had so long counselled as their 'Guide'. An English translation of the Black Book that gave a statistical analysis of officials' origins can be found on the JEM website, http://www.sudanjem.com. The ruling National Congress Party, made up of members of the National Islamic Front, who staged the coup in 1989, is completely controlled by members of the Shaigiya, Jaalin and Danagla clans from three towns north of Khartoum. A perceptive discussion of the relation between Turabi and his epigones can be found in Prunier (2005), 82–6.

3 See de Waal (1995) and the indictment of the International Citizens' Tribunal on Sudan, part of which is posted at http://www.judgmentongenocide.org (accessed 21 June 2008). The text of the indictment can be downloaded from http://weaversofthewind.org/docs/2009-02-09/2009_Darfur_Report/08-Brochure_-Final_Solution.doc.

4 Prunier (2005, 125–30) who discusses the way Darfur emerged as a story. As far as I know Prunier is the only outsider who has seen this film. With their journalists under threat of severe reprisals if they publish stories the GoS finds objectionable, *Al Jazeera*'s coverage of the Darfur disaster has been not much more frequent or extensive than that of the three (unthreatened) American TV networks, themselves decidedly uninterested in Darfur, as has been demonstrated by *New York Times* columnist Nicholas Kristof. In the print media researchers have so far not been able to uncover any Middle Eastern journalist who regularly reports about Darfur, with the exception of the British-born Julie Flint, who publishes in English in the Beirut *Star*. Recent surveys by American polling firms have indicated, however, that the Darfur disaster has not gone unnoticed in Middle Eastern countries: a majority of respondents are said to favor 'consensual' actions such as the deployment of the AU/UN hybrid force after it has accepted the restrictions imposed by Sudan in the negotiations following the passage of UN Resolution 1769 (31 July 2007). It should also be mentioned here that a project launched by the American Save Darfur Coalition and led by SDC staffer Allyn Brooks-LaSure took a score of African and Arab journalists to Chad EDP camps in February 2008. Brooks-LaSure told activist leaders in the US that his initial follow-up research revealed that the journalists' first direct access to victims turned their reporting in a distinctly more critical direction.

5 Scholars such as Douglas Johnson have pointed out that the elaboration of bureaucratic structures and the tactics of bureaucratic warfare constitute a legacy of British and Egyptian administration in Sudan, just as is the failure to broaden the number of educated officials to include Sudanese not part of the riverain Arab elite.

6 The Elders group was formed by Nelson Mandela in association with British businessman Richard Branson and rock star Peter Gabriel. In includes Lakhdar Brahimi, Jimmy Carter, Graca Machel, and Desmond Tutu.

7 The starting point of the story chosen by narrators had a great influence upon interpretations of its nature. If one started with the JEM/SLA attack on the El Fashir air base in April 2003, then the conflict was always framed in military terms, the armed revolt and its commanders occupying center stage, the GoS actions appearing as a *reaction* (or over-reaction) to armed attacks. This approach, and such an April 2003 starting date, has dominated the 'background' accounts of journalists; American, UN, and European officials; humanitarian organizations, and even some rescuer activist groups. Attention to the combination of neglect, political repression, manipulation, and negotiation in bad faith that the GoS had served up to Darfur since its first months in power has remained largely confined to scholarly accounts such as Johnson (2004), Daly (2007), Burr and Collins (2006) and Prunier (2005) or the August 2004 issue of the journal *Parliamentary Brief.*

8 The suggestion of a moral equivalence between government war crimes and rebel war crimes has drawn constant fire from analyst Eric Reeves. Along with his hundreds of postings about Sudan and Darfur at http://www.sudanreeves.org/, his *A Long Day's Dying: Critical Moments in the Darfur Genocide* (2007) deserves attention.

9 The cease-fire which the intervening troops were supposedly monitoring was signed in N'Djamena in March 2004. LeBor (2006, 188–9) concludes that 'the truth was that [the African Union Mission in Sudan] was a completely inadequate response to the carnage in Darfur, but it provided a useful and politically correct alibi for both Western and African countries'.

10 Rice is a former Assistant Secretary of State for African affairs. It was also at this time that American and European diplomats and political analysts began to claim that the genocide had ended.

11 Power (2002, 83), noting that the OAU pledged 'total solidarity' with the genocidal Burundian government in 1972 , also showed that American diplomacy had already established a pattern of avoiding effective measures to stop such slaughters. There was in fact an institutional bias in the opposite direction: one top State Department official responded to a junior's call for action by asking 'Do you know any official whose career has been advanced because he spoke out for human rights?' Confirmation of the dominance of this culture of indifference to atrocity crimes within the State Department can be found in the Clinton Administration's risk-averse bystandership in Bosnia, which four young Foreign Service officers were only able to expose by resigning, and its insistence during

the run-up to the Rwandan genocide that the UN *withdraw* most of its forces from the country. Ibid., 247–390.

12 Jeffrey Gettleman reports on how the Bashir regime has found a way to combine its profits from food import fees collected from aid agencies (and the elimination of any need to provide its own food aid to the Darfuri people) with profits from its industrialized agriculture in a time of spiking prices: 'Even as it receives a billion pounds of free food from international donors, Sudan is growing and selling vast quantities of its own crops to other countries, capitalizing on high global food prices at a time when millions of people in its war-riddled region of Darfur barely have enough to eat' (*New York Times*, 8 August 2008).

13 Interview with a highly placed employee of one of the companies, a retired American general, Ithaca, New York, 3 April 2008.

14 Elizabeth Neuffer (2001) shows how genocide victims place justice above material needs such as food, shelter, or security in T*he Key to My Neighbor's House: Seeking Justice in Bosnia and Rwanda.*

15 A listing: Armenians in World War I; Iraqi Assyrians of Seyfo in World War I and Simele in 1933; Ukrainians in the 1930s terror famine; Jews in the Holocaust; Cambodians; Kurds in the 1988 Anfal campaign; Marsh Arabs in Iraq; Hutu in Burundi; Tutsis in Rwanda; Bosnian Muslims of Srebrenica and elsewhere; Beja in Eastern Sudan; Nuba mountains tribes in central Sudan; and the Dinka in Southern Sudan.

16 In including for the first time a section on stopping genocide, however, the *National Security Strategy of the United States*, (March 2006, 17), quotes the Convention definition but then describes it as a 'moral imperative' and states flatly that 'where perpetrators of mass killing defy all attempts at peaceful intervention, armed intervention may be required, preferably by the forces of several nations working together under appropriate regional or international auspices'. It also confronts, in part, the problem of language: 'We must not allow the legal debate over the technical definition of "genocide" to excuse inaction. The world must act in cases of mass atrocities and mass killing that will eventually lead to genocide even if the local parties are not prepared for peace.'

17 The following statement appears on page 2 of the Report: 'Based on a thorough analysis of the information gathered in the course of its investigations, the Commission established that the Government of the Sudan and the Janjaweed are responsible for serious violations of international human rights and humanitarian law amounting to crimes under international law. In particular, the Commission found that Government forces and militias conducted indiscriminate attacks, including killing of civilians, torture, enforced disappearances, destruction of villages, rape and other forms of sexual violence, pillaging and forced displacement, throughout Darfur. These acts were conducted on a widespread and systematic basis, and therefore may amount to crimes against humanity.'

18 Gareth Evans, co-author of *The Responsibility to Protect* and until recently president of the International Crisis Group, provides one of the most important examples. The *Responsibility* document advocates armed intervention 'as a last

resort'. But when questioned at a conference on conflict prevention held at the Trudeau Centre for Peace and Conflict Studies in May 2007, he claimed that in the case of Darfur there were many resorts that had not been tried. He also questioned the nature of the atrocity crime: 'This is not Rwanda'. Since that time Evans' speeches and writings have sketched a careful, complicated attempt to define the conditions under which strong enforcement actions under R2P must be taken. A graphing of these statements closely resembles a curve approaching an asymptote, continuously drawing nearer to the line of military intervention without ever touching it.

19 The actual wording of Article I: 'The Contracting Parties confirm that genocide, whether committed in time of peace or in time of war, is a crime under international law which they undertake to prevent and to punish.' Certain scholars such as Norman Naimark have joined Colin Powell in finding that the Convention does not specify any particular actions that a state party should take in order to prevent or punish, however.

20 Ignatieff (2000, 44–7), points out the culture-specific element in notions of human rights in the course of a critical analysis of the human rights movement.

21 Thirty-three per cent of the 1,136 randomly selected respondents interviewed in the summer of 2004 reported hearing racial epithets.

22 Haggar (2007, 121–37), which publishes important Arab Gathering documents. See also Flint and de Waal (2008), 36–7 et al.

23 The discovery of this pattern by journalists newly assigned to Sudan can produce stories such as that filed by Heba Aly (2008) from the town of Dongola near Khartoum.

24 For a detailed account of the Government's unsuccessful efforts to recruit the large Beni Halba tribe in order to counter an expected international intervention after the passage of UN Resolution 1706 in 2006, see ICG (2007). The largest tribal grouping, the Southern Rizeigat, consistently refused to join in the fight against Darfuri rebels.

25 A full-length study in English is de Waal (1995). The study opens with a listing of the 'components of genocide', including rape, abduction, and the use of concentration camps, and concludes with the judgment that what the GoS accomplished in the remarkably diverse Nuba Mountains was 'genocide by attrition'.

26 This was the title of the article in the *London Review of Books* of 5 August 2004. De Waal later published it in *Review of African Political Economy* (2004).

27 Testimony at the International Citizens Tribunal on Sudan, summaries of which are available at www.judgmentongenocide.org (accessed 21 June 2008), is one source of evidence for the fact that the militias regularly chose to attack undefended villages rather than armed rebel groups known to be in the area. For International Criminal Court Prosecutor Luis Moreno-Ocampo, the conflict in terminology is easily resolved in the text of his request for the indictment of Bashir: 'His pretext was counterinsurgency. His intent was genocide' (ICC Office of the Prosecutor, Situation in Sudan Summary of the Case, 3).

28 As did the minder/driver assigned to the British-Sudanese documentary filmmaker Taghreed Elsanhouri in her 2005 film *All About Darfur*.
29 Enough Project authors John Prendergast and Gayle Smith have pointed out that no more than six rebel factions are of any significance, despite UN and Western diplomats' citing of estimates like 'more than twenty' or 'a host of' or 'more than a score' that make negotiation efforts seem hopeless.
30 There is also a contingent of about 250 Chinese engineers.
31 The latest example appears in a story by Lydia Polgreen in the *New York Times* of 25 August 2008 reporting about an attack on the huge Kalma camp: 'The United Nations said that it was 'gravely concerned' about reports of attacks on civilians in the camp. But aid officials and displaced people expressed dismay that nearby peacekeeping troops, part of a joint mission of the United Nations and the African Union, did not intervene.'
32 This despite the fact that NATO's Kosovo intervention of 1999, the only action that ever stopped a genocide-in-the-making, never received authorization from the UN. What the Martin government, the succeeding Harper government, and the Ministry of External Affairs have refused to do, think outside the UN box, a group of distinguished officials, political figures, humanitarian leaders, and heads of activist organizations has in fact done. See this group's 'Proposal to the European Union' and accompanying documents at http://www.weaversofthewind.org.
33 For example, see the proposal for a federal Sudan posted by the Justice and Equality Movement in August 2005 at http://www.sudanjem.com/2009/ar/.
34 The budget of the National Democratic Institute's initiatives to survey public political attitudes (through focus groups) and civic education, begun in 2005, could not be determined at this time. The scale of operations seems relatively modest: in the 'Three Areas' of Southern Kordofan, Abyei, and Blue Nile State, they held 41 focus group meetings in 2006 with the participation of 447 persons. Their activities were made possible by the Comprehensive Peace Agreement between North and South, which did not include Darfur. See http://www.ndl.org/worldwide/safrica/sudan_pf.asp.
35 Flint and de Waal conclude this latest joint publication on a pessimistic note, however, framing the 'politics of exhaustion' with 'endless chaos'.
36 Such was the goal of the Darfur Liberation Front and its successor, the Sudan Liberation Movement, according to Daly (2007, 280).

References

Aly, Heba (2008), 'Sudanese: "What Arab-African Rift?"', *Christian Science Monitor* 22 August.

Collins, Robert (2004), 'Disaster in Darfur', *African Geopolitics* 15/16: 51–73.

Commission of Inquiry on Darfur (2005), Report of the Commission of Inquiry on Darfur appointed pursuant to UN Resolution 1564, submitted 25 January.

Daly, Martin W. (2007), *Darfur's Sorrow: A History of Destruction and Genocide* (Cambridge: Cambridge University Press).

Fadul, Abdul-Jabbar and Tanner, Victor (2007), 'Darfur after Abuja: A View from the Ground', in Alex de Waal (ed.), *War in Darfur and the Search for Peace* (Cambridge, MA: Harvard University Press).

Flint, Julie (2007), 'A Seismic Political Shift is Taking Place in Darfur', *Daily Star* (Beirut), 31 December.

Flint, Julie and Waal, Alex de (2008), *Darfur: A New History of a Long War* (New York: Zed Books).

Haggar, Ali (2007), 'The Origins and Organization of the Janjawiid in Darfur', in Alex de Waal (ed.), *War in Darfur and the Search for Peace* (Cambridge, MA: Harvard University Press).

Ignatieff, Michael (2000), *The Rights Revolution* (Toronto: Anansi Press).

Ignatieff, Michael (2002), 'Intervention and State Failure', in Nicholas Mills and Kira Brunner (eds), *The New Killing Fields: Massacre and the Politics of Intervention.* (New York: Basic Books, 2002).

International Crisis Group (ICC) (2007), 'Darfur's New Security Reality', Africa Report No. 134, 26 November.

Johnson, Douglas (2004), *The Root Causes of Sudan's Civil Wars* (Bloomington, IN: James Currey).

Kristof, Nicholas (2005), PBS *News Hour with Jim Lehrer*, 10 June.

LeBor, Adam (2006), *'Complicity with Evil': The United Nations in the Age of Modern Genocide* (New Haven, CT: Yale University Press).

Millard Burr, J. and Collins, Robert (2006), *Darfur: The Long Road to Disaster* (Princeton, NJ: Markus Weiner).

Neuffer, Elizabeth (2001), *The Key to My Neighbor's House: Seeking Justice in Bosnia and Rwanda* (New York: Picador).

Nordlinger, Eric (1981), *On the Autonomy of the Democratic State* (Cambridge, MA: Harvard University Press).

Power, Samantha (2002), *'A Problem from Hell': America in the Age of Genocide* (New York: Basic Books).

Prendergast, John and Cheadle, Don (2007), *Not on Our Watch: The Mission to End Genocide in Darfur and Beyond* (New York: Hyperion Books).

Prunier, Gérard)2005), *Darfur: The Ambiguous Genocide* (Ithaca, NY: Cornell University Press).

Reeves, Eric (2007), *A Long Day's Dying: Critical Moments in the Darfur Genocide* (Toronto: The Key Publishing House).

Rice, Susan, 'Why Darfur Can't Be Left to Africa', *Washington Post*, 7 August, B4.
Totten, Samuel (2006), 'The US Investigation into the Darfur Crisis and Its Determination of Genocide: A Critical Analysis', in Samuel Totten and Eric Markusen (eds), *Genocide in Darfur: Investigating the Atrocities in Sudan* (New York: Routledge).
US Senate Foreign Relations Committee (2004), *Hearings*, 9 September.
Waal, Alex de (1995), *Facing Genocide: The Nuba of Sudan* (London: African Rights).
Waal, Alex de (2004), Counterinsurgency on the Cheap', *Review of African Political Economy* 31(102) (December), 716–25.

CHAPTER FIVE

WARS ACROSS STATES AND STATE COLLAPSE IN AFRICA

James J. Hentz

Introduction

The study of state collapse in Africa has focused largely on the internal dynamics of collapse. Generally, the argument is that after decades of post-colonial domestic political decay, some states are no longer able to supply the public goods expected of a functioning state. All collapsed states have failed to deliver the requisite public goods (Rotberg 2002, 132), with security being the most important (Rotberg 2004, 2–3). By most accepted definitions, they no longer function as *de facto* states. Nonetheless, state collapse remains relatively rare. The classic cases include: Somalia, Liberia, and the Democratic Republic of Congo (DRC).

This chapter argues for an outside-in complement to the weak state argument. We can use the metaphor of a deflated basketball sitting on a desktop to paint the picture. It will look fine on the outside, but collapse when someone picks it up putting pressure on it from the outside. It is almost a truism that Africa is dotted with weak and failing states, although not all equally so (van de Walle 2004, 101); few, nonetheless have collapsed. After years of hollowing out, it usually takes pressure from the outside to trigger collapse; I argue from the state's periphery, which includes the penumbras of contiguous states.

The remainder of this chapter proceeds in three parts. First, it will briefly discuss what we mean by collapsed states and briefly explain the inside-out explanations of collapse. The following two sections then make up the heart of the paper. The next section introduces the outside-in explanation. The argument here is that state collapse in Africa has been triggered by *wars across states*. Furthermore, these wars have an inherent regional dimension that cannot be captured by a state-centric analysis, although the state remains an essential element in the explanation of these wars. The chapter will conclude by applying the notion of *wars across states* and the possibility of state collapse to the situation surrounding Darfur.

Weak, Failed and Collapsed States in Africa

Robert Zartman offers a three-pronged definition of state collapse related to three functions a state should, but in the case of state failure, does not meet: the state as sovereign authority, the state as the security guarantor for a populated territory, and the state as an institution (Zartman 1995, 5). Zartman also notes that state collapse is a long-term degenerative disease (ibid., 8). William Rotberg accepts this definition, but adds more specificity concerning which functions of a state are critical, and he argues that that we must do a better job in distinguishing among and between weak states, failing and failed states, and collapsed states (Rotberg 2004, 43).[1] Most importantly, Rotberg acknowledges a dynamic relationship among state weakness, failure and collapse.

The implication of Rotberg's typology, as with Zartman's framework, is that there is a progression from weak states through failed states to state collapse.[2] However, while the literature on state failure and collapse does a good job explaining how state weakness leads to failure and collapse, the causal link in the linear progression from failure to collapse is less clear. Rotberg (2004, 9) defines a 'collapsed' state as a 'rare and extreme version of a failed state'.[3] Reno (1998, 5) seems to make a similar argument by including in 'the distinctive political logic of weak states' a process that in extreme cases engenders warlord politics and ultimately, or possibly, collapsed states. In Rotberg and Reno, as well as implied in Zartman, collapse seems to be a matter of degree, rather than a change in kind.[4] The Failed States project at Purdue University suffers from a similar weakness. It argues that state failure and state collapse are when institutions of the state are so weakened that it can no longer maintain authority or political order beyond the capital (Esty et al. 1993, 1). But the conditions that mark this failure '… may precede or follow the institutional collapse of the state; sometimes they are instrumental in causing it …' (ibid.). As John Heilbrunn (2006, 141) notes, '… a proposition that weakness predicts failure and potential collapse neglects to analyse why a state is weak. Weak states are the antecedent condition that may or may not lead to state failure and/or collapse (Widner 1995). Furthermore, weaknesses can come in many forms and some may be more critical to state survival than others.

Therefore, there are two problems to deal with here. First, as John Heilbrunn (2006, 142) continues, there is a problematic circularity in the argument that weak states fail because they are weak. One of the better volumes on state collapses poses and answers the question: 'Why do states collapse? Because they can no longer perform the functions required for them to pass as states' (Zartman 1995, 5). But earlier in this article it stated: state collapse is: '… a situation where the structure, authority (legitimate power), law, and political order have fallen apart …' (ibid., 1). What is described is also doing the explaining. Nonetheless, the internal dynamics of state collapse remain relatively well founded.[6]

The second problem that comes from conflating cause and effect in explanations of state collapse is how we calibrate the contribution of violence to state collapse. In almost any depiction or definition of state collapse, violence and conflict are an essential component; but at what level, or better, what kind of violence contributes to or is indicative of state collapse?

The argument here is that to understand how states go from failure to collapse we need to more closely examine the dimension of violence. Most of the literature on state collapse (as distinct from state failure) includes a heightened level of violence. But it is not just the level of violence, but the form the violence takes that matters. The two most common forms of conflict in Africa are insurgencies and civil wars.

Christopher Clapham (1998, 6–7) lists four types of insurgencies, liberation, separatists, reform, and warlord and he adds that we must distinguish between state-consolidating and state-subverting insurgencies. Warlord insurgencies are most often associated with state collapse. But they are, nonetheless, a poor predictor of state collapse.[7] For instance the northern penumbra of Uganda has had a long running conflict fuelled by the Joseph Kony's Lord's Resistance Army, which has spilled over into neighbouring countries (see Dunn 2007). Uganda, nonetheless, remains a relatively strong state. There are far more insurgencies, including warlord insurgencies, in Africa than there are collapsed states.

Civil war and state collapse are often used as either substitutes or proxies for each other. But a civil war may lead to a strong state, i.e. the United States, or to a collapsed state, i.e. Liberia.[8] In Iraq, state collapse could lead to civil war. As will be argued below, Angola suffered from a long civil war, but never went from state failure to state collapse. State collapse in Africa is a product of state weakness and conflict. But both conditions are endemic in Sub-Sahara Africa, so we need to explore how the two relate to each other, and why and how they combine to trigger state collapse.

Wars across States in Africa

State weakness, a long process of the hollowing out of the state, can lead to state failure. This is an inside-out process. State collapse, on the other hand has an outside-in complement. The conflict that causes state collapse is typically a *war across states*. A state's periphery plays the central role in this kind of conflict.

While the literature on state failure and collapse usually notes the importance of weak peripheries and unstable borderlands, it does not go nearly far enough in using those conditions to explain state collapse. For instance, Zartman (1995, 9) states that '... the political space – the territory where politics is played – of the collapsing state is broader than its borders'. Rotberg (2004, 8) notes that failed states often cannot extend authority beyond their capital city. Reno (1998, 2) makes a similar point, noting that because a weak state is not only reflected in a weak bureaucracy, but is the existence of informal parallel networks; ones that are more likely to flourish the further they are away for the seat of power.[9] In fact, he adds, that control over commerce is more important than control over territory. The Purdue project includes threatening the security of surrounding states and region in its explanation of state failure (Rotberg 2004, 43), but more as effect than cause.

The classic cases of state collapse, the DRC and Liberia, were embedded in a 'war across states'. In both the cases, insurgencies that started in the periphery, relatively quickly captured the capital. In both cases, they left a shell of a state in their wake. In both cases, the remnants of various armies fractured into warlord armies: in Liberia, the Independent National Patriotic Front of Liberia (INPFL) led by Prince Yourmie Johnson split off from Charles Taylor's National Patriotic Front of Liberia (NPFL). In 1990, many Krahns and Mandingos fled to Sierra Leone and Guiana to form the United Liberation Movement for Democracy (ULIMO), which continued to fight across the border in Liberia.

Originally supported by a united Uganda–Rwanda front, in June 1999, the rebel movement in the DRC split into three groups. And, in fact, the Uganda and Rwanda backed forces battled each other deep inside the DRC (Latham et al. 2001, 3). As Koen Vlassenroot (2006, 49) argues, '... the end of Mobutism was not the result of state collapse but was caused by local and regional dynamics that fell completely outside the zone of control of the central government'.

State collapse is driven as much by regional dynamics as it is by state dynamics. Curiously, although the literature on state development in Africa usually begins by acknowledging the artificial borders bequeathed to Africa by the Berlin Conference of 1884/85, those same borders proscribe our analysis of regional conflict in Africa. It is not the weaknesses of the state alone that leads to collapse, but rather how those weakness do or do not affect the spaces that traverse those inherited borders. That, in turn, is explained by the structural weaknesses of states and the kind of conflict those weaknesses engender.

State weakness is broadly defined by a lack of 'stateness'. In extreme cases, states lose the ability to govern through bureaucracies (Ellis 2003b, 37), which typically reflects corruption, poor economic performance, and an inability to broadcast authority throughout the country. States fail when a weak state becomes racked by violence, usually instigated by out-groups who resent the shrinking ambit of privilege controlled by the elite in power and their clients (Bøås 2004, 14).

Sub-Saharan African states were born handicapped. Partly as a legacy of colonial rule, the newly minted regimes of post-colonial Africa had difficulty projecting authority into their hinterlands.[10] This was exacerbated by the fact that the newly established regimes had a strong urban bias and typically transferred wealth from the countryside to the urban areas. Robert Bates' (1981) classic study on states and markets in Africa explains this process. Most Africa countries had monopsonistic markets that used marketing boards (themselves a legacy of colonial rule) to generate rents for patrimonial networks. This not only contributed to the polarization of society, but, as well, by keeping producer prices artificially low contributed to the poverty of the regions distant from the urban areas.

The institutional and structural legacy of Africa's state development, therefore, has made it difficult for them to project authority into their hinterland. Aristide Zolberg (1968, 71) talked about *syncretic* societies where the centre of a newly independent state in Africa had not expanded sufficiently to create an integrated society – they could not reach out to their periphery. Stathis Kalyvas notes that actors at the centre seeking power in Sub-Saharan Africa formed alliances with peripheral actors.[11] But, as the ability of the state to project power beyond their base of support, typically clustered in and nearby the capital city progressively atrophied, the peripheries of these countries become detached from the centre, and in extreme cases became no-man's-lands. But, weakness followed by failure does not necessarily lead to state collapse. In fact, many failed states live side-by-side with collapsed states. The tipping point for collapse is a *war across states*.

Sub-Sahara Africa almost never has the type wars that created and shaped the modern Westphalia nation state and which concomitantly provided a context for understanding modern war (see Tilly 1985, 169).[12] In a classical act of war, the state and its agents are the central players throughout the drama. In *wars across states*, the state may become almost irrelevant or only a bit player. As well, the staging of these wars are different than that of a classic war. Rather than conflict either between states (international) or within states (civil), these wars occur across state borders. They rarely have a discernible centre of gravity, at least in the classical sense of fighting over the proverbial line drawn in the sand. In a *war across states*, large tracts of territory bleeding across state borders provide the staging. As Paul Richards (2005, 13) has related, the new wars of the post-Cold War era occur on the margins of weak and retreating states. The players are primarily non-state actors.

Because interstate war is rare in Africa, many of its conflicts are labeled civil wars. As well, civil war is often conflated with state collapse. For instance, Jennifer Widner (1995 139) described state collapse as when '… the government is under siege or has disintegrated completely into civil war'. In Collier and Hoeffler's (2001, 21–2) groundbreaking work on conflict in Africa, Liberia and Sierra Leone's conflicts are treated as two distinct civil wars. The first civil war in Liberia lasted from December 1989 until November 1991 and its second civil war from October 1992 until November 1996. Sierra Leone had two civil wars, March 1991 to November 1996 and May 1997 until July 1999. In 1991, Charles Taylor, who led the first insurgency as leader of the National Patriotic Front of Liberia (NPFL) expanded the conflict from Liberia into Sierra Leone to gain that country's diamond fields (see Reno 2000, 56). That year, Foday Sankoh, as the leader of the Revolutionary United Front (RUF), started a war in Sierra Leone with the backing of Charles Taylor along the Liberian border. The relationship between Sankoh and Taylor had begun in the 1980s when both men were in Libya. Sankoh later traded diamonds to Taylor for guns. The first Sierra Leone conflict funded the second Liberian conflict. The two are listed separately only because the state is the analytical prism for studying conflict. Treating them as separate conflicts is like treating the eastern and western fronts in Europe during the World Wars as distinct conflicts. There were not two civil wars centred on, respectively, Liberia and Sierra Leone, there was one war. The conflict had a regional logic independent of a struggle over the dispensation of the state imbedded in what Pugh and Cooper (2004) see as regional economic, military, political, and social networks. These kinds of wars break the classic mould.

The notion of resistance means active resistance by two sides, one side being the state. It implies the war is over control of the state or for what can become a new state; this is not the case in a *war across states.* In both the Liberia/Sierra Leone and the DRC conflicts, the wars continued, intensified, and spread even after the capital was captured and a new regime replaced the old; the insurgents no longer necessarily engaged a force representative of the state. Early in these two conflicts, the national governments were active participants but they later lost what control over their military and then became as much a bystander as a participant. When a state did remain an active player it was often a contiguous state rather than the state ostensibly hosting the conflict. In eastern DRC, Rwanda and Uganda became more central to the conflict than was the Kisangani regime. But the states agents involved in the conflict do not necessarily represent state interests. Combatants may have national loyalties, at least on paper, but they do not fight for national causes.

In Africa, what may begin as a civil war, often takes on a life of its own. The geopolitical terrain of Africa determines the path of those conflicts. They rarely follow the well trodden path of a conventional civil war. In fact, with a closer look, civil war is not as common as typically thought; many would be better labelled *wars across states*.

A civil war is any armed conflict that involves: military action internal to the country and effective resistance by two sides, one which represents the national government. A civil war, therefore, is simply a war over the state itself. Either a new regime replaces an old regime or a new regime (and state) is created by succession.[13] A *war across states* is something different. It is a war about the state.

The military action in a *war across states* is not internal to the country. Fighting certainly occurs within a state, but this represents only part of the conflict. Unlike civil wars, in these conflicts effective resistance by the government disappears and the government's military fractures into competing militias fighting among themselves and against, or sometimes with, insurgents.[14] There are more than two sides and it is often difficult to distinguish government forces from militias.[15] The term 'sobels', for instance, was coined to describe the combatants in Sierra Leone – it signifies soldiers by night and rebels by day.

A *war across states* makes it difficult to reconstitute the sovereign state because it is the catalytic effect creating a new political order in the overlapping penumbra of failed and collapsed states. Christopher Clapham (1996, 222) summarizes:

> As the administrative reach of African states declined, with the shrinking of their revenue base and the spread of armed challenges to their power, so the number and size of such zones increased … in the process creating a new international relations of statelessness.

Clapham adds that insurgencies themselves can be regarded as quasi-states (ibid.). The question is, how and why do *wars across states* breakout? They, and concomitant state collapse, remain relatively rare.

Wars across states occur because of a particular regional logic. Björn Hettne (2000, 16) noted that failed states create 'black holes'. Reno notes that the three cases of failure he examines (Liberia, Sierra Leone, DRC), occurred within 'zones of conflict' (Reno 1998). Holsti (1996, 141) calls them 'zones of war'. These zones constitute the geographical space of a *war across states*. It is the articulation of border areas that explain state collapse.

Jeffrey Herbst (2000) has differentiated three classes of states that are more to less prone to problems related to the inability to project power into the periphery. First are the 'challenged states'. These states have pockets of high population density separated by vast areas of sparsely populated areas. This makes it difficult for the centre (one area of high population density) to connect with outlying areas (with pockets of high population density). As well, these states are susceptible to ethnic fractionalization (ibid., 146). The second category is 'hinterland' states, characterized by vast empty hinterlands and small pockets of people scattered around the country. These countries have trouble projecting authority into the periphery, but most people live in the city so it is not necessarily destabilizing. The third category is 'countries with favorable geography', where the highest concentration of power is found in one area – usually around the capital (ibid., 154).

Herbst states that geography is not destiny, noting in particular that Sierra Leone, in the 'favourable' category, failed because it could not contain the civil war that spread form Liberia (ibid., 159). This is telling, because if we replace the state-centric analytical prism with a regional prism that focuses on the overlapping penumbras, we get a different picture. There are, therefore, two missing elements to Herbst's important typology: a regional dimension and a dynamic dimension. To understand how weakness, in the form of favourable or unfavourable geography, can lead to a *war across states*, we have to look at the nature of the antecedent conflicts and, in particular, their regional effects. By way of example we can contrast the DRC and Angola.

The DRC and Angola are both classified by Herbst as 'challenged states'. The former has collapsed and is part of a *war across states* and the latter, after a long civil war while at one time possibly a failed state, has not collapsed. Angola certainly does not represent a 'war across states'. The collapse of the DRC was precipitated by the influx of refugees from neighbouring conflicts, in particular the influx of refugees after the 1994 genocide in Rwanda.[16] As seen in Figure 5-1, the large influx of refugees extended along the entire border of Eastern DRC with Rwanda and Burundi (UNHCR 1994).

During the Cold War, Angola also allowed nationalist liberation groups from neighbouring countries to set up military bases on its territory, which could launch attacks against the remaining colonial regimes outside of Angola (Kreike 2004, 9). The South West African People's Organization (SWAPO), for instance, had its base in Angola and launched attacks for the liberation of

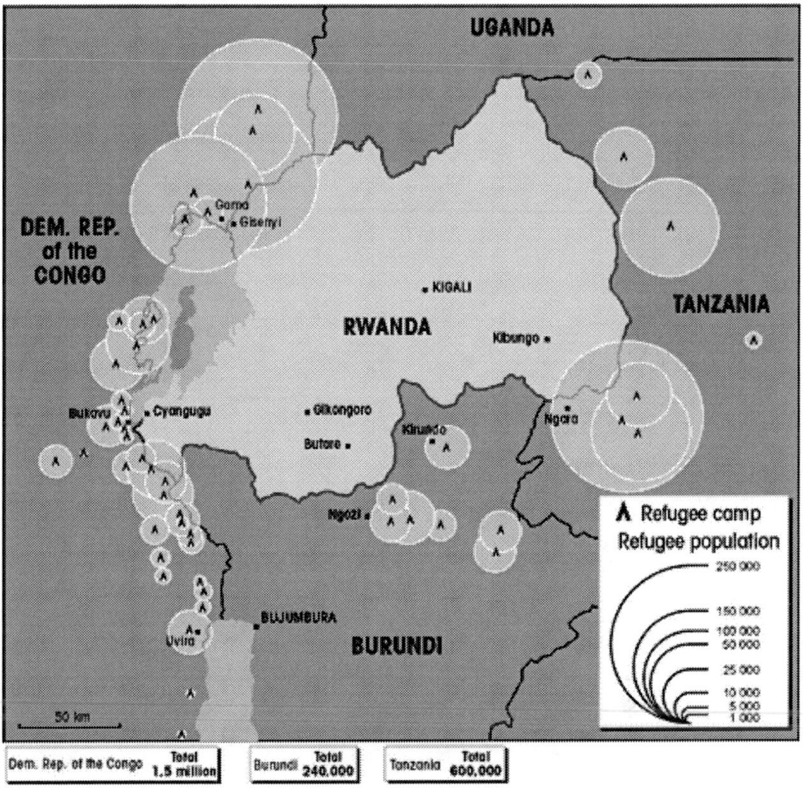

Figure 5-1 Refugee camp populations, December 1994

Source: UNHCR, 1994, http://www.reliefweb.int/mapc/afr_east/gl_reg/gl_ref94.html.

Namibia. South Africa retaliated by sending its much superior SADF (South African Defense Forces) into Angola to target the rebels. In order to thwart the rebel attacks coming from within Angola, SADF began to implement special buffer zones, which they cleared of populations and their resource bases, effectively stabilizing the border.

Unlike in the case of Burundi and Rwanda, where more than two million refugees fled across the border into the DRC, Angolan refugees moved primarily into the interior of the country. Most of the camps, in the case of Angola, were set up in central and western parts of the country (OCHA 2004). As seen in Figure 5-2, the majority of refugees did not move out into peripheries, or across the state's borders, but instead dispersed within Angola (OCHA 2001). Refugees were prevented from moving westward into the country by locals, who were afraid that refugees would bring the conflict into their homeland (Rutter 1996). In fact, the population dispersion more closely resembles what the literature on civil war hypothesizes – that rebels will use rough terrain, to hide.

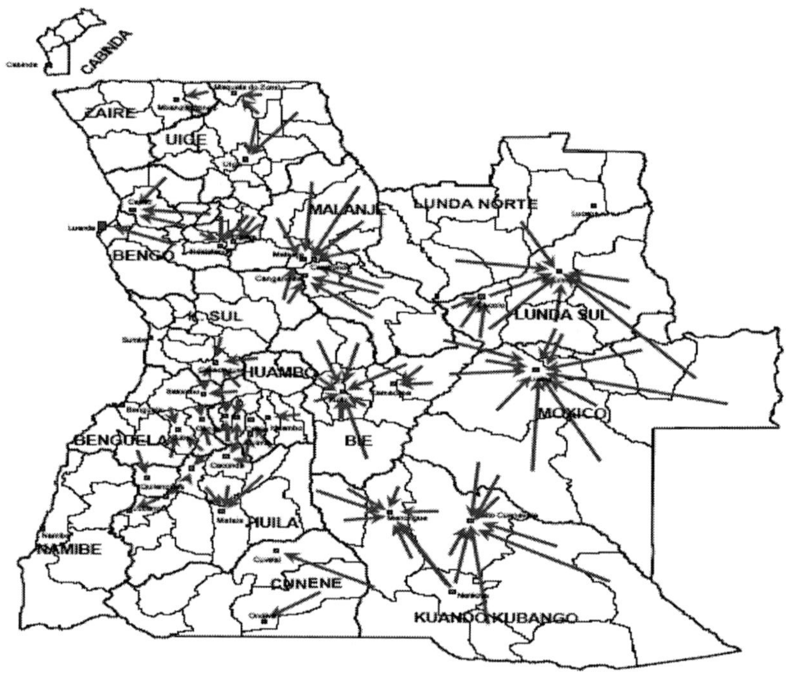

Figure 5-2 Population displacements in Angola

Source: author.

The DRC and Angolan cases are far more complex than can be summarized here. The point, nonetheless, is that state weakness, or more precisely how weakness related to the ability to control border areas, is partially defined by the regional context and the nature of the conflict. For instance, while Chad is listed a 'hinterland' state, the possibility for a *war across states* has increased with the crisis in Darfur (Sudan) (see

Polgreen 2006). We must look at the specific effects of coups, civil wars and insurgencies within a regional context. We need to see each conflict in its regional context.

The *War across States* in Darfur

At least 200,000 people – and perhaps as many as 400,000 – have been killed in Darfur since 2003.[17] The conflict in Darfur is a humanitarian crisis, most wars are. But its strategic context is being ignored. It must be understood in a broader geographical and historical context and as part of an evolving regional conflict. Like the DRC and Liberia, the conflict in Darfur is imbedded in a complex historical, geographical, and political context. It has serious international security implications and has become a *war across states*.

Weak, Failed and Collapsing States: Chad and Sudan

Dar Fur (modern day Darfur), was an independent sultanate for three hundred years, until 1916 when it was forced into Anglo-Egyptian Sudan. While it is formally part of Sudan, it lays historically, geographically, and in the sense of *de facto* sovereignty, between Sudan and Chad. An area larger than France, many of its people straddle Chad and Sudan (Jooma 2006, 2). Ruth Iyob and Gilbert Khadiagala (2006, 133) call it a 'geographical frontier' within the larger Sudanese state.

While the internal weaknesses of both states cannot be ignored in explaining the conflict, as in other 'wars across states', the regional logic may shape the conflict.[18] Iyod and Gilbert (2006, 27) have characterized it as 'interlocking regional conflicts'. Both Chad and Sudan are weak states and both have been racked by long civil wars (see Woodward 2003, 156). Chad has been called Africa's first collapsed state. Throughout the 1970s and 1980s it was failing. At the time, only the political centre in the capital city of N'djamena maintained a semblance of authority, and only because of outside assistance such as from the French, resisting Libya's regional ambitions. After 15 years of civil war, in William Foltz's (1995, 15) words: '[S]tate authority collapsed definitively ....' *Le Monde* (30 December 1980) stated: 'the modern state inherited from the colonial period no longer exists.' In 1982, Hissein Habre's Forces Armees du Nord (FAN) gained control of the capital (defeating a loose alliance of militias known as the second GUNT). Habre's personalized rule, however, alienated many, including some in his own military and he was overthrown in November 1990 by Idriss Deby, Habre's former army commander. Deby had used Darfur to regroup, twice, before capturing the Chadian capital (with support from Libya and Sudan) (Foltz 1995, 160).[19]

Chad's institutional and structural weaknesses, as elsewhere in Africa, have retarded the development of a strong state. It contains between 72 and 110 different language groups (ibid., 16). Rule is traditionally highly segmented, which means it is difficult for even a broadly defined ethnic group to unite. Traditionally, fractions of the same ethnic group may align with factions of neighbouring ethnic groups. This fractionalization spills over into the military forces. For instance, when the FAN began its siege of N'djamena it was only one of 17 politico-military factions (ibid., 17).

Sudan is a slightly different case. Although it too is a weak state wracked by years of civil war, it may have failed but has not collapsed. Gérard Prunier and Rachel M. Gisselquist have labelled it 'a successfully failed state'.[20] In fact, while Sudan has fought two civil wars in its south and insurgencies in its East and West, the central government has ruled under one regime since the National Islamic Front (NIF) came to power through a coup d'etat in 1989.[21] Nonetheless, like most of Africa, the ability or willingness of the central government in Sudan to provide public goods in the periphery (Darfur) was limited, and of course had been exacerbated by their civil war in the South, itself partially a product of the centre of the country alienating the peripheral areas (Woodward 2003, 41).[22] The Khartoum government has governed for the benefit of a narrow elite (Woodward 2003, 21; see also Jooma 2006, 3–4). The inability to project power into Darfur was evidenced by its failure to deal with the famine of 1984/85. This famine was, in part, triggered by the movement of peoples from the North to South during the 1970s because of a decline in rainfall affecting, at first, Northern Darfur, and later the south. As competition for land in Darfur intensified in the 1980s, Khartoum largely ignored it (Power 2004, 61).

Although both Chad and Sudan could be labelled weak states, the bleeding penumbras of Chad and Sudan are more important than the juxtaposition of two weak states for understanding Darfur. Jeffrey Herbst (2000, 147) explains that because the small areas of highly population densities are scattered over the vast country of Sudan, it is not surprising that it has a long history of civil war.[23] Chad, on the other hand, is what Herbst (ibid., 152) labels a *hinterland state*. These are states with high and medium population density in relatively small areas of the country with vast hinterlands that are sparsely populated.[24] However, the more populated periphery of this *hinterland state*, in fact, sits astride Darfur. So, in effect, you have a penumbra of two weak states far from the centre of either county. 'The permeability of Darfur to the political upheavals on its borderlands with Chad and Libya engendered transborder ethnic alliances that put the juridical identity of Sudan and Chad at risk' (Iyob and Khadiagala 2006, 136).

Darfur has long been the centre of regional conflicts. It was from there that Gaddafi's *Islamic Legion* troops staged an attack on Chad in 1987 for control of the Aouzou strip. It has remained stubbornly independent of the regime in Khartoum and a refuge and recruiting ground for Chadian rebels since that country's first post-colonial war that began in 1965. For centuries, the Masalit villages, where some of the worse humanitarian attacks have taken place, were in the political no-man's lands between Dar Fur and the Wadai Sultanate, in what is today eastern Chad (Flint and de Waal 2006, 8).

The conflict in Darfur, therefore, rests at the interstices of two conflicts, the one in Chad and the civil war in Sudan. However, while an explanation of the conflict in Darfur cannot be divorced from its antecedents, it can take on a life of its own developing into a *war across states*. The current conflict in Darfur started when the Darfur Liberation Front attacked a Sudanese army outpost in Gola in February 2003.[25] Sudan responded by licensing the Arab Janjaweed militias to attack those groups in Darfur fighting for a larger slice of the national economic pie. The conflict is often labelled a struggle between African pastoralist and Arab herders. Jan Eliasson, a special envoy for the UN has called it a 'fight over grass' (Atlantic Council of the United States 2007, 5).[26] The environmental degradation of the northern pasturelands led to polarization between cattle and camel nomads and sedentary farmers.[27]

As Douglas Johnson (2006, 95) clearly shows, the conflict in Darfur has played out against Sudan's second civil war in the South, which broke out in 1983. Sudan was initially colonized as two different regions – North and the South. In 1946, the British combined the two regions, which immediately triggered conflict between the mostly Muslim north and Christian south. Sudan became independent on 1 January 1956, and was soon dominated by the Muslim North. The Sudanese People's Liberation Army (SPLA) subsequently resisted northern dominance and fought for a separate state, or later for more say in the government. But the discovery of oil in the south only heightened the importance of the south to the rulers in the capital of Khartoum. Africa's longest running civil war came to a formal close on 9 January 2005, with the signing of the 'Comprehensive Peace Agreement'.

But, the insurgency that was already two years old in Darfur was not part of the North–South agreement. This, despite the fact that a least part of the insurgency in Darfur had ties with the SPLA (*New York Times* 2004, A3). Abububaker Hamid Nour, then general coordinator of the rebel group Justice and Equality Movement (JEM), stated 'No peace will come in Sudan if we leave the marginalized areas in Sudan and make peace in the South' (ibid.). The peace, such as it was, between the North and the South exacerbated the conflict in the West (Darfur).

The current conflict has already bled into Chad, which confronts its own simmering insurgency (Associated Press 2007). And Chad's civil war between an Arab minority in the north and an African majority in the south contributed to the Pan-Arab movement in Darfur (Johnson 2006, 94). The Janjaweed have expanded their reach from Sudan in Shamal Darfur (Northern Darfur) hundreds of miles into Chad, or more accurately, into Gharb Darfur (Western Darfur). For instance, Janjaweed leader, Abdalla Hila, drew recruits from his Um Jalul clans in Chad (Flint and de Waal 2006, 45).[28] The first violent displacement of Fur occurred at the refugee camp at Anjikoti (teeming with refugees from Chad's conflicts) adjacent to the border market of Foro Baranga – the biggest mercantile centre in the border zone (ibid. 54). There is a symbiotic relationship between Janjaweed attacks in Darfur and the Chadian rebel attacks across Chad. While the Chadian army is preoccupied with the rebels, the Janjaweed have a free hand in Darfur. Chadian rebels who want to overthrow President Idriss Deby use the no-man's-lands of Darfur created by the Janjaweed's ethnic cleansing to renew their fight. Mohamed Nour, President of the Chadian rebel group, Rally for Democracy and Liberty in Chad, claims President Idriss Deby's removal is their goal. He comes from the Tama tribe which crisscrosses the Chad-Sudan border. He took part in the 1990 rebellion that overthrew Chadian president, Hissene Habre and replaced him with Deby. In October 2007, the Chadian government recalled troops to protect the capital. Some government troops had already deserted to fight with the rebels in Darfur (France 24, 2007; Fisher 2005).

Chad and Sudan have both suffered from civil wars. Those wars, however, are contained with the vessel of the post-colonial state. The conflict in Darfur is neither between two states (international) nor within one state (civil). The military action no longer can be described as internal to a particular state (i.e. Sudan or Chad); the active participation of national government is eclipsed by the role of militias; and the notion of resistance by both sides belies a reality where defining sides is almost impossible. Possibly the most serious harbinger of a war across states and state collapse is the fracturing of rebel movements – creating new actors and shaping the trans-regional morphology of the conflict – a new stage.

The fracturing of the conflict in Darfur has deep historical roots in Chad and Sudan. Iyob and Khadiagala (2006, 26) trace the roots of the conflict at least as far back as the process of Arabization and Islamization that began in the second half of the first millennium. This long process led to *awlad al-balad* (children of the land) of the Arabized/Islamized riverain communities dominating Sudan. The Government of Sudan (GoS) supported Arab ethnic groups through the 1980s, culminating in the Fur-Arab war that in mid-1989. Figure 5-3 depicts the GoS conflict with its peripheries.

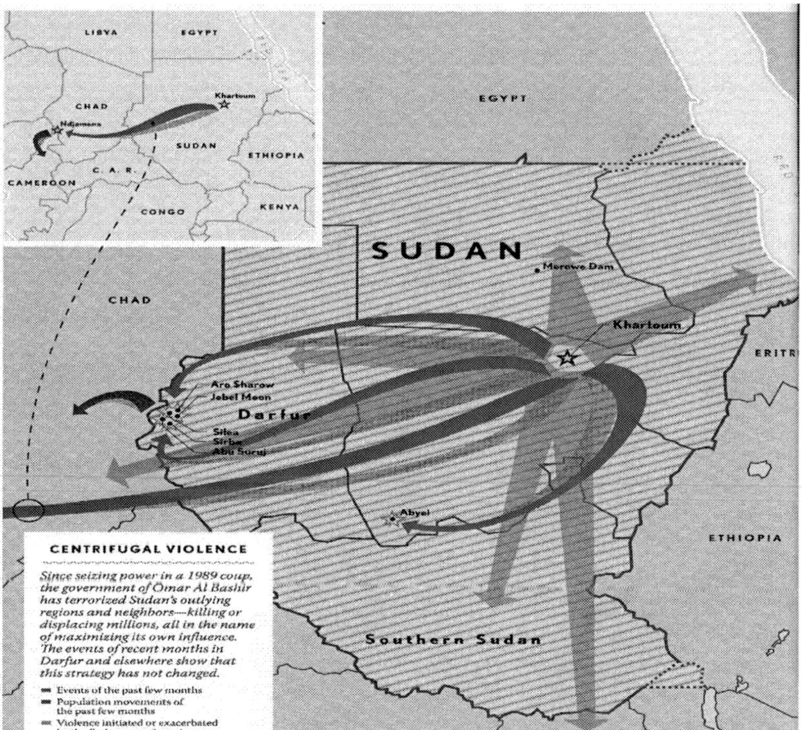

Figure 5-3 Government of Sudan conflict and its peripheries

Source: UNHCR, 1994, http://www.reliefweb.int/mapc/afr_east/gl_reg/gl_ref94.html.

In *Dar fur* ('domain of the fur'), the sultanate included three main African groups, the Fur, Zaghawa and the Masalit, sometimes collectively called the *awlad al-garb* ('children of the west'). To weaken the *awlad al-garb*, the GoS in 1994 divided Darfur into three regions: North Darfur, West Darfur and South Darfur. Ironically, the Zaghawa, once aligned with the GoS, therefore were pulled toward an alliance with the Fur. The Masalit had also begun to organize.

The Sudan Liberation Movement/Army (SLM/A), which evolved out of the Darfur resistance, originally presented a united front: The Chairman was to be a Fur; the Chief of Staff a Zaghawa; and the Deputy Chair a Masalit. But there are fault lines imbedded in the SLM/A. The Justice and Equality Movement (JEM), as part of the umbrella group, is a neo-Islamist movement that was started in Sudan in the mid-1990s within the government (Brosché 2008, 12). It is mainly Zaghawa. The SLM was dominated by the Fur.

The split became open when the JEM, led by Minni Acru Minnawi (from the Zaghawa), signed the 5 May Darfur Peace Agreement (DPA) with the GoS. Minnawi became Chief Advisor to the GoS President under the DPA. But this ultimately led to a split within the JEM when a group led by Khalil Ibrahim left in 2007 and formed the Justice and Equality Movement-Collective Leadership (LEM-CL). The larger faction led by Abdul Wahid al-Nur (from the Fur), the founder of the SLA, refused to sign the agreement. Nonetheless, his participation in the Abuja talks leading up to the DPA, triggered a split led by Khamees called G 19 (ibid., 25).

This fracturing has continued. In July 2007, a new umbrella group, the United Front for Liberation and Development, made up of five splinter groups including two splinters of the Sudan Liberation Movement Army, was formed in Eritrea. As many as 16 rebel groups are now fighting – spurring as in the DRC and Liberia/Sierra Leone, a *war across states*. Finally, if and when Khartoum stops supporting the Janjaweed, there is little guarantee they will stop the killing. As much as 50 per cent of Janjaweed may come from neighbouring countries, putting them outside the control of Khartoum (ibid., 76). Upon her return from Chad in January 2007, Marcia Dam from UNHCR noted: 'It seemed to us, the different rebel groups were changing their hats so fast that is was hard to know who they were' (Atlantic Council of the United States 2007, 11).

The regionalization of the conflict is not confined to the Chad-Sudan border. Just as the conflict in Liberia was tied not only to the conflict in its northern neighbour, Sierra Leone, but to the conflict in its southern neighbour, Côte d'Ivoire, the conflict in Darfur is also connected to the crisis in the Central African Republic (CAR), to the south of Sudan and Chad. About 50,000 people from the northwest have fled that two-year old-conflict into Chad (Polgreen 2007). The rebellion in the CAR has ties to Sudan's government and to rebels seeking to overthrow Chad's government.

The proliferation of actors and the expanding trans-regional stage creates a new drama. The movements of people; as triggered by the Rwanda genocide, which destabilized and militarized eastern DRC; as triggered by the war in Liberia, which helped destabilize Côte d'Ivoire, as well as Guinea and Sierra Leone, is now happening in Darfur. There are 444,000 refugees and 120,000 displaced persons inside Chad. There are millions of refugees and displaced people in Darfur. Demographics will fuel the conflict – but one whose unique political topography as defined by Africa's institutional and structural legacy, will define its shape.

The central geopolitical question in Darfur should be: is what many consider a civil war really a *war across states?* The spreading conflict would destabilize the region in general, and neighbouring Chad in particular. A destabilized, to say nothing of a collapsed Chad, would create a regional black hole where anti-Western terrorists could set up shop. The importance of Chad in this regard in reflected in its central place in the US Pan Sahel Initiative (PSI). As well, Chad, since the completion of the oil pipeline connecting it to Cameroon (the Chad-Cameroon oil development and pipeline project is the largest private investment project in Africa), is a significant oil producer. From a regional perspective, the US expects to get as much as 25 per cent of its oil from West Africa over the next 10 years. The contagion effects of a destabilized or collapsed Chad could bleed into neighbouring oil producers in West Africa.

A close look at the conflict centred on Darfur reveals many similarities to the ones in the DRC and Liberia/Sierra Leone. The actors and staging of this conflict point to a new *war across states*. A war with a distinct logic from the classical wars of the last century.

Notes

1 Jennifer Widner (1995, 131) also argued for distinguishing between cases of collapse and failure.

2 Jean-Germain Gros (1996) offers a similar 'imaginary continuum' with a taxonomy that has five signpost: anarchic states, mirage states, anaemic states, captured states, and *in vitro* failed states. These are useful and interesting descriptions but tell us little about causation.

3 The authors in the first part of Rotberg's edited volume do not distinguish between failure and collapse. And they tend, as well, to operate within matters of degree. For instance, Kasfir (2004, 57) talks about a 'continuum' (his quotations marks) of decreasing government effectiveness.

4 Heilbrunn (2006, 137) makes a clearer distinction, 'A weak state fails when it inadequately delivers services throughout its territory and is incapable of mediating factional interests; a failed state collapses when its bureaucracy ceases to function, public services are unavailable, and violence becomes commonplace'. But it still reads like a continuum.

5 Because the 'extreme' case is relatively rare, the Purdue project created a dependent variable for their quantitative analysis that includes states that have collapsed completely and those in the process of failing (Esty et al. 1991, 2).

6 There is a vast literature on state weakness in Africa. A good place to start is Jackson and Rosberg (1982).

7 Clapham's list of 10 African insurgencies – Burundi, DRC, Eritrea, Ethiopia, Liberia, Rwanda, Sierra Leone, Somalia, Sudan and Uganda (1998, 1) – includes four collapsed states (DRC, Liberia, Sierra Leone and Somalia), and Rwanda and Uganda, which are part of the *war across states* centred on the DRC (ibid.).

8 Jennifer Widner (1995, 129) relates that emergence of pressure groups in the US after the Civil War brought about fundamental changes that led to state building that you do not find after civil wars in Africa. This is quite similar to Reno's contrasting Tilly's description of the alliance between the commercial and manufacturing classes with Nobles in Europe that stimulated a strong state, and absence of such classes in Africa.

9 Janet MacGaffey's (1987) prescient, and now classic, study of Zaire's informal economy examined the effects of the decline of the administrative capacity of the state. Her focus was on the peripheral areas of Upper Zaire and North Kivu, as well as Kisangani.

10 Historically, in much of pre-colonial Africa, groups escaped authority by moving farther away from what was perceived as oppressive authority. The control of people and resources was typically more important than the control over territory (Vansina 1966, 82).

11 Kalyvas (2003, 486) notes that civil wars are a transformation of centre and periphery quest for power.

12 Historically, in much of pre-colonial Africa, groups escaped authority by moving farther away from what was perceived as oppressive authority. The control of people and resources was typically more important than the control over territory (Herbst 1990).

13 Almost all scholars emphasize that civil wars are internal conflicts. See Brown (1996). Small and Singer's study *Resort to Arms* contains an accepted definition of civil war that focuses on the intrastate characteristics of those wars (Sambanis 2004, 816).

14 Will Reno (2006, 29) has convincingly argued that, in fact, incumbent rulers in Africa's weak states purposefully try to avoid centralizing military command and, rather, try to manipulate factional conflicts with the military to their own advantage.

15 For instance, Stephen Ellis (2001, 80–87) notes that early in Liberian civil war splits in Charles Taylor's NPFL were evident. It later spawned the proliferation of warlord groups, as many as seven by 1997 (Ellis 2003a, 154).

16 The conflict centred on the DRC is part of a long-running struggle fuelled by a competition over land, regional political power and access to patrimonial resources in the provinces of North Kivu and South Kivu, between *autochtones* ('indigenous' Congolese) and Kinyarwanda speakers (people who trace their heritage to Rwanda) living in eastern DRC. See Tull (2003, 102).

17 There is some debate over these numbers. *The New Republic* (2008) puts the total at 400,000.

18 In fact, the juxtaposition of a relatively strong state, Sudan, with a weaker state, Chad, may be a better predictor of regional instability than two weak states side-by-side. This is similar to the Rwanda/Uganda/DRC case. An ascendant Rwanda (with Uganda support) successfully projected power into its periphery, which in turn destabilized the weak periphery of DRC.

19 Sudan's Prime Minister Sadiq el-Mahid gave Libya a free rein in western Darfur to support Idris Deby against Hissein Habre.

20 This is the title of their chapter ('The Sudan: A Successfully Failed State'), in Rotberg 2003), p. 101.

21 The NIF became the National Congress Party (NCP).

22 The SPLM fighting for autonomy in the South encouraged the creation of the SLA (Jooma 2006, 6).

23 Sudan is what he calls a 'state challenged by geography', the category that contains the states most prone to failure.

24 These states are also challenged, but given the capital is more able to control the country because the population is not as dispersed.

25 The post-colonial conflict in Darfur goes back, at least, to the Darfur Resistance Front founded by Ahmed Ibrahim Draige, founded in the 1960s and the *Sooni* and Red Fame insurgencies of the 1960s.

26 It should be noted, however, that the conflict in Darfur did not begin as an ethnic contest between African and Arab. Pastoralists displaced by the 1970s' drought included Arabs and Africans and, originally, the non-Arab Zaghawa (pastoralists) clashed with the African Fur (agriculturalist), who later joined forces to fight the Arabs.

27 Conflict triggered by environmental deterioration has a long history in the region. S.P. Reyna (1990) relates how historical 'environmental reversals' have triggered conflict between herders and cereal producers. The latter typically conducted offensive warfare while the latter conducted defensive warfare.

28 General Mohammed Mohammed Alseladhi from the Fur council stated that 50 per cent of the Janjaweed come from outside of Sudan (Brosché 2008, 76).

References

Associated Press (2007),'Security Worsens in Eight African States', 18 June.

Atlantic Council of the United States Global Leadership Series (2007), 'Remarks by Jan Eliasson, UN Special Envoy to Darfur', 16 May, Washington, DC.

Bates, Robert (1981), *Markets and States in Tropical Africa: The Political Basis of Agricultural Policy* (Berkeley, CA: University of California Press).

Bøås, Morten (2004), 'Africa's Young Guerrillas: Rebels with a Cause', *Current History* May, 211–14.

Brosché, Johan (2008), *Darfur: Dimensions and Dilemmas of a Complex Situation* (Oslo: Uppsala University, Department of Peace and Conflict Research).

Brown, Michael (ed.) (1996), *Ethnic Conflict and International Conflict* (Princeton, NJ: Princeton University Press).

Clapham, Christopher (1996), *Africa and the International System: The Politics of State Survival* (New York: Cambridge University Press).

Clapham, Christopher (1998), 'Introduction: Analysing African Insurgencies', in Christopher Clapham (ed.), *African Guerrillas* (Bloomington, IN: Indiana University Press).

Collier, Paul and Hoeffler, Anke (2001), *Greed and Grievance in Civil War*, (Washington, DC: World Bank).

Dunn, Kevin (2007), 'Uganda: The Resistance Army', in Morten Bøås and Kevin Dunn (eds), *African Guerrillas: Raging against the Machine* (Boulder, CO: Lynne Rienner).

Ellis, Stephen (2001), *The Masks of Anarchy* (New York: New York University Press).

Ellis, Stephen (2003a), 'Liberia's Warlord Insurgency', in Christopher Clapham (ed.), *African Guerrillas* (Bloomington, IN: Indiana University Press).

Ellis, Stephen (2003b), 'The Old Roots of Africa's New Wars', *International Politics and Society* 2, 29–43.

Esty, Daniel, Goldstone, Jack, Gurr, Ted, Hariff, Barbara, Surko, Pamela, Unger, Alan and Chen, Robert (1998), 'Failed States and International Security: Causes, Prospects and Consequences', Purdue University,http://www.ippu.purdue.edu/failed_states/1998/papers/gurr.html.

Fisher, Jonah (2005), 'Sudan Attacks Chadian Deserters' *BBC* 19 November, http://news.bbc.co.uk/2/hi/africa/4453120.stm.

Flint, Julie and Waal, Alex de (2006), *Darfur: A Short History of a Long War* (New York: Zed Books).

Foltz, William (1995), 'Reconstructing the State of Chad', in I. William Zartman (ed.), *Collapsed States: The Disintegration and Restoration of Legitimate Authority* (Boulder, CO: Lynne Rienner).

France 24 International News 24/7 (2007), http://www.france24.com/france24Public/en/archives/news/world/20071012-Chad-rebels-desertion-sudan-border-rfi.php.

Gros, Jean-Germain (1996), 'Towards a Taxonomy of Failed States in the New World Order', *Third World Quarterly* 17(3), 455–72.

Heilbrunn, John (2006), 'Paying the Price for Failure: Reconstructing Failed and Collapsed States in Africa and Central Asia: A Review Essay', *Perspectives on Politics* 4(1), 135–50.

Herbst, Jeffrey (1990), 'War and State in Africa', *International Security* 14(4), 117–39.

Herbst, Jeffrey (2000), *States and Power in Africa* (Princeton, NJ: Princeton University Press).

Hettne, Björn (2000), 'Globalization and the New Regionalism: The Second Great Transformation', in Björn Hettne, András Inotai and Osvaldo Sunkel (eds), *Globalism and the New Regionalism* (New York: Macmillan Press).

Holsti, Kalevi J. (1996), *The State, War, and the State of War* (Princeton, NJ: Princeton University Press).

Jackson, Robert and Rosberg, Carl (1982), 'Why Africa's Weak States Persist: The Empirical and Juridical in Statehood', *World Politics* 35(1), 1–24.

Johnson, Douglas (2006), 'Darfur: Peace, Genocide and Crimes against Humanity in Sudan', in Preben Kaarsholm (ed.), *Violence, Political Culture and Development in Africa* (Athens, OH: Ohio University Press).

Iyob, Ruth and Khadiagala, Gilbert (2006), *Sudan: The Elusive Quest for Peace* (Boulder, CO: Lynne Rienner).

Jooma Mariam Bibi (2006), 'Darfur and the Battle for Khartoum', *Institute for Security Studies Situation Report* (Pretoria: ISS).

Kalyvas, Stathis (2003), 'The Ontology of "Political Violence": Action and Identity in Civil Wars', *Perspectives on Politics* 1(3), 475–94.

Kreike, Emmanuel (2004), 'War and the Environmental Effects of Displacement in Southern Africa (1970s–1990s)', in William Moseley and B. Ikubolajeh Logan (eds), *African Environment and Development* (Burlington, VT: Ashgate).

Latham, Robert, Kassimir, Ronald, and Callaghy, Thomas (2001), 'Introduction: Transboundary Formation, Intervention, Order, and Authority', in Robert Latham, Ronald Kassimir and Thomas Callaghy (eds), *Intervention and Transnationalism in Africa: Global-Local Networks of Power* (New York: Cambridge University Press).

Kasfir, Nelson (2004),' Domestic Anarchy, Security Dilemmas, and Violent Predation', in Robert Rotberg (ed.), *When States Fail* (New York: Princeton University Press).

MacGaffey, Janet (1987), *Entrepreneurs and Parasites: The Struggle for Indigenous Capitalism in Zaire* (New York: Cambridge University Press).

The New Republic (2008) 9 April.

The New York Times (2004), 'War in Western Sudan Overshadows Peace in the South', 17 January.

OCHA (2001), 'Angola. Population Displacements', http://www.reliefweb.int/w/fullMaps_Af.nsf/luFullMap/22E7A4C5190B3BD285256A630050C9F4/$File/an_displace0401.pdf?OpenElement, accessed 8 July 2004.

OCHA (2004), 'Angola. IDPs in Camps and Transit Centers', http://www.reliefweb.int/w/fullMaps_Af.nsf/lufullMap/D8D218B23213D78E852569FB0073081E/$File/ang_idp_camp.pdf?OpenElement, accessed 8 July 2004.

Polgreen, Lydia (2006), 'Refugee Crisis Grows as Darfur War Crosses a Border', *New York Times*, 28 February.

Polgreen, Lydia (2007), 'Wedged Amid African Crises, a Neglected Nation Suffers', *New York Times*, 2 April.

Power, Samantha (2004), 'Dying in Darfur', *The New Yorker*, 30 August.

Prunier, Gérard and Gisselquist,Rachel M. (2003), 'The Sudan: A Successfully Failed State', in Robert Rotberg (ed.), *State Failure and State Weakness in a Time of Terrror* (Washington, DC: Brookings Institution Press).

Pugh, Michael and Cooper, Neil (2004), *War Economies in a Regional Context: Challenges of Transition* (Boulder, CO: Lynne Rienner).

Reno, Will (1998), *Warlord Politics and African States* (Boulder, CO: Lynne Rienner).

Reno, Will (2000), 'Shadow States and the Political Economy of Civil Wars', in Mats Berdal and David Malone (eds), *Greed and Grievance: Economic Agendas in Civil Wars* (Boulder, CO: Lynne Rienner).

Reno, Will (2006), 'Insurgencies in the Shadow of State Collapse', in Preben Kaarsholm (ed.), *Violence, Political Culture and Development in Africa* (Athens, OH: Ohio University Press).

Reyna, S.P. (1990), *War Without End: The Political Economy of a Precolonial African State* (Hanover, NE: University Press of New England).

Richards, Paul (2005), 'New War: An Ethnographic Approach', in Paul Richards (ed.), *No Peace, No War: An Anthropology of Contemporary Armed Conflict* (Athens, OH: Ohio University Press).

Rotberg, Robert (2002), 'Failed States in a World of Terror', *Foreign Affairs* 81(4), 127–40.

Rotberg, Robert (2004), 'The Failure and Collapse of Nation-States: Breakdown, Prevention and Repair', in Robert Rotberg (ed.), *When States Fail: Causes and Consequences* (Princeton, NJ: Princeton University Press).

Rutter, Jill, (1996), *We Left Because We Had To* (London, Refugee Council, http://www.unhcr.org.uk/pdfs/lessonplans_history/plan_12.pdf.

Sambanis, Nicholas (2004), 'What is Civil War', *Journal of Conflict Resolution* 48(6), 259–82.

Tilly, Charles (1985), 'War Making and State Making as Organized Crime', in Peter Evans, Dietrich Rueschemeyer and Theda Skopal (eds), *Bringing the State Back In* (New York: Cambridge University Press).

Tull, Denis (2003), 'A Reconfiguration of Political Order? The State of the State in North Kivu (DR Congo)', *African Affairs* 102(408), 429–46.

Vansina, Jan (1966), *Kingdoms of the Savanna* (Madison, WI: University of Wisconsin Press).

Vlassenroot, Koen (2006), 'A Societal View on Violence and War: Conflict and Militia Formation in Eastern Congo', in Preben Kaarsholm (ed.), *Violence, Political Culture and Development in Africa* (Athens, OH: Ohio University Press).

Walle, Nicolas van de (2004) 'The Economic Correlates of State Failure', in Robert Rotberg (ed.), *When States Fail* (New York: Princeton University Press).

Widner, Jennifer (1995), 'States and Statelessness in late Twentieth-Century Africa', *Daedalus* 124(3), 129–53.

Woodward, Peter (2003), *The Horn of Africa: Politics and International Relations* (New York: I.B. Tauris).

Zartman, I. William (1995), 'Introduction: Posing the Problem of State Collapse', in I. William Zartman (ed.), *Collapsed States: The Disintegration and Restoration of Legitimate Authority* (Boulder, CO: Lynne Rienner).

Zolberg, Aristide (1968), 'The Structure of Political Conflict in the New States of Africa', *American Political Science Review*, 62(1), 70–87.

Chapter Six

State Fiscal Capacity and State Failure in Sub-Saharan Africa

Cameron G. Thies

Introduction

The problem of state failure began to occupy global attention soon after the end of the Cold War. Spectacular failures like Somalia and Liberia called out for solutions. Why do states fail and what can we do to stop it from happening? The initial enthusiasm among social scientists for systematically investigating the causes of state failure was dampened by methodological criticism of the quantitative techniques used by the State Failure Task Force. Further investigation then moved to qualitative studies of individual cases and small-*n* comparisons of state failure. Recently, Robert Bates has reinvigorated the quantitative study of state failure. Bates grounds his approach to state failure in a fable played out by a ruler interacting with two patrons representing groups of citizens. While fables often serve as models for the origins of political order in the state building literature, this fable is also grounded in a formal model that yields deductive insights. The insights that Bates highlights include the key importance of the level of public revenues, the benefits of predation, and the discount factor of incumbent rulers. When public revenues declined, the benefits of predation on natural resources increased, and the discount rate for autocratic rulers rose during democratization, state failure was a logical and all too often real world result in Africa.

I build on Bates's fable by making explicit connections to the literature on the predatory theory of the state as well as the current quantitative civil war literature. This allows me to test Bates's arguments controlling for a variety of factors normally associated with civil conflict. In this case, the civil war literature is harnessed to explain state failure onset. I am able to consider the role of state fiscal capacity highlighted by Bates, as well as the role of natural resources as a source of predation for rulers (and rebels as in the civil war literature) in the production of state failure onset. This is accomplished through the use of a two-stage least squares technique that appropriately models the endogeneity that accompanies the incorporation of state fiscal capacity into a model of state failure onset.

The results are intriguing. State fiscal capacity deters state failure onset. A variety of factors normally associated with state fiscal capacity and state failure onset are significant in the models. The role of natural resources is similar to what Bates would expect: natural resources mostly affect state fiscal capacity and do not substantially affect state failure onset directly. Oil, in particular, is virtually inconsequential to either state fiscal capacity or state failure onset. Diamonds, which have also drawn much attention in civil war literature, exert their affects on state fiscal capacity. The discount rate of rulers does not have significant effects on state failure onset or state fiscal capacity as measured by the levels of democracy.

Why do States Fail?

The quantitative study of state failure has had its ups and downs. The State Failure Task Force, now known as the Political Instability Task Force (PITF), was set up in 1994 at the behest of the US government with the express purpose of trying to quantitatively forecast state failures (Esty et al. 1995; Esty et al. 1998a; Esty et al. 1998b; Goldstone et al. 2000; Bates et al. 2003). According to the PITF, a 'state failure' consists of revolutionary wars,[1] ethnic wars,[2] adverse regime changes[3] and genocides or politicides[4] (Marshall et al. 2001). Most political scientists were introduced to the work of the task force through a stinging methodological critique published by Gary King and Langche Zeng (2001). Unfortunately, King and Zeng's critique seemed to have discouraged many social scientists from pursuing the quantitative study of state failures. The PITF continued its work nonetheless, and many qualitatively oriented social scientists continued to make contributions to the literature (e.g., Beissinger and Young 2002; Rotberg 2003a and 2003b; Fukuyama 2004; Chesterman et al. 2005).

Recently, Robert Bates has led a revival of the quantitative study of state failure in Sub-Saharan Africa. Bates (2008a: 5) grounds his work in a formal model of political order, which he rightly notes '*cannot* be treated as a given'. The formal model itself is a product of a stylized fable (Bates et al. 2002; Bates 2008a). In this fable, a community contains a ruler, or 'specialist in violence', as well as two groups of citizens led by patrons. The ruler derives income through seizing the wealth of citizens or charging citizens for protection. The citizens are shielded to some extent by their patrons, who may also mobilize them to seize the wealth of others or defend the wealth they generate from their productive labour. The ruler and the patrons interact repeatedly through time. Political order that gives rise to the state is an equilibrium outcome when the ruler uses the means of violence to protect citizens and those citizens devote themselves to producing wealth, taking a portion of that wealth to pay the ruler for such protection. Should either the ruler switch from protection to predation, or the patrons withhold tax payments or prey upon each other, then the equilibrium of political order breaks down.

The expected payoff to the ruler of returns from predation and returns from taxation largely determines whether the ruler will continue to protect its citizens or engage in predation, which then triggers the citizenry and their patrons to take up arms against the ruler. As a result, political order is affected by the level of tax revenues, the benefits of predation, and the ruler's discount rate. If tax revenues are too low, the immediate benefits of predation too high, and/or the ruler discounts the future heavily because he is greedy or insecure, then state failure is quite likely. As Bates (2008a: 20–29) notes, all of these conditions were met in late twentieth-century Africa. The global recession induced by the oil shocks of the 1970s reduced the demand for African exports. Since most African states relied heavily on taxes on trade, a crisis in public revenues ensued. By the late 1980s a wave of democratization had spread through Africa, leaving many authoritarian rulers with increased, unanticipated political risk; hence, they began to discount the future heavily. Finally, African states contain many precious commodities, including oil, minerals and gemstones which provided a tempting target for ruler predation. The fable seems to eerily predict reality, as rulers began to prey upon the citizenry, and patrons organized the citizenry to take up arms against the rulers in retaliation. According to Bates (2008a: 124–5):

> Public revenues declined, political elites became insecure, and the temptation to engage in predation therefore rose in Africa, amidst abundant opportunities to do so. In the face of increased threats from above, citizens found reason to search for patrons who could help them to safeguard life and property. While inflicting widespread costs, disorder also offered attractive prospects for those willing to invest in the building of political organizations.

Political disorder–state failure, is thus the product of a crisis in public revenues. The ruler's turn to predation engenders the rise of rival patrons. Ethnic conflict is also a product of political disorder, as patrons turn to land rights and regional claims on central government revenue to organize their opposition. Since ethnic groups often occupy distinct territories, clashes over land rights and regional redistribution of revenues take on the guise of ethnicity. In contradiction to many claims in the qualitative civil war literature, ethnicity is thus not the cause of state failure, but may be correlated with it as ethnic tensions rise during periods of state failure (Bates 2008a: 134). Qualitative accounts that link the presence of natural resources to the onset of civil war also have the causal order mistaken in this account. According to Bates (2008a: 135), the state fails first, then rival patrons attempt to seize control of natural resource wealth. Quantitative accounts that fail to find robust correlations between ethnicity and civil war, and natural resources and civil war therefore suffer from a lack of strong theoretical foundations to guide their understanding of the causal connections.

Bates is certainly not the only theorist to centre his account of the production of political order on the ruler's desire for revenue. Douglass North (1981: 21) defines the state as 'an organization with a comparative advantage in violence, extending over a geographic area whose boundaries are determined by its power to tax constituents'. This definition, or something like it, is central to all analyses of state behaviour in the predatory theory tradition. North (1981: 23) developed a model of the state as a wealth-maximizing ruler based on three characteristics: the state trades services such as protection and justice in exchange for revenue, the state discriminates among groups of its constituents to devise property rights that best maximize its revenue, and the state's revenue extraction is constrained by the opportunity costs posed by potential rival rulers both within the state and outside of it. Charles Tilly (1992: 96–7) identifies a similar model of the state that engages in the following activities: statemaking, to attack and check potential rival rulers from within the territory claimed by the state; warmaking, to attack and check potential rival rulers from outside of the territory claimed by the state; protection, to attack and check rivals to the ruler's allies both inside and outside of the territorial state; and, most importantly, extraction of resources from its subject population to support the aforementioned activities.

Olson's (1993) fable of roving versus stationary bandits also portrays the stark differences between rulers who invest in their population's productive capacity and provide protection and those who solely consume its resources until they are exhausted. This version of the fable highlights the true nature of the problem in Africa. In Olson's fable, roving bandits consume all of the resources of a population, then move on to the next locale. Substituting Olson's terms in Bates's fable, we see that once a stationary bandit, who previously took only a portion of the population's resources, switches to predation, they remain stationary. The only defence against a stationary bandit who acts like a roving bandit is poverty. The population has no incentive to invest for the future because they known that the fruits of their production will be taken from them. Olson's fable as seen through Bates's fable demonstrates the desperate plight of Africans living under conditions of state failure. All theorists in the predatory tradition would undoubtedly come to the same conclusion.

Some scholars question whether predatory theories of the state developed from the European experience are applicable to Africa and other contemporary developing states (e.g., Centeno 2002; Herbst 2000; Desch 1996; Clapham 1996; Lustick 1997; Jackson and Rosberg 1982). They suggest that internal conflicts in developing countries reflect the absence of international competitors and the inability of states to centralize power domestically. The limited interstate wars fought by developing countries have not provided the opportunity for rulers to increase their extraction from society and centralize power (c.f. Thies 2007). The frequent civil wars have only served to undermine attempts to build the state. Recent quantitative analyses, such as Thies (2005; 2006) confirm a significant, negative relationship between civil war incidence and tax revenue extraction. Of course, civil wars are not necessarily conceptually or operationally the same type of event as state failure, but they are related phenomenon. Bates (2008b: 2–4) notes that not all civil wars originate in failed states, but the close correspondence between the two means that we can explore state failure with recourse to many of the same explanatory variables used in the civil war literature. In fact, since there has been so little systematic, quantitative research conducted on state failure, we must turn to the civil war literature for assistance in building our statistical models.

Rather than the top-down approach to state failure that focuses on the 'incumbents', most of the quantitative civil war literature takes a bottom-up approach focused on the 'insurgents' (Bates 2008a: 131–2). The same issues are at stake in both perspectives: public revenues, the benefits of predation, and the discount rate of the key actors. For example, Collier and Hoeffler (1998) originally formulated a model in which rebel greed drives rebellion. The objective of rebellion in their analytical framework is either to capture the state or secede from it. The incentive to rebel is a product of the probability of victory and the state's capacity to defend itself as a function of its ability to tax. Thus, if the rebels' goal is to capture the state, then state revenues serve as an incentive to greedy rebels as well as an impediment to their success.

The cost of rebellion is modelled as a function of per capita income. These costs also increase as the conflict endures, which is a function of the state's capacity to defend itself. The problem, as Collier and Hoeffler (1998: 564) note, is that taxation and military expenditure (or any similar measure of state capacity) are endogenous to the risk of rebellion. Collier and Hoeffler (1998:

566) choose to proxy taxable capacity with per capita income and the natural resource endowment. They find that per capita income reduces the risk of civil war, which suggests that wealthier states are better able to defend themselves from rebellion than poorer states, consistent with many subsequent studies (Hegre and Sambanis 2006). The effect of natural resources initially increases civil war incidence (*sxp*), but then reduces it (sxp^2), indicating that only an abundance of natural resources allows the state to deter rebellion. Ethno-linguistic fractionalization (ELF) and its squared term were not consistently significant across their statistical models. Bates (2008a; 2008b) also fails to find empirical support for the effect of ethnic diversity on state failure in the subset of African cases; however, other contributions to the literature find evidence of the curvilinear relationship (Bates 2000; Collier and Hoeffler 2004). Finally, larger populations increased the risk of civil war, which is consistent with many studies (Hegre and Sambanis 2006). These findings were provocative enough to launch much of the recent literature on civil war and primary commodities.

Rather than focus on rebel greed, Fearon and Laitin (2003) argue that weak central governments increase the probability of insurgency as a result of their inability to effectively manage potential counter-insurgent practices at the local level. Without robust and efficient administrative, military and police apparatuses, the state is a sitting target for rebels regardless of motive. In keeping with the spirit of predatory theory, they suggest that 'where states are relatively weak and capricious, both fears and opportunities encourage the rise of would-be rulers who supply a rough local justice while arrogating the power to 'tax' for themselves and, often, for a larger cause' (Fearon and Laitin 2003, 76). This argument complements Bates's (2008a) in many ways. In order to test their argument, they substitute per capita income as a proxy for state strength, much like Collier and Hoeffler (1998). Their findings support the argument that states with higher incomes per capita are at significantly less risk for civil war than those with lower incomes (see also Goldstone et al. 2003; Hegre and Sambanis 2006). This finding, along with the significantly increased risk associated with large populations, political instability, being a new state or an oil exporter are more important than grievance indicators like ethnic or religious diversity, the lack of democracy or civil liberties, economic inequality or linguistic and religious discrimination. Other studies suggest that the impact of democracy on civil war onset is better captured as an 'inverted-U' relationship (Hegre et al. 2001; Bates 2008b). With the exception of the oil exporter dummy variable, Fearon and Laitin (2003) do not find evidence that supports Collier and Hoeffler's (1998) earlier findings about the importance of primary commodity exports as source of greed-based rebellion. Bates (2008a; 2008b) arrives at a similar conclusion for Africa, suggesting that the link between oil revenues and state failure must run through rulers rather than rebels.

Fearon (2005) later expanded the argument in Fearon and Laitin (2003) that state dependence on oil rents produces weaker administrative and bureaucratic structures by suggesting that dependence on primary commodities more generally will produce weak states. While large oil revenues may increase the prize of the state, the measure of primary commodities (*sxp*) advocated by Collier and Hoeffler (1998; 2004) consisting of cash crops and fuel exports is not likely to be much of a prize, since rebels lack the national distribution system to exploit these resources. Further, even if rebels are able to tax primary commodities to fund their start-up costs, those same commodities provide a relative easy source of tax revenue for the government. Fearon (2005: 502) then poses a critical question: 'Why should rebels be more favored by this source of revenue than the government?'

This is *the* crucial question left unanswered in the civil war literature, and one raised by Bates's (2008) fable, and indeed is a question that would be asked by any of the aforementioned predatory theories of the state. Resource rents are often argued to be the cause of corruption, underperforming state institutions, poor economic growth and governance, and a variety of other factors commonly known as the 'resource curse' (Karl 1997; Ross 2001). Le Billon (2001: 567) summarizes these findings by suggesting that resource rents allow rulers to avoid the need for broad-based taxation in a diversified economy. Instead, resource rents finance a repressive security apparatus and reward individuals and groups that support the ruler (Reno 1998). Violence often becomes the only option available to redress both greed and grievance issues in such a system. In sum, 'resource dependent countries thus tend to have predatory governments serving sectional interests' (Le Billon 2001: 567). Therefore, natural resources are just as attractive to rulers as rebels, despite the potentially damaging effects they may have on the state.

Yet, the conventional wisdom on the impact of natural resources on the state is being modified. Snyder (2006) argues that lootable wealth does not have to lead to disorder. Instead,

> If rulers are able to forge institutions of extraction that give them control of revenue generated by lootable resources, these resources can actually contribute to the maintenance of order by providing the income with which to govern. In contrast, the breakdown or absence of such institutions can produce instability in two ways: first, by causing a fiscal crisis that renders

> the state vulnerable to collapse and second, by making it easier for rebels to organize. (Snyder 2006: 947)

Rulers prefer public extraction, such as state-owned mining and oil companies that maximize rents while minimizing transaction and agency costs associated with monitoring and enforcing contracts (Levi 1988: 30–32). Private actors prefer private extraction because it maximizes their income by denying the rulers a share of the wealth. Joint extraction and no extraction are also possibilities depending on the tools at the ruler's disposal. This is critical, since under the right conditions, 'rulers, not rebels, will control the income generated by lootable resources' (Snyder and Bhavnani 2005). Recent work by Luong and Weinthal (2006) on ownership structures, and Dunning (2005) ruler incentives to diversify their economies pushes us to reconsider resource abundance as a 'structural variable willfully exerting its own effects' (Smith 2004: 243).

Smith (2004), for example, finds evidence that oil-rich states were less likely to suffer regime failure or civil war onset than states without oil wealth. He suggests that rulers may have forged robust social coalitions and built state institutions that were able to deal effectively with opposition. In sum, the current resource curse literature based on the examination of a few outlier cases may have overstated the case for the weakening of state institutions and legitimacy that Fearon and Laitin (2003) and Bates (2008a) assume along with most of the resource curse literature.

I adopt Bates's (2008a) fable as my guide to understanding the sources of state failure. I recognize that many of his insights are rooted in the predatory theory of the state tradition, and that these insights have often been challenged by those writing about the developing world. I also incorporate the systematic knowledge gleaned from the civil war literature. By integrating a top-down approach that starts with the ruler and a bottom-up approach that starts with rebels, we have a more theoretically informed and empirically fleshed out model of state failure. This approach considers carefully the three variables that affect state failure mentioned by Bates (2008a): public revenues, the benefits of predation, and the discount rate of rulers. These are operationalized by tax revenues, the presence of a variety of natural resources, and democracy, much as Bates (2008a) has suggested. Finally, including a measure of state fiscal capacity like tax revenues introduces endogeneity problems that must be appropriately addressed as recognized by Bates (2007; 2008a: 168), since state failure may affect tax revenues, just as tax revenues may affect state failure. Hegre and Sambanis (2006: 513) note that endogeneity is one of the serious, but largely unaddressed issues in the civil war literature. Bates (2008a: 168) is not especially clear about his resolution of the endogeneity problem.

In sum, I expect that higher levels of tax revenue should decrease the likelihood of state failure onset. State failure onset may also exert a negative impact on tax revenues, though tax revenues would more likely be impacted if we were looking at the duration or incidence of state failure. The presence of natural resources should exert direct effects on levels of tax revenue. If natural resources produce rents for the state, then the relationship should be negative since rents are a substitute for taxation. Unfortunately, the data does not discriminate between different types of ownership structures, so some natural resources may actually augment tax revenues. In either case, I expect that natural resources will affect the revenues of the state, rather than state failure onset directly. Finally, I test for the 'inverted-U' shaped relationship between democracy and state failure, which provides some indication of the discount rate for rulers. Democracy is also known to affect the level of tax revenue collection, though the direction of this impact is inconsistent in the literature.

Data and Method

There are two endogenous equations in this model. One represents the onset of state failure and the other the fiscal capacity of the state. The technique I use to analyze this system of equations was originally developed by Maddala (1983) and more practically implemented by Keshk (2003). This method is designed for simultaneous equation models where one of the endogenous variables is continuous and the other is dichotomous. This two-stage estimation technique creates instruments for the endogenous variables and then substitutes them for their endogenous counterparts in the structural equations. The continuous variable is estimated with OLS and the dichotomous variable with probit in both the first and second stages of estimation. It has previously been applied to studies of trade and conflict (Keshk et al. 2004), and democracy and conflict (Reuveny and Li 2003), among other efforts.

The State Failure Onset Equation

The state failure onset equation starts with the model developed by Fearon and Laitin (2003). This model is frequently used as a baseline by many subsequent studies that have offered conceptual or methodological innovations in the civil war literature (e.g., Humphreys 2005; Lujala et al. 2005; Cederman and Girardin 2007). Due to data limitations present in the state fiscal capacity equation, I use Fearon and Laitin's (2003) data for 1960–1999. My approach to modeling state failure onset is thus quite different from what Bates (2008a: 169) implemented, though not necessarily from what he recommended (Bates 2008b: 2–3). Bates (2008a) develops a single equation model with the existence of militias serving as a proxy for state failure onset. His model also fails to include many of the variables normally associated with civil conflict onset. My two-stage least squares approach will therefore serve as a useful robustness check on his central finding that higher public revenues lessen the probability of state failure.

The variables used in my equation for state failure onset are drawn from those used in Fearon and Laitin's (2003: 76) basic model with a few additions suggested by the aforementioned analyses. *State failure onset* is coded dichotomously according to the PITF criteria for revolutionary war, ethnic war, adverse regime changes, and genocides or politicides (Marshall et al. 2001). *Per capita income* is measured in thousands of 1985 US dollars and lagged one year. *Population* is the logged population size, which is lagged one year. *Mountainous terrain* is measured as the logged share of a state's terrain covered by mountains. *Noncontiguous state* is a dichotomous variable that captures the effect of having noncontiguous territory, such as islands or enclaves. *Oil exporter* is a dummy variable for states that obtain more than one-third of their export revenues from oil exports. *Instability* is a dummy variable that indicates whether the state had a change of three or greater in the Polity IV regime index in any of the prior three years. *Democracy* is a lagged Polity IV value derived from the polity2 score that varies between –10 (most autocratic) and +10 (most democratic). *Democracy*^{2} is the squared value of democracy to test for the inverted-U shaped relationship. *Ethnic fractionalization* is represented by the commonly used ELF index of ethnolinguistic fractionalization, which ranges from 0 (complete ethnic homogeneity) to 100 (complete ethnic heterogeneity) by measuring the probability that two randomly chosen individuals belong to different ethnolinguistic groups. *Ethnic fractionalization*^{2} is the squared value of ethnic fractionalization to test for non-linear effects of this variable. *Religious fractionalization* is a measure that Fearon and Laitin (2003) construct along similar lines to the ELF index to represent religious diversity.

The state failure onset model is identified by the exclusion condition (e.g., Greene 2003; Gujarati 2003). There are four variables that are unique to the state failure onset equations, including population, instability, mountainous terrain, and noncontiguous state. I also employ the technique developed by

Beck, Katz and Tucker (1998) to address the problem of serial correlation. The state failure onset equation is estimated with a counter for the number of years that a state has been at peace and three cubic splines to account for the effect of autocorrelation. Their inclusion has no appreciable effect, much as found by Fearon and Laitin (2003: 83) in their model of civil war onset.

The State Fiscal Capacity Equation

The measurement of state capacity is inherently problematic and has been subject to a great deal of debate through the years. I adopt what is considered a fiscal sociology approach to the measurement of state capacity, which is also quite common in political science (e.g., Campbell 1993; Lieberman 2002) and consistent with Bates's (2008a; 2008b) argument. As Lieberman (2002: 95) notes, when using taxation data the researcher must be careful about the 'fit between the indicator(s) and the particular concept under investigation'. In our case, the concept of state capacity could be proxied by any number of indicators. Fearon and Laitin (2003) and Collier and Hoeffler (1998) proxy state capacity with per capita income. Collier and Hoeffler (1998) are clear that they would rather use an indicator of taxation, but do not because it is endogenous to the risk of rebellion. Since I will employ a statistical technique to deal with that endogeneity, I can reasonably use a measure of tax revenue.

The chapter uses the *tax ratio* to capture state fiscal capacity, which is the state's tax revenue as a percentage of GDP. The tax ratio is the conventional gauge of the state's extractive capacity (e.g., Campbell 1993; Chaudhry 1997; Cheibub 1998; Fauvelle-Aymar 1999; Tsai 1999; Centeno 2002; Thies 2005 2007). Taxation and the development of bureaucracies that support regularized extraction activities are fundamental to the survival of the modern state. For Bates (2008a) it represents the equilibrium of political order as the normal source of revenue for the state. The data is from an ongoing collection effort by Johnson and Rabinowitz (2005).

The state fiscal capacity equation uses a number of standard control variables for predictions of the tax ratio. A number of the control variables overlap with those found in the civil war equation, including oil exporter, democracy, democracy^2, ethnic fractionalization, ethnic fractionalization^2 and religious fractionalization. Being an *oil exporter* has long been identified as a source of the 'resource curse' faced by many developing countries that may have prevented development. According to Fearon and Laitin (2003), it is the primary culprit in their argument that weak states are a target for insurgents. Oil could hypothetically have either positive or negative effects on our various measures of state fiscal capacity, depending upon the ownership structure. If oil produces rents (tax revenue) for the state, then it will probably have negative (positive) effects on measures based on tax revenues. Unfortunately, this is impossible to sort out with existing data.

Predatory theory based on the European experience expects a negative relationship between *democracy* and tax-based measures of state capacity (e.g., Tilly 1985; Olson 1993), although previous empirical studies find mixed evidence for this proposition in the developing world (e.g., Cheibub 1998; Thies 2004). *Ethnic fractionalization* or *religious fractionalization* that might potentially lead to violence may serve as a focal point for bargaining with the state over relative shares of the tax burden that ultimately reduces state extraction. Ethnic and religious diversity serve as a type of transaction cost as suggested by Collier and Hoeffler (1998).

I also control for several other indicators of the transaction costs associated with taxation, including per capita income, trade openness and inflation (e.g., Cheibub 1998). The impact of national wealth and economic development on the tax ratio is assessed with *per capita income*. *Trade openness* measured as imports and exports as a percentage of GDP is expected to be positively related to tax revenues as international trade is relatively easy to tax as it moves through a limited number of ports. Reliance on customs duties is especially common in developing countries, including Africa. Data on trade openness is from the Penn World Tables 6.2 (Heston et al. 2006). *Inflation* is expected to be negatively associated with government revenues, since poor monetary policy is likely to have a negative impact of the functioning of the economy and consequent tax collection efforts.

Official development assistance (ODA) as a percentage of total revenue, and public and publicly guaranteed *debt* as a percentage of GDP are both included in the model as the literature suggests that these sources of international funds have prevented developing states from augmenting their domestic resource extraction capabilities (e.g., Snider 1990; Bates 2001; Remmer 2004). Both variables should be negatively associated with the tax ratio, since they are substitutes for taxable income. The data on ODA is from the OECD, while the data on debt is from the World Development Indicators.

Finally, I control for the effect that fiscal *federalism* may have on central government revenue extraction. Subnational units in federal political systems that have the authority to raise taxes may crowd out the central government, thus reducing the federal government's portion of revenues. This variable is based on the dichotomous 'author' variable from the Database of Political Institutions described in Beck et al. (2001), which indicates whether 'subnational governments have extensive taxing, spending, or regulatory authority'. Missing data is augmented by drawing upon several other sources (e.g., Wibbels 2005).

The model of state fiscal capacity is identified by the exclusion condition. There are five variables that are unique to the state capacity equation, including trade openness, debt, ODA, inflation and federalism. Serial correlation is a potential problem in the state fiscal capacity equation. It is addressed by the use of robust standard errors, which are adjusted for clustering on countries (White 1980; Newey and West 1987). These standard errors are consistent in the face of serial correlation and heteroskedasticity of a general type (Keshk 2003).

Additional Considerations for Testing the Effects of Primary Commodities

Since Collier and Hoeffler (1998) originally posited a link between primary commodities and civil war, a great deal of effort has been spent trying to determine what types of commodities may be linked to civil war, how they should be measured, how to model the linkage, and what causal logic may explain the linkage. Bates (2008a) is also interested in the role that primary commodities may play as an easy source of predation for rulers. In the first set of models, I simply replicate the inclusion of Fearon and Laitin's (2003) *oil exporter* dummy variable to see how it affects the relationship between state failure onset and state capacity. Yet, a wide variety of measures for oil and other primary commodities have been developed in the attempt to understand their impact on civil war. We also know that primary commodities directly affect the state's capacity. In fact, Bates (2008a; 2008b) expects natural resources to have their primary effects on the state, rather than on rebels. In order to provide a robust test of the effects of primary commodities on both endogenous variables, I test a variety of indicators present in the literature. In each case I rerun the statistical analysis by substituting these additional measures of natural resources for the oil exporter variable in the original analysis. I begin with a measure of *fuel exports* as a percentage of GDP measured on a yearly basis from Fearon (2005). I also test Humphreys's (2005) measure of *oil production* in barrels per capita per day. All measures of oil production should be positively related to state failure onset. The effect on state capacity is uncertain, depending upon whether oil produces rents or revenues.

Along with oil, diamond production has drawn a lot of attention, especially with regard to the 'conflict diamonds' that are thought to contribute to the onset and duration of African civil wars. I test Humphreys' (2005) measure of *diamond production* in carats per capita, which he demonstrates is positively related to civil war onset. The effect of diamond production on state capacity is somewhat indeterminate as it is a function of ownership arrangements that are not captured by this measure. I also replicate Lujala et al. (2005) by including dummy variables for the production of *primary diamonds* (kimberlite and laprolite) and *secondary diamonds* (alluvial) from the DIADATA dataset produced by (Gilmore et al. 2005). Lujala et al.(2005) expect that primary diamonds will have no effect on civil war onset, since most of the revenues from primary diamonds will accrue to the state in some form. Secondary diamonds will produce a higher risk of civil war onset and incidence. Finally, I include a variable *secondary x conflict zone* from Gilmore et al. (2005) that captures whether secondary diamond production is occurring in areas of conflict. Secondary diamond production in conflict zones is expected to spur civil war onset. Secondary diamonds should diminish government revenues, as they are more readily extracted without government regulation. The interactive term may similarly diminish revenue extraction or one could even imagine the opposite as well-financed internal rivals may pose a greater threat to the state than their poorly financed counterparts, thereby stimulating extraction from other sources. In all of these cases, we can expect that their posited effects on civil war onset may be the same as on state failure onset. In order to test Collier and Hoeffler's (1998; 2004) finding that primary commodities in general should stimulate civil conflict, I include *sxp* and sxp^2, and separately the *log of sxp* from Fearon (2005). These are the version of the measure that has been interpolated from five year observations to yearly observations. The measure includes food and live animals, beverages and tobacco, textiles, rubber, wood products, oil, coal, natural gas, animal and vegetable oils, fats, waxes, and nonferrous metals like silver, copper, nickel, aluminum, lead and tin (Fearon 2005: 491). Collier and Hoeffler (2004: 574) argue that the impact of *sxp* is positive on civil war onset until it peaks at around 33 percent of GDP, when it begins to decline. This is why both *sxp* and its squared term are typically included in the model. Fearon and Laitin (2003) and Fearon (2005) do not find support for this finding. Fearon (2005) actually finds better empirical support for the simple log of *sxp*. Since *sxp* is composed of mainly cash crops and fuel exports, Fearon (2005: 500) suggests that the type of distribution system required to take advantage of these resources is rarely available to rebels. Hence, Fearon does not expect *sxp* to be related to civil war onset. Instead, it provides the government with an easy source of tax revenue, potentially increasing state capacity. Conversely, *sxp* may also tap into the 'resource curse' if the government fails to develop administrative capacity beyond the distribution and taxation of primary commodities.

I test two final blunt measures of primary commodities: mining as a percentage of GDP and non-tax revenue as a percentage of GDP. Many studies of tax revenue include *mining* as a percentage of GDP, but the empirical results have proven inconclusive. Fauvelle-Aymar (1999) and Cheibub (1998) both found an unexpected negative association between mining and the tax ratio. As Leiberman (2002, 98) points out, this is likely due to the fact that some types of mineral production, such as oil, are rents and therefore classified as non-tax revenue for the state. Finally, Ross (2006: 288) includes *non-tax revenue* in a prediction of civil war onset, which fails to achieve significance. Since non-tax revenue is a substitute for tax revenue, we would expect it to be negatively related to the tax ratio. Both should be positively related to state failure.

Analysis

The use of the two-stage estimation technique for the system of simultaneous equations modelling state failure onset and state fiscal capacity as endogenous variables produces some intriguing results. In all models, the instrumented variables produced in the first stage estimation exhibit reasonably good fit as indicated by relatively high R^2 values. The quality of these instruments is also reinforced by the fact that there is virtually no difference between the standard errors produced by the Maddala (1983) procedure or the White (1980) and Newey and West (1987). I only present the White/Newey and West standard errors produced in the second stage of the estimation in the tables discussed below. Tables 6-1 and 6-2 present the results from the simultaneous equation model of state fiscal capacity and state failure onset. Table 6-1 presents the first half of the model by demonstrating the effect of state fiscal capacity on state failure onset. The second half of these equations reveals the effects of state failure onset on state fiscal capacity in Table 6-2.

The results presented in Table 6-1 indicate that higher levels of tax revenue reduce the likelihood of state failure onset. This is exactly as Bates and other predatory theorists would expect – African states that are more fiscally capable are less likely to experience internal breakdown. It also replicates Bates's (2008a: 169) statistical finding, despite his use of a different dependent variable to proxy state failure onset. This finding also supports arguments posed by Fearon and Laitin (2003) and Fearon (2005) that strong states can deter rebel opportunism, while weak states provide opportunities for rebellion.

Table 6-1 The effect of state fiscal capacity on state failure onset

Variables	Coefficient	Standard Error
Tax ratio	–6.200**	2.748
Per capita income	.243***	.090
Population	.001	.069
Mountainous terrain	.139**	.064
Noncontiguous state	1.506*	.890
Oil exporter	.013	.273
Instability	–.257	.184
Democracy	–.006	.013
Democracy^2	–.005*	.003
Ethnic fractionalization	3.313***	1.391
Ethnic fractionalization^2	–2.972**	1.305
Religious fractionalization	–.493	.486
N	1448	
LR X^2	21.62***	

Note: Coefficients for peace years, cubic splines and constant are not shown.
Two-tailed test: *p<.10, **p<.05, ***p<.01

Yet, the oil exporter dummy is not significantly related to state failure onset in Africa. What we are able to demonstrate with this modelling technique is that the effect of oil exports is separable from that of state fiscal capacity.

Income per capita is positive and significantly related to state failure. It should also be clear that income per capita is also separable from state capacity, despite its frequent use as a surrogate measure in previous studies. This is not the effect that we would expect to find. In Africa, at least, states with higher income levels are more likely than their less prosperous counterparts to experience state failure onset. Mountainous terrain and noncontiguous state are also positive and significant predictors of state failure as expected. Instability is not a significant predictor of state failure onset, as instability may be just as likely to occur in countries that do and do not experience

Table 6-2 The effect of state failure onset on state fiscal capacity

Variables	Coefficient	Standard Error
State failure	.034*	.017
Trade openness	.085***	.014
Per capita income	–.001	.005
Debt	.026***	.007
ODA	–.089***	.018
Oil exporter	.006	.013
Democracy	.001**	.000
Democracy^2	.001**	.000
Federalism	.012	.013
Ethnic fractionalization	–.046	.063
Ethnic fractionalization^2	.093	.066
Religious fractionalization	–.080***	.018
N	1448	
F	22.65***	

Note: Coefficient for constant is not shown.
Two-tailed test: *p<.10, **p<.05, ***p<.01

state failure. Democracy, while negative at the lower and upper ends of the scale, is only significant at high levels, suggesting the 'inverted-U' found in previous studies. Ethnic fractionalization has a positive effect on state failure at lower levels, but a negative effect at higher levels, consistent with some previous findings (e.g., Elbadwi and Sambanis 2000). This suggests that in Africa, highly fractionalized societies do not provide opportunities to mobilize for rebellion. Religious fractionalization is not significantly related to state failure onset.

In Table 6-2, we can see that state failure onset actually increases the extraction of taxes, which is not exactly what one might expect. Thies (2004) also found a similar positive effect of state failure incidence on the tax ratio in a cross-regional sample of developing countries, which when decomposed into political and ethnic challenges demonstrated that ethnic challenges to the state prompt increases in revenue extraction. This may reflect the instrumental use of ethnicity by the ruler as a tool to increase revenue extraction from ethnic groups that would support his continued rule.[5] Democracy and its squared term both have positive, significant effects on the tax ratio in African states. This does not support Bates's (2008a: 137) story about the discount rate for autocrats facing the transition to democracy, but as he notes, we probably do not have enough data points to fully sort out this relationship yet. ODA is negatively related to the tax ratio, as would be expected as a substitute for tax revenue. Debt is positively related to the tax ratio, which suggests that debt may have helped to build infrastructure to further tax collection efforts. Trade openness is positively related to the tax ratio as expected given the heavy reliance of African states on trade taxes. Federalism, income per capita, and the ethnic fractionalization measures are not significantly related to the tax ratio. Religious fractionalization has a negative effect on the tax ratio, which is what we would expect as a type of transaction cost or the basis for some grievance. The oil exporter dummy variable is not significantly related to the tax ratio, which suggests that state revenue extraction is not substituted for oil rents, nor does oil contribute significantly to the tax base.

Primary Commodities

Table 6-3 tests the effects of a variety of measures of primary commodities found in the literature. In order to conduct these tests, I replaced the oil exporter dummy in the previous models with various configurations of these alternative variables as indicated by the numbers in parenthesis on the left side of Table 6-3. I only report the sign and the significance level for the coefficients. The substitution of these and other measures of primary commodities does not substantially affect the results from the previous equations. What is most stunning about Table 6-3 is the general absence of significant relationships between primary commodities and state failure onset. Only the oil production per capita and mining as a percentage of GDP measures have significant, positive effects on state failure onset. As Bates (2008a) has argued, qualitative studies that suggest a close connection between primary commodities and state failure onset appear mistaken. Instead of affecting state failure onset, primary commodities are more directly related to state fiscal capacity, which is exactly what Bates and other predatory theorists would expect.

Table 6-3 The effect of primary commodities on state failure and state fiscal capacity

Variable	State failure onset	State fiscal capacity
(1) Oil exporter	+	+
(2) Fuel exports/GDP	–	+
(3) Oil production per capita	+**	–
Diamond production per capita	+	+***
(4) Primary Diamond Production	+	+*
Secondary Diamond Production	+	+**
Secondary × Conflict Zone	–	–
(5) sxp	+	+***
sxp^2	–	_***
(6) sxp (log)	+	–
(7) Mining/GDP	+***	+***
(8) Nontax revenue/GDP	+	+*

Let me briefly review the findings from substituting different measures of primary commodities into the state fiscal capacity equation. Neither the oil exporter dummy, fuel exports/GDP nor oil production per capita exhibit a significant effect on the tax ratio. These findings question the notion of a resource curse – at least as it impacts state fiscal capacity. The lack of robust findings about the effect of oil in either the state failure onset or state fiscal capacity equation suggests that much of the literature fails to speak to the African experience.

Diamond production is another matter altogether. Diamond production per capita, and the dummy variables for primary and secondary diamond production all exert significant, positive effects on the tax ratio. These findings suggest that diamond production is largely taxed by the state, as opposed to being a source of rents – including secondary production, which is often thought to fuel civil wars.

The Collier and Hoeffler (1998; 2004) measure of primary commodities, *sxp* and sxp^2, is found to significantly affect state fiscal capacity in a curvilinear manner. Low levels of primary commodity production increase state fiscal capacity, but excessive reliance on primary commodities at high levels reduce state fiscal capacity. Ultimately, Collier and Hoeffler (1998; 2004) are correct in arguing that primary commodities are important, just not in the way that they originally thought. Fearon's (2005) conjecture that the cash crops and fuel exports represented by this measure provide the government with a relatively easy source of tax revenue is consistent with the data. However, the log of *sxp* is not significantly related to the tax ratio.

Finally, in separate tests I include mining as a percentage of GDP and nontax revenue as a percentage of GDP. Mining is positively related to the tax ratio, suggesting that the state is able to capture many of the revenues generated by mining from taxes. Nontax revenue as a percentage of GDP also has a positive effect on the tax ratio, which is not what one would expect if the ruler were substituting nontax revenue for tax revenue. Overall, Bates's (2008a) argument that natural resources should primarily affect the incumbents rather than the insurgents seems to be born out in this data. A variety of measures of primary commodities have direct effects on state fiscal capacity, but few measures directly affect state failure onset.

Conclusion

Bates (2008a) argued that political order can disintegrate depending upon the level of public revenues, the benefits of predation on natural resources, and the discount rates of rulers. The evidence presented in this analysis suggests that rulers at the helms of states with higher levels of tax revenue were less likely to suffer state failure onset than rulers with lower levels of tax revenue. The effect of natural resources on rulers is not exactly what Bates would expect. Oil appears to have no effect on rulers and no robust effect on rebels with the possible exception of oil production per capita. The lack of robust findings across all measures of oil production calls that finding into question as well. In Africa, it appears that oil is not consequential to either state fiscal capacity or state failure onset. Diamond production does not appear to fuel state failure onset, though it does appear to augment the ruler's tax revenue extraction. Although some African rulers notably turned to predation of diamond resources, in the more general African context diamonds continue to support public revenues. Collier and Hoeffler's (1998) broader measure of primary commodities, *sxp* and sxp^2, do not exhibit the expected nonlinear effects on state failure onset. They do have the expected effect on state tax revenues, with low levels supporting tax revenue extraction, but high levels serving to undermine such extraction. The effect of rulers' discount rates is not especially clear from the data. High levels of democracy reduce state failure onset and increase state fiscal capacity. We do not observe increased state failure onset or decreased state fiscal capacity at low levels of democracy.

These results are provocative for they suggest that natural resources are not the problem in Africa, in contradiction to much of the civil war and resource curse literature. The problem of state failure in Africa is driven by crises in public revenues, as Bates has argued theoretically and demonstrated empirically. Efforts by the World Bank and others to augment the capacity of the state are on target and should be supported. Strong states are sometimes seen as a threat to the population in Africa, but this is another case of viewing the state in the aftermath of state failure when the tools of the state are used oppressively. Fiscally capable states provide rulers with the revenues they need to produce political order and investments in the future productive wealth of a country. When states are able to adequately administer systems of taxation, there is no need to prey upon natural resources or the wealth of the population. There is no need for patrons to organize citizens to take up arms against the ruler in order to protect their own wealth or loot wealth from others. As Bates (2008a: 5) notes, 'political order *cannot* be treated as a given'. It is the product of circumstance and choice. The goal for those interested in preventing future state failures is to ensure that the circumstances that produce choices that lead to political disorder are avoided. At a minimum, this means building the fiscal capacity of the state.

Notes

1 'Episodes of violent conflict between governments and politically organized groups (political challengers) that seek to overthrow the central government, to replace its leaders, or to seize power in one region' (Marshall et al. 2001).

2 'Episodes of violent conflict between governments and national, ethnic, religious, or other communal minorities (ethnic challengers) in which the challengers seek major changes in their status' (Marshall et al. 2001).

3 'Adverse shifts in patterns of governance, including major and abrupt shifts away from more open, electoral systems to more closed, authoritarian systems; revolutionary changes in political elites and the mode of governance; contested dissolution of federated states or secession of a substantial area of a state by extrajudicial means; and complete or near-total collapse of central state authority and the ability to govern' (Marshall et al. 2001).

4 'The promotion, execution, and/or implied consent of sustained policies by governing elites or their agents or in the case of civil war, either of the contending authorities that result in the deaths of a substantial portion of a communal group or politicized non communal group' (Marshall et al. 2001).

5 The finding may also reflect the fact that during a state failure episode, GDP declines dramatically while tax revenues take some time to fall off. If this is the

case, then the positive finding is a statistical artifact of a short-term adjustment in the political economy.

References

Bates, Robert H. (2000), 'Ethnicity and Development in Africa', *American Economic Review* 90: 131–4.

Bates, Robert H. (2001), *Prosperity and Violence: The Political Economy of Development* (New York: W.W. Norton).

Bates, Robert H. (2007), 'Political Conflict and State Failure', in Benno Ndulu, Stephen O'Connell, Robert Bates, Paul Collier and Charles Soludo (eds), *The Political Economy of Economic Growth in Africa, 1960–2000* (Cambridge: Cambridge University Press).

Bates, Robert H. (2008a), *When Things Fell Apart: State Failure in Late-Century Africa* (New York: Cambridge University Press).

Bates, Robert H. (2008b), 'State Failure', *Annual Review of Political Science* 11: 1–12.

Bates, Robert H., Greif, Avner and Singh, Smita (2002), 'Organizing Violence', *Journal of Conflict Resolution* 46(5): 599–628.

Bates, Robert H., Epstein, David L., Goldstone, Jack A., Gurr, Ted Robert, Harff, Barbara, Kahl, Colin H., Knight, Kristen, Levy, Marc A., Lustik, Michael, Marshall, Monty G., Parris, Thomas M., Ulfelder, Jay and Woodward, Mark R. (2003), *Political Instability Task Force Report: Phase IV Findings* (McLean, VA: Science Applications International Corporation).

Beck, Nathaniel, Katz, Jonathan N. and Tucker, Robert (1998), 'Taking Time Seriously: Time-Series Cross-Section Analysis Within a Binary Dependent Variable', *American Journal of Political Science* 42(4): 1260–89.

Beck, Thorsten, Clarke, George, Groff, Alberto, Keefer, Philip and Walsh, Patrick (2001), 'New Tools in Comparative Political Economy: The Database of Political Institutions', *World Bank Economic Review* 15(1): 165–76.

Beissinger, Mark R. and Young, Crawford (eds) (2002), *Beyond State Crisis? Postcolonial Africa and Post-Soviet Eurasia in Comparative Perspective* (Washington, DC: Woodrow Wilson Center Press).

Campbell, John L. (1993), 'The State and Fiscal Sociology', *Annual Review of Sociology* 19: 163–85.

Cederman, Lars-Erik and Girardin, Luc (2007), 'Beyond Fractionalization: Mapping Ethnicity onto Nationalist Insurgencies', *American Political Science Review* 101(1): 173–85.

Centeno, Miguel Angel (2002), *Blood and Debt: War and the Nation-State in Latin America* (University Park, PA: Pennsylvania State University Press).

Chaudhry, Kiren Aziz (1997), *The Price of Wealth: Economies and Institutions in the Middle East* (Ithaca, NY: Cornell University Press).

Cheibub, Jose Antonio (1998), 'Political Regimes and the Extractive Capacity of Governments: Taxation in Democracies and Dictatorships', *World Politics* 50: 349–76.

Chesterman, Simon, Ignatieff, Michael and Thakur, Ramesh (2005), *Making States Work: State Failure and the Crisis and Governance* (Tokyo: United Nations University Press).

Clapham, Christopher (1996), *Africa and the International System: The Politics of State Survival* (Cambridge: Cambridge University Press).

Collier, Paul and Hoeffler, Anke (1998), 'On Economic Causes of Civil War', *Oxford Economic Papers* 50(4): 563–73.

Collier, Paul and Hoeffler, Anke (2004), 'Greed and Grievance in Civil War', *Oxford Economic Papers* 56: 563–95.

Desch, Michael C. (1996), 'War and Strong States, Peace and Weak States?', *International Organization* 50: 237–68.

Dunning, Thad (2005), 'Resource Dependence, Economic Performance, and Political Stability', *Journal of Conflict Resolution* 49(4): 451–82.

Elbadwi, Ibrahim and Sambanis, Nicholas (2000), 'Why Are There So Many Civil Wars in Africa? Understanding and Preventing Violent Conflict', *Journal of African Economies* 9(3): 244–69.

Esty, Daniel C., Goldstone, Jack A., Gurr, Ted Robert, Surko, Pamela T. and Unger, Alan N. (1995), *Working Papers: State Failure Task Force Report* (McLean, VA: Science Applications International Corporation).

Esty, Daniel C., Goldstone, Jack, Gurr, Ted Robert, Harff, Barbara, Surko, Pamela T., Unger, Alan N. and Chen, Robert (1998a), 'The State Failure Project: Early Warning Research for US Foreign Policy Planning', in John L. Davies and Ted Robert Gurr (eds), *Preventive Measures: Building Risk Assessment and Crisis Early Warning Systems* (Boulder, CO and Totowa, NJ: Rowman and Littlefield).

Esty, Daniel C., Goldstone, Jack A., Gurr, Ted Robert, Harff, Barbara, Levy, Marc, Dabelko, Geoffrey D., Surko, Pamela T. and Unger, Alan N. (1998b), *State Failure Task Force Report: Phase II Findings* (McLean, VA: Science Applications International Corporation).

Fauvelle-Aymar, Christine (1999), 'The Political and Tax Capacity of Government in Developing Countries', *Kyklos* 52: 391–413.

Fearon, James D. (2005), 'Primary Commodity Exports and Civil War', *Journal of Conflict Resolution* 49(4): 483–507.

Fearon, James D. and Laitin, David D. (2003), 'Ethnicity, Insurgency, and Civil War', *American Political Science Review* 97(1): 75–90.

Fukuyama, Francis (2004), *State-Building: Governance and World Order in the Twenty-first Century* (Ithaca, NY: Cornell University Press).

Gilmore, Elizabeth, Gleditsch, Nils Peter, Lujala, Paivi and Rod, Jan Ketil (2005), 'Conflict Diamonds: A New Dataset', *Conflict Management and Peace Science* 22(3): 257–72.

Goldstone, Jack A., Gurr, Ted Robert, Harff, Barbara, Levy, Marc A., Marshall, Monty G., Bates, Robert H., Epstein, David L., Kahl, Colin H., Surko, Pamela T., Ulfelder, John C. and Unger, Alan N. in consultation with Christenson, Matthew, Dabelko, Geoffrey D., Esty, Daniel C. and Parris, Thomas M. (2000), *State Failure Task Force Report: Phase III Findings* (McLean, VA: Science Applications International Corporation).

Greene, William H. (2003), *Econometric Analysis*, 5th edn (Upper Saddle River, NJ: Prentice Hall).

Gujarati, Damodar N. (2003), *Basic Econometrics*, 4th edn (New York: McGraw-Hill Irwin).

Hegre, Havard, Gates, Scott and Gleditsch, Nils Petr (2001), 'Toward a Democratic Civil Peace? Democracy, Political Change and Civil War, 1816–1992', *American Political Science Review* 95: 33–48.

Hegre, Havard and Sambanis, Nicholas (2006), 'Sensitivity Analysis of Empirical Results on Civil War Onset', *Journal of Conflict Resolution* 50(4): 508–35.

Herbst, Jeffrey (2000), *States and Power in Africa: Comparative Lessons in Authority and Control* (Princeton, NJ: Princeton University Press).

Heston, Alan, Summers, Robert and Aten, Bettina (2006), Penn World Table Version 6.2, Center for International Comparisons of Production, Income and Prices at the University of Pennsylvania.

Humphreys, Macartan (2005), 'Natural Resources, Conflict, and Conflict Resolution: Uncovering the Mechanisms', *Journal of Conflict Resolution* 49(4): 508–37.

Jackson, Robert H. and Rosberg, Carl G. (1982), 'Why Africa's Weak States Persist: The Empirical and the Juridical in Statehood', *World Politics* 35: 1–24.

Johnson, Kristin and Rabinowitz, Marina Arbetman (2005), 'Relative Political Capacity Model and Data Description', paper prepared for the Workshop on Political Economy, Claremont Graduate University, 7 October.

Karl, Terry L. (1997), *The Paradox of Plenty: Oil Booms, Venezuela, and Other Petro-States* (Berkeley, CA: University of California Press).

Keshk, Omar M.G. (2003), 'CDSIMEQ: A Program to Implement Two-Stage Probit Least Squares', *The State Journal* 3: 157–67.

Keshk, Omar, Pollins, Brian M. and Reuveny, Rafael (2004), 'Trade Still Follows the Flag: The Primacy of Politics in a Simultaneous Model of Interdependence and Armed Conflict', *Journal of Politics* 66(4): 1155–79.

King, Gary and Zeng, Langche (2001), 'Improving Forecasts of State Failure', *World Politics* 53(4): 623–58.

Le Billon, Philippe (2001), 'The Political Ecology of War: Natural Resources and Armed Conflicts', *Political Geography* 20: 561–84.

Levi, Margaret (1988), *Of Rule and Revenue* (Berkeley, CA: University of California Press).

Lieberman, Evan S. (2002), 'Taxation Data as Indicators of State-Society Relations: Possibilities and Pitfalls in Cross-National Research', *Studies in Comparative and International Development* 36(4): 89–115.

Luong, Pauline Jones and Weinthal, Erika (2006), 'Rethinking the Resource Curse: Ownership Structure, Institutional Capacity, and Domestic Constraints', *Annual Review of Political Science* 9: 241–63.

Lujala, Paivi, Gleditsch, Nils Petter, and Gilmore, Elisabeth (2005), 'A Diamond Curse? Civil War and a Lootable Resource', *Journal of Conflict Resolution* 49(4): 538–62.

Lustick, Ian (1997), 'The Absence of Middle Eastern Great Powers: Political "Backwardness" in Historical Perspective', *International Organization* 51: 653–83.

Maddala, G.S. (1983), *Limited Dependent and Qualitative Variables in Econometrics* (Cambridge: Cambridge University Press).

Marshall, Monty G., Gurr, Ted Robert and Harff, Barbara (2001), *Political Instability Task Force Problem Set Codebook* (McLean, VA: Science Applications International Corporation).

Newey, W. and West, K. (1987), 'A Simple Positive Semi-Definite, Heteroscedasticity and Autocorrelation Consistent Covariance Matrix', *Econometrica* 55: 703–78.

North, Douglass C. (1981), *Structure and Change in Economic History* (New York: W.W. Norton).

Olson, Mancur (1993), 'Dictatorship, Democracy, and Development', *American Political Science Review* 87: 567–76.

Organski, A.F.K. and Kugler, Jacek (1980), *The War Ledger* (Chicago: University of Chicago Press).

Remmer, Karen (2004), 'Does Foreign Aid Promote the Expansion of Government?', *American Journal of Political Science* 48: 77–92.

Reno, William (1998), *Warlord Politics and African States* (Boulder, CO: Lynne Rienner).

Reuveny, Rafael and Li, Quan (2003), 'The Joint Democracy-Dyadic Conflict Nexus: A Simultaneous Equations Model', *International Studies Quarterly* 47(3): 325–46.

Ross, Michael L. (2001), 'Does Oil Hinder Democracy?', *World Politics* 53(3): 325–61.

Ross, Michael L. (2006), 'A Closer Look at Oil, Diamonds, and Civil War', *Annual Review of Political Science* 9: 265–300.

Rotberg, Robert I. (ed.) (2003a), *When States Fail: Causes and Consequences* (Princeton, NJ: Princeton University Press).

Rotberg, Robert I. (ed.) (2003b), *State Failure and State Weakness in a Time of Terror* (Washington, DC: Brookings Institution Press).

Sambanis, Nicholas (2001), 'Do Ethnic and Nonethnic Civil Wars Have the Same Causes?: A Theoretical and Empirical Inquiry (Part 1)', *Journal of Conflict Resolution* 45(3): 259–82.

Smith, Benjamin (2004), 'Oil Wealth and Regime Survival in the Developing World, 1960–1999', *American Journal of Political Science* 48(2): 232–46.

Snider, Lewis (1990), 'The Political Performances of Third World Governments and the Debt Crisis', *American Political Science Review* 84: 1263–80.

Snyder, Richard (2006), 'Does Lootable Wealth Breed Disorder? A Political Economy of Extraction Framework', *Comparative Political Studies* 39(8): 943–68.

Snyder, Richard and Bhavnani, Ravi (2005), 'Diamonds, Blood, and Taxes: A Revenue-Centered Framework for Explaining Political Order', *Journal of Conflict Resolution* 49(4): 563–97.

Tsai, Ming-Chang (1999), 'State Power, State Embeddedness, and National Development in Less Developed Countries: A Cross-National Analysis', *Studies in Comparative and International Development* 33(4): 66–88.

Thies, Cameron G. (2004), 'State Building, Interstate and Intrastate Rivalry: A Study of Post-Colonial Developing Country Extractive Efforts, 1975–2000', *International Studies Quarterly* 48(1): 53–72.

Thies, Cameron G. (2005), 'War, Rivalry, and State Building in Latin America', *American Journal of Political Science* 49(3): 451–65.

Thies, Cameron G. (2006), 'Public Violence and State Building in Central America', *Comparative Political Studies* 39(10):1263–82.

Thies, Cameron G. (2007), 'The Political Economy of State Building in Sub-Saharan Africa', *Journal of Politics* 69(3): 716–31.

Tilly, Charles (1985), 'War Making and State Making as Organized Crime', in P. Evans, D. Rueschemeyer, and T. Skocpol (eds), *Bringing the State Back In* (Cambridge: Cambridge University Press).
Tilly, Charles (1992), *Coercion, Capital, and European States, AD 990–1992* (Cambridge, MA: Blackwell).
White, H. (1980), 'A Heteroscedasticity-Consistent Covariance Matrix Estimator and a Direct Test for Heteroscedasticity', *Econometrica* 48: 817–38.
Wibbels, Erik (2005), *Federalism and the Market: Intergovernmental Conflict and Economic Reform in the Developing World* (New York: Cambridge University Press).

Chapter Seven

Neopatrimonial Crises and the Strategy of Ethnic Violence: Darfur and Beyond

Pablo Yanguas

All cruelty springs from weakness. (Seneca)

Massacres do not happen spontaneously. If only for the basic reason that most people, most of the time, would prefer not to kill, massacres should be among the most improbable of social phenomena in times of peace. However, the 1990s and 2000s have witnessed some truly horrendous forms of collective violence take place in sub-Saharan Africa, with Rwanda and Darfur becoming tragically familiar names around the world. This begs the question, if massacres seldom arise out of spontaneous social action, of whether there is someone who stands to benefit from promoting such violence, someone who would see collective violence as a means to achieving certain ends. History tells us that in times of crisis there are indeed many different ways in which entrepreneurs of death can push ordinary people into committing the worst kinds of atrocities. This chapter focuses on one such mechanism.

My argument can be summarized thus: in African post-colonial states ethnic violence is likely to be a crisis-management tool deployed by neopatrimonial elites who stand to lose from change. This proposition, as it should be clear from its formulation, does not aspire to be a covering law of human behaviour. Instead, it is a hypothesis intimately tied to the specific ways in which African states have developed since independence. And it is not an entirely new idea either. Quite on the opposite, the aim of this chapter is to conceptualize in an explicit manner a mechanism that research on ethnic conflict in Africa has often relied on implicitly. In the pages that follow the first section deals with concept-building, specifically regarding the main historical components of my argument. The second section takes these concepts and builds them into a mechanism of strategic choice. The third section attempts to illustrate some implications of the argument in brief case studies of ethnic violence in Darfur, Kenya, and Rwanda. The fourth and concluding section deals with structural consequences of the mechanism and some basic implications.

Even controlling for rhetorical liberties, the opening quote by classical philosopher Seneca is loaded with sociological insights. We normally think of cruelty as an individual aberration, belonging to the domain of psychopathy. However, Seneca tells us, there is also a relational aspect to cruelty – weakness. And for a person to be weak, by necessity there has to be another person who is powerful. It is as a reaction to this power imbalance that cruelty may appear. The ideas that I articulate here follow similar assumptions, but at a collective instead of individual level. The gist of it can be loosely summarized by taking Seneca's words and substituting 'ethnic violence' for 'cruelty' and 'threat' for 'weakness'. I do not think that all ethnic violence originates in this way, but I argue that in sub-Saharan Africa a substantial portion of it does.

The Weight of History: Power, Resources and Identity

I propose that at least some of the instances of ethnic violence in recent African history have resulted from purposeful manipulation by neopatrimonial elites trying to maintain a status quo that ensures their position of power. The actual workings of the mechanism that accounts for this outcome will be spelled out in the next section. But first, for the argument to function three necessary components have to be explored: a) a power structure that benefits the elite; b) a threat to this structure by non-elite actors; and c) the means whereby the elite can instigate and channel ethnic violence.

The Post-colonial State and Neopatrimonialism

If there is a strong consensus among students of post-colonial African politics, it is the categorization of most African states as neopatrimonial. The term 'neopatrimonialism' was first used for African cases in the 1980s to define a special kind of political system in which 'the bureaucratic logic was artificially applied to a patrimonial logic' (Medard 1982, 179). Other terms have been used that refer roughly to the same phenomenon, such as 'patrimonial bureaucracy' (Zolberg 1966) or 'patrimonial administrative state' (Callaghy 1984), but all of them have in common a number of core features, and they all build upon Weberian concepts.

Max Weber distinguished between three ideal-typical bases of domination – charismatic, traditional, and bureaucratic. Patrimonialism is a type of traditional domination that expands the 'household' model of domination to the whole polity, creating an extended form of patriarchal order whereby the ruler owns the public domain. Officials are chosen on a personal basis by the ruler, according to their loyalty and dependence more than to their expertise or reliability. They are thus extensions of him, their authority and position subject to his arbitrariness, and their loyalty is maintained through material rewards and access to positions of predation upon society. Patrimonialism is characterized by a constant tension between the arbitrariness of the ruler and the limitations of tradition. To avoid this tension legitimation is achieved through certain ideological tools, such as that of 'enlightened absolutism', which often portray an ideal glorified by collective legends (Weber 1968, 1006–69).

If one defines a modern power structure as one which is structured around the principles of Weberian bureaucratic logic, i.e. the regularization and institutionalization of an impersonal and rational system of administration (ibid., 1393), neopatrimonialism appears then as a nonmodern power structure. Still by its very nature it is 'a contemporary phenomenon closely bound to modernization' (Medard 1982, 179), since it represents the merging of a modern logic with a patrimonial one. It is not purely a patrimonial system, but a hybrid regime product of a limited modernization. Its roots can be traced back to pre-colonial modes of authority, but also to the colonial state, and to the particularities of post-colonial political design. It is not a totally irrational order, in the Weberian sense, for at the core lies a political machine based on 'a fairly rational distributive system', but one 'which is based on other than rational-legal norms' (Zolberg 1966, 160–61).

The transition from the colonial to the post-colonial state in Africa was a key moment in the formation of current neopatrimonial regimes, in that it reflected a double trend of continuity and change. Continuity was reflected in the inherited institutional and regulative architecture of the colonial state seized by the new African elites. This institutional heritage included the late colonial notion of the state as 'manager of transformation, at once architect of development and its primary theologian', together with its high degree of intervention in economic and political affairs (Young 2004). Change manifested itself through an expansion of this notion, fuelled by a growing confidence in a model of state-led development that was supported both by socialist and welfare-capitalist doctrines at the time. Throughout the continent governments seized foreign ownership of economic resources, beginning a process of nationalization and indigenization aimed especially at commodity- and fuel-exporting sectors. As it gained control of the economy, the state was tilting the system against the development of private enterprises (against Weberian rationality) and towards the public or parastatal sector.

Neopatrimonialism thus linked a nonproductive socioeconomic logic with a state-level political logic that turned the state into 'the major avenue of upward mobility and accumulation' (Callaghy 1988), truly 'the prime instrument with which a class can hope to become a ruling class' (Fatton 1988, 254). The long-term rationality of economic development has been constantly displaced by the short-term logic of enrichment and patronage, and entrepreneurial activity outside patrimonial capitalism was virtually non-existent beyond the small-scale informal economy (Van de Walle 2001).

In the political sphere, unity took precedence over competition, and the single-party state became the dominant political system in Africa, aspiring to engulf the whole polity in its developmental project. Patrimonial authoritarianism has been defined as a synthesis of three forms of state: the 'colonial state', characterized by its command over society and its high degree of intervention; the 'integral state', characterized by state tutelage of the masses; and the 'prebendal state', characterized by rent-seeking, clientelism, and corruption, which undermines the other two (Young 1994). State incapacity is thus one of the fundamental consequences of this synthesis. The state is 'quasi-omnipresent, but not anywhere near omnipotent;' its power 'is not unlimited, but rather unsupervised' (Callaghy 1988, 81). Even though the patrimonial administrative state was born of this attempt at state-building, it was ultimately plagued by a lack of capacity combined with a multi-layered interplay of authorities, both internal and external, traditional and modern (Callaghy 1984, 34–68).

In essence, neopatrimonialism stems from 'the absence of distinction between public and private domains, or rather the privatization of the public sector' (Medard 1982, 177). While at the core of Western societies there is a distinction between the public and private realms, both grounded on a common moral foundation, African societies present two distinct public realms, a civic one and a primordial one (Ekeh 1975). The former relates to the colonial legacy of rational-legal institutions; the latter relates to the traditional form of legitimacy, the same set of norms that sustains the private realm. As a result the civic public realm is deprived from effective authority and does not embody any kind of public interest. Instead, it is 'a place from which one seeks to gain' for patrimonial purposes, be it public or private (Hyden 1983, 39). And those who hijack the public sphere naturally rise to the top of the power structure.

The question of political-economic elites in Africa is probably one of the most undisputed elements of scholarly research. As John Dunn summarizes it, 'the one social category in Africa which is by common consent rather successful in representing itself is the membership of the higher echelons of the state apparatus; career politicians, senior civil servants (particularly when involved in the regulation of international trade or the award of major public contracts), senior army officers, and managers of state sector economic enterprises' (Dunn 1986, 164). Indeed, through their access to the state, they have become 'the ultimate and decisive builders of clienteles' (Fatton 1988, 261). Instead of a rational-legal bureaucracy, the state is dominated by a 'bureaucratic gentry', 'a class based not on their relation to property but on their relation to the state apparatus', which engages in policies of economic redistribution for its own enrichment (Zolberg 1966, 142). This 'political aristocracy' (Callaghy 1984, 184–94) that comprises the state elite enjoys a certain degree of autonomy from both infra- and supra-state groups and organizations; it is able to manoeuvre between a society characterized by little political participation and foreign sponsors more concerned about security than about the returns to their economic aid. Since societies have remained largely rural and illiterate, and since they are not horizontally structured along class or corporatist lines, but vertically along ethnic and clientelistic networks, the ruling elite can count on a collective action problem or outright ignorance on the part of a society indifferent to civic values.

What this 'theoretical history' of the post-colonial African state does is providing the setting in which all of my argument is rooted. Especially when the state controls most – if not all – of economic activity, directly through the fiscal process and indirectly through regulation, those who control the state enjoy a privileged position atop a power structure from which they are able to organize social relations to their own benefit. Naturally, when someone comes forth and challenges their privileged position, neopatrimonial elites are bound to be, at the very least, irritated.

The Fundamental Threat of Distributive Challenges

By distributive challenge I mean a political initiative seeking redress of some kind of distributive imbalance. The neopatrimonial regime is built on stark inequalities, and it is not at all uncommon for it to privilege one region over another, or one particular tribe, or one set of families within a tribe. It is only logical that excluded groups will resent their limited access to resources in the regime. However, this resentment may never materialize politically. One of the great political feats of neopatrimonial leaders has been to de-link popular participation from political decision-making, relegating it to the domain of symbolism (Chazan 1982). Therefore it can be difficult for the disenfranchised to even address the neopatrimonial regime. Inequality does not necessarily breed protest. But it does carry the seeds of it.

There are several ways in which such grievances may come to the political arena in times of crisis, such as conflict in a neighbouring country, a rearrangement of the political elite, or donor-promoted multi-party elections. The causal effect of such critical events is not to magically organize and mobilize the disenfranchised and underprivileged. Such a task requires political entrepreneurs whose agenda may or may not prosper. What critical junctures do is to make visible that which is normally invisible, thinkable what is normally unthinkable, political what is normally apolitical. As Bourdieu put it, '[e]very established order tends to produce (to very different degrees and with very different means) the naturalization of its own arbitrariness' (1977, 164). However, when orthodoxy needs to assert itself, it has already lost its hegemonic power. It is in such times of crisis that resources are stretched, accountability is strained, and dissent finds its own breathing space – the opportunity for distributive challenges arises. Considering the inherent imbalances of neopatrimonialism, the articulation and politicization of inequality is very likely to prosper during critical junctures. Which means that, given enough time, distributive challenges are virtually inevitable.

Two interconnected features of the distributive challenge are particularly important. First, it amounts to an exercise of voice. Albert Hirschman (1970) theorized the three possible courses of action in the face of organizational decline: loyalty, voice, or exit. Distributive challenges are symptomatic of a collapse of loyalty to the neopatrimonial regime, but more often than not they represent instances of voice, not exit – the challengers do not 'want out', they 'want in', they demand their share of the resource pool. Second, this voice is exercised through extra-institutional channels. Due to state capture by the ruling elites, state institutions have no legitimacy or trust in the eyes of the challengers, who will be reluctant to seek redress in administrative or judicial fora. Instead, they are likely to take their grievances beyond the regulated arena of institutions into the open arena of politics.

What neopatrimonialism does, through the merging of private and public spheres and the reproduction of structural inequality, is to transform every dispute over resource distribution into a dispute over the nature of the regime. This explains why a distributive challenge constitutes an explicit threat to the dominant position of neopatrimonial elites. The next section will address the strategies with which they can respond to this threat, but first I will explore the tools which they can deploy in their reaction.

Ethnopatronage Networks as Instruments of Mobilization

Once a distributive challenge arises, I hypothesize that a likely course of action by the threatened patrimonial elite will be to incite ethnic violence. This proposition is based on the presence of ethnopatronage networks, a combination of two interconnected legacies that facilitate ethnic mobilization – politicized ethnicity and patron-client networks.

While the first component, politicized ethnicity, seems straightforward enough, I believe it merits some careful consideration. Most crucially, it is important to stress at the outset that politicized ethnicity is not equivalent to ethnic heterogeneity (Posner 2004). There are two main reasons for this. First, ethnicity is not *the* social cleavage, but *a* social cleavage. In any given society individuals have more than one identity at any given time. Ethnicity belongs to the category of collective markers, which includes nation, class, profession, political ideology, party, etc. Second, ethnicity becomes relevant only when it is made relevant, when it trumps all other forms of identity and becomes the major political cleavage in society. As Max Weber wrote, 'it is primarily the political community, no matter how artificially organized, that inspires the belief in common ethnicity' (1968, 389). Therefore we may restate the first structural legacy as a political history in which ethnicity has been made relevant as a form of legitimate representation.

Ethnicity is an extension of kinship based on the shared belief on a common ancestry, regardless of whether or not an objective blood relationship exists. As psychological and cognitive studies have shown, people have an innate tendency to categorize themselves and others as members of groups, adopting collective positions that are more polarized than their own preferences and engaging in constant intergroup comparison (Tajfel 1981; Horowitz 1985, 142ff; Zeruvabel 1997). As one among multiple, overlapping categories for self- and other-categorization, ethnicity is a presumed identity that contains the potential for group formation, but does not constitute the group (Brubaker 2004). Ethnic trust may actually find itself at odds with other forms of political identity, such as class or professional affiliation. This is so because ethnicity is a form of intrinsic community, in which membership is based on ascriptive characteristics related to birth, as opposed to extrinsic communities based on common interests and choice (Horowitz 1985, 55). For this reason, the rise of a particular communal marker entails some sort of instrumentality (Posner 2005), but I posit that the crystallization of politicized ethnicity has less to do with individuals choosing from identity repertoires, and more with ethnic entrepreneurs putting forward group-making projects (Brubaker 2004). However, as David Laitin (1986, 177) wrote of culture, identity is both 'internally dynamic and politically embedded', which means that manipulation by ethnic entrepreneurs is possible within the boundaries of shared conceptions of identity.

In neopatrimonial regimes social trust is to a large extent articulated through ethnic communities, and embedded in clientelistic networks (Berman 2004). Ethnicity is politicized to the extent that kinship groups are considered to be the building blocks of society, replacing the state-individual relationship that lies at the core of Western notions. Peter Ekeh (2004) provides an interesting historical explanation for the prevalence of kinship in Africa, starting from what he calls the 'Hobbesian complex'. In his view, a state that from pre-colonial times has been indifferent or even inimical to individuals' basic security needs cannot command the loyalty that would breed civic trust. Instead, ethnicity and kinship have an important role to play in contexts of state incapacity, inefficiency, indifference, or outright predation. The civic bond between the citizen and the state is thus replaced with the ethnic bond between community members, and between these and community leaders.

African ethnic groups are understood in an external sense as the collective actors of competitive politics, in what has been termed political tribalism, but also as the 'internal discursive political arena, through which ethnic identities have emerged out of multiple, selective imaginings of 'tradition', culture, and identity from European as well as African sources', what has been termed moral ethnicity (Berman 2006, 9). These conceptions were entrenched by the colonial system of indirect rule, which based its strategy of political control on the empowerment as clients of 'traditional' leaders who would oversee 'tribal' communities, understood as the fundamental building blocks of social organization. Through their link to the state, traditional leaders became the key to state resources and authority, and after independence they ended up merging with the central elite, which has used a policy of redistribution to organize their political base around ethnic and clientelistic lines. The result has been the racialization of a citizen that has often become an ethnic subject (Mamdani 1996).

Together with politicized ethnicity, the second legacy that facilitates ethnic mobilization is the pervasiveness of patron-client networks, which are often singled out as the main channels of accountability and sources of societal cohesion in post-colonial Africa (Chabal and Daloz 1999; Berman 2004). They entail a reciprocal contract that ties both patron and client, which generates expectations towards both sides. Accountability is thus understood, not strictly in terms of representation, but in terms of redistribution. 'If a big man is able to help, he will expect a thanksgiving gift or personal service from the recipient at a later date. In addition, and perhaps more important, the recipient will sing the praises of his benefactor in the community' (Dixon 1991, 69). This utilitarian rationale of reciprocity has pervaded politics in Africa, and it has been sustained by the presence of norms emphasizing the principles of patriarchalism and redistribution (Schatzberg 2001). As a vertical logic, in addition, clientelism prevents the formation of horizontal solidarities, such as those of class and professional occupation, thus fundamentally hindering the chances of interest groups and political parties that are not constituted along patronage lines. It is precisely for this reason that political entrepreneurs usually play the identitarian card in order to gain access to power; if they can prove that they represent a significant group, they will be offered co-option.

The patrimonial politics of ethnicity in post-colonial Africa, therefore, stems both from the structure of access to state resources, with a political aristocracy at its top, and from the set of underlying norms of accountability and redistribution. This is a question of social hierarchy because, as Bruce Berman stresses, in the post-colonial period the dominant discourses of ethnicity have indeed come from 'those groups who gained the most from colonialism – the indigenous authorities of the colonial state and the educated elite – and interpreted tradition to justify their gains and maintain control over networks of patronage that provided access for others to the resources of modernity' (1998, 327).

Managing the Crisis: Dilemmas, Strategies, and Violence

My argument is based on the concepts just explored. Atop neopatrimonial states are political elites whose power is based on controlling access to economic resources and redistributing them in support of their clientelistic base. This kind of political-economic regime is both self-perpetuating and self-destructive. On the one hand, it perpetuates itself through the de-politicization of participation and the organization of citizens into ethnic constituencies linked to elite members. On the other hand, it undermines itself through an imbalanced power distribution, manifest in the form of unequal access to resources, which is bound to be contested by excluded groups in times of crisis. When a distributive challenge arises, it presents the neopatrimonial elite with a dilemma. In theorizing about such dilemma, my argument draws from rational choice approaches to ethnic violence (Bates 1983; Fearon and Laitin 1996), while keeping in mind social-psychological theories (Kaufman 2006). The intent of my own approach is to bring insights from both schools closer to the specific macro-institutional features of neopatrimonialism. In so doing I attempt to reconcile structure, culture, and choice in African instances of ethnic violence.

Elite Dilemmas: Choosing the Right Strategy

In light of a distributive challenge, the neopatrimonial aristocracy has to confront the dilemmas of reconciling two conflicting objectives: 1) maintaining the power distribution, and 2) demobilizing the challenge. Ideally, they would achieve the former without making any concessions to the latter. But the uncertainty of a distributive crisis guarantees that there will be trade-offs involved.

In principle, the elite has a choice of three core strategies: co-option, redress, and confrontation. Co-option is a well-known practice based on clear rules and a predictable outcome: the elite invites the leadership of the challenging constituency into the regime, in exchange for an end to the challenge. In essence, they just need to put a few more chairs at the table, granting the leaders of the distributive challenge access to the state, and thus offering the aggrieved populations some kind of indirect redress. Actual redress, in contrast, entails granting resources to the aggrieved constituency, in the form of offices, budget transfers, service provision, etc. It is a costly matter, in so far as the resource pool has to be resized and renegotiated, and history has shown that most regimes are not concerned about service provision or redistributive policies. Confrontation, finally, entails facing the challenge in security terms, commanding police, paramilitary, and/or military forces to repress dissent. In the case of regimes with strong coercive capacity and close links to the security services, confrontation might be a viable choice. However, in many African countries terrain is a paramount impediment to counterinsurgency operations, the costs of which cannot be accurately predicted and can actually end up weakening the regime. Just like redress is undesirable because of its elevated costs, confrontation is much too uncertain to be a safe strategy.

Under normal circumstances, then, the elite is likely to choose co-option, or bargaining. James Fearon (1995) developed a rational choice model to explain why the most likely outcome of the prospect of war should be a negotiated settlement. He assumes that (a) both sides stand to lose from a conflict, and (b) under conditions of perfect information it is easy to tell who will win in the end. The expected losing side will foresee that it can actually stand to lose less from compromising than fighting, in which case the incentives for it to negotiate are strong. Unless there is private information or an inability to commit, therefore, the prospect of war should logically lead to a bargained settlement instead of actual war.

One of the assumptions of Fearon's model that matters for neo-patrimonialism concerns the divisibility of the issue at stake. Money, ministries, and offices are all divisible, so that disputes over them offer a good prospect of settlement. In some instances, nonetheless, bargaining might just not be possible due to the indivisibility of the issue of contention. Perhaps the challengers of neopatrimonial regimes will not accept anything short of structural reform, or perhaps the costs of their demands are so great to the elites that meeting them would equal relinquishing their control of resources and power. These are but two of the hypothetical conditions under which compromises are unlikely, and it is under such circumstances that the uncertain outcome of confrontation may be seen as a less costly strategy than co-option.

Elite Choices: Strategic Ethnicization and Violence

The central theoretical point of my argument is that if the neopatrimonial elite chooses confrontation over co-option, a process of strategic ethnicization is likely to ensue. Strategic ethnicization is the process by which the elite emphasizes those identity cleavages that would weaken the challengers and strengthen their own position. This theory builds upon the idea that different cleavages benefit different actors at different levels of scale (Posner 2005), and it elaborates on the concept of in-group policing (Laitin 1995). The mechanism works in the following manner: when a distributive challenge garners its support by appealing to a particular identity, it is in the interest of the threatened elite to attack that support base through the promotion of a different identitarian cleavage, particularly if the latter strengthens their own support base. A couple of examples can illustrate the rationale behind this strategy. Against a programmatic, interethnic challenge, this strategy would call for shifting the politics from horizontal to vertical cleavages, for instance categorizing the challenge as a covert hegemonic initiative by one of the ethnicities, with two objectives: first and foremost making some of the challengers question their allies' intentions, but also preventing defections from the elite's own ethnic group. Against a region-based challenge, in contrast, strategic ethnicization would shift the politics to such identitarian scale as it favours the ruling elite. Such a challenge may be portrayed as a ploy by one of the sub-regional groups to achieve supremacy. In both cases, the desired outcome of the ethnicization strategy is to break up the challengers into smaller, competing groups.

Strategic ethnicization is possible because of the two tools for social mobilization that I have already presented – politicized ethnicity and patron-client networks. In neopatrimonial regimes certain forms of identity are constantly actualized to the detriment of others, even if it is in a latent manner. The politicization of certain frames is feasible because the whole system of political accountability as access to resources is based on such frames. The most powerful frame of political mobilization that leaders have is the one that keeps their patron-client relations legitimate. Therefore, in the wake of a distributive crisis that threatens the distribution of power, the elite will try to use their patronage networks to exacerbate certain ethnic affiliations in order to counter multi-ethnic, class, or regional challenges. And the most efficient way of shifting the fault line of conflict is by inciting ethnic distrust and violence. The cognitive frames of collective identity are already embedded in the political-economic system, making any kind of mobilization easier – it is not a process of construction, but of intensification. This argument is thus a logical prediction of the research on neopatrimonialism – a political aristocracy whose power base is at stake will try to reinforce ethnic differences in order to maintain its control of the state.

An interesting implication is that, in contrast to non-patrimonial cases, ethnic violence in neopatrimonial regimes is likely to result in – instead of being the result of – a heightening of ethnic differentiation and hatred, with ideologies reframing – instead of constructing – the threat. At first violence is likely to come from the core clients of the threatened elite and, as the confrontation spreads to the entire polity, non-patrimonial coalitions will face increasing challenges to its constituent members, who will eventually be dragged into their collective identities because of the security dilemma (Posen 1993; Kasfir 2004). As distrust, confrontation, and violence spread away from core clients into society, collective and individual motivations for ethnic cleansing will gradually rise to the fore (Mann 2005). However, it is important to locate the trigger in a threatened elite trying to manage a distributive challenge. At best, this mechanism of crisis management will result in isolated episodes of violence and the dissolution of opposition organizations. At worst, it will pit ethnic groups against each other, with dire consequences for those that do not enjoy the support of neopatrimonial patrons within the regime (Berman 1998, 336). It is here that the process of escalation can take place due to a variety of contextual reasons, such as democratization, economic crisis or civil war, turning ethnic confrontation into persecution, expulsion or outright genocide.

Illustrating the Mechanism: Tribal Militias, Ethnic Clashes, Genocide

Theories that deal with such imperfectly measurable variables as identitarian cleavages and informal networks are always difficult to explore. However, the mechanism that I have outlined in the previous section does produce some observable implications that we should look for in empirical instances of ethnic violence. First, ethnicization understood as an ethnic-based discourse of confrontation will originate in threatened elites, not in challengers. Second, elites are likely to promote non-state actors, officially detached from the regime, to initiate the kind of cleavage violence that aims to disrupt the challengers. Third, ethnic violence is likely to spread from core neopatrimonial clients, so that the first perpetrators should be direct supporters of the threatened elite. Fourth, as the discourse and practice of confrontation propagates, interethnic coalitions are likely to collapse due to the security dilemma. Fifth, as a result of conflict the identitarian agenda will trump the original distributive agenda, turning the challenge into a tradtional patrimonial conflict.

A good research design should be able to operationalize the data in such a way as to prove or disprove these and other possible observable implications. However, for the purposes of this chapter my interest is that of illustrating the inner workings of the mechanism. To that end I have selected three seemingly different instances of ethnic violence in recent African history: the tribal conflict in the Sudanese region of Darfur since 2003; the ethnic clashes around multi-party elections in Kenya in the 1990s; and the genocide of Rwanda in 1994. With these cases I seek to illustrate the internal logic and key components of the argument – neopatrimonial regime, politicized ethnicity, patron-client accountability, a distributive challenge, and the response by a threatened elite in the form of strategic ethnicization. My aim is not to minimize the specificity of each country's situation, but to highlight the kind of empirical regularities that warrant further comparative research.

Tribal Militias in Darfur

The Sudan is a tragically archetypal case of neopatrimonial regime. A 'successfully failed state', Sudan's government and economy are dominated by a narrow segment of the population coming from the Northern, Arab-identified regions of the country, and who benefits from a regime that plays on the ethnic divisions and the localized isolation of the rest of society (Prunier and Gisselquist 2003). This 'Riverine Arab' political elite is organized as a network of families connected by intermarriage, whose members are 'sons of the country', as opposed to the rest of Sudanese, who would implicitly be second-class citizens (Prunier 2005, 172 n. 36). They are a neopatrimonial elite with a *de facto* monopoly over political and economic power in Sudan.

For the purposes of enforcing this monopoly they have such tools of social mobilization as I have conceptualized above. In terms of politicized identity, the country is yet another case of precolonial identities being racialized by the colonial state, from the inherent flexibility of cultural practice to the rigid boundaries of political institutionalization. The policy of indirect rule by British administrators fragmented local people into imagined and constructed 'native authorities with different sets of customary law or tribal law' (Idris 2005: 40). Especially relevant was the Victorian evolutionary worldview that categorized Sudanese communities into civilizing 'Arabs' and tribal 'Africans', a distinction whose political repercussions would be paramount in the days to come (Prunier and Gisselquist, 112). Independence would further institutionalize this divide, consolidating the political hegemony of the north against marginalized black Muslims in the western regions and nilotic Christian and Animist populations of the South. In a common neopatrimonial practice, the various Sudanese regimes have included 'token members' of these minorities in their governments, while guaranteeing that the party system is based exclusively on sectarian and tribal alliances (ibid., 114).

Such a political arrangement has facilitated the exercise of control through ethnopatronage networks that have managed to survive apparently substantive regime change. Indeed, despite the revolution of 1989 that expelled president Nimeiri and installed an Islamist regime, the main resorts of power have remained largely associated with a small group of people traceable to the central areas of the country, from which all leaders have emerged. Although policies of Islamization and Arabization have fed into the identitarian divide between 'Arabs' and 'Africans', central authorities have followed a policy of ensuring control of the regions by replacing local officials with loyal clients (Kasfir 2005). Family, clan, sectarian and ethnopatronage networks are thus the main resorts of power, in a pattern that illustrates the neopatrimonial logic.

In 1983 a revolt started in the South to confront this status quo, posing the first big distributive challenge to the regime. The Sudanese People's Liberation Army/Movement (SPLA/M) crafted itself not as a separatist movement, but as a state-wide challenge to the regime, seeking to unite the whole country along political lines transcending regional, ethnic, and racial interests. In Sudan, the regime's response to this kind of challenge has usually been to arm tribal militias recruited from the 'Arab' regional clients. In order to ensure its grip to power and resources, the elite has resorted to an implicit intensification of ethnic confrontation, so that tribal militias have prospered in post-colonial times – with direct or indirect support from the government – where they did not exist in precolonial times, and their role has been significant in the conflict with the SPLA/M. This retribalization has shrunk the political arena, signalling a shift from building modern institutions to reinforcing ethnic tendencies in political action (Salih 1989). Ethnic militias have served the purpose of 'splitting local populations on cultural rather than uniting them on economic grounds' (Kasfir 2005, 199).

The region of Darfur in western Sudan has been even more neglected in economic policy than the East and South of the country (Idris 2005; Daly 2007). The history of the region is too complex to be made justice here, and the traditional, low-intensity conflicts between communities over natural resources complicate any analysis of the root causes of confrontation. But it is fair to say that systematic ethnic violence originated in the mid-1980s as the Government of Sudan armed Arab militias with the aim of disrupting the popular bases of support for the SPLA in Darfur. This process led to the 1987–1989 conflict between the Fur and the Arabs, in which Khartoum propaganda ended up reinforcing the fault line along this identitarian cleavage. A similar strategy was used after the 1992–1993 SPLA incursion in Southern Darfur, as well as during the government-sponsored war on the Massalit, creating resentment and fears among non-Arabs that the government was enacting a policy of ethnic cleansing (Crisis Group 2004; Daly 2007, 261ff).

Eventually, a settlement over the conflict in Southern Sudan was reached. The lesson that Darfuris learned from the peace negotiations in the South, focused on wealth and power sharing, was that 'rebellion pays', to use Nelson Kasfir's words. As a result, it was reasonable to expect groups like the Sudanese Liberation Army/Movement (SLM/A) and the Justice and Equality Movement (JEM) to eventually arise. When they did, they started a armed revolt with a political discourse of programmatic aims and a broad tribal base (UN 2005, 23, 38–9; Prunier 2005, 93–4). To counter this new challenge, the central government relied once more on the recruitment of paramilitary Arab militias to suppress the rebellion. The political use of ethnicity in Darfur was even more blatant than in the South, given that the Darfurian tribes had previously been considered 'Northerners', and therefore 'Arabs' (Idris 2005). By recruiting its militias from some tribes but not others, and by identifying the rebels with the Fur and Massalit tribes, the government achieved the strategic ethnicization of the conflict, thus undermining the economic projection of the rebellion. Even though the Janjaweed are essentially the economic equals of the rebels, the mobilization of ethnopatronage networks has 'retribalized' the threat in order to protect the elites' power while reinforcing the loyalty of their clients. The whole process of other-categorization and the ensuing atrocities have been well documented by international teams investigating the international crimes committed during the conflict (UN 2005; HRW 2005a; HRW 2005b; ICC 2007).

The conflict in Darfur, which started primarily as a challenge to the neopatrimonial elite ruling the country, has been turned into a case of murderous ethnic violence. Hundreds of thousands have died so far, and millions have been displaced from the region. Nevertheless, ethnic cleansing – and potentially genocide – was never a 'deliberate well-thought out policy', but a strategy to keep together a system of minority domination (Prunier 2005, 105). In the meantime, Arab militias are taking over the land as a reward for their allegiance (HRW 2005a, 10), further reinforcing the strength of the regime's patrimonial basis of support. It is not the purpose of this brief case study to diminish the importance of identitarian claims and the role of Islamization and Arabization in the colonial and post-colonial history of Sudan. But it is indisputable that ethnic mobilization in Darfur was a consequence of – and not a cause for – the challenge to the regime. The elite's ethnopatronage networks made possible a swift repression of the threat, despite the increasing risks of genocide. In the way the crisis was handled by the authorities, the significance of neopatrimonial structures cannot be denied.

Ethnic Clashes in Kenya

My second case is Kenya during the 1990s, when recurrent 'ethnic clashes' targeted members of the Kikuyu ethnicity during the country's transition to democracy. For much of its history, Kenya was a single-party state, with the Kenya National African Union (KANU) channelling all political influence. KANU was founded as an alliance of the Kikuyu and Luo ethnicicties against the Kenya African Democratic Union (KADU) of the Kalenjin, Maasai, Turkana and Samburu. But KADU dissolved itself and joined KANU a year after independence. Until 1982 Kenya would be a *de facto* single-party regime; the constitutional amendment of that year would turn KANU into the only legal political formation. The process was one of increasing centralization of power in the hands of the president and the provincial administration, a patrimonial regime that became increasingly absolutist (Widner 1992). When Daniel arap Moi succeeded Kenyatta within KANU, the major shift involved was a mere realignment of the particular ethnic coalitions.

In precolonial Kenya, writes John Lonsdale, tribes did not exist 'in the sense of self-contained, externally bounded, collective groups' (2004, 77). Indeed, as in many other African societies, ethnicity was not a clear-cut system for social differentiation, but a complex pattern of relations whose constituent units were fluid and had porous borders, spanning different socioeconomic roles and political units. 'Ethnic consciousness unquestionably became sharper in colonial times', when British administration established its system of indirect rule, privileging the formation of distinct tribal units according to the native 'tradition', each one under the control of a tribal leader that would be accountable to the colonial administration in exchange for wealth and institutional security (ibid., 78).

This model was largely reproduced by the national hero, Jomo Kenyatta, after independence in 1963. The new state was essentially 'a compromise of ethnic claims to power or resources' (Muigai 2004, 200). Kinship remained the locus of political loyalty in the absence of an alternative national ideology. First as prime minister, and later on as president, Kenyatta constructed his own power base through a policy of 'ethnic feudalism', which would eventually devolve into an absolutist patrimonial regime which 'relied for loyalty on political tribalisms that competed for an abject dependence on the state' (Lonsdale 2004, 91). He broadened his support base by creating a complex patronage network with designated ethnic chiefs, 'mostly sons of colonial chiefs who owed direct loyalty to him and assured him the support of their various ethnic groups' (Muigai 2004, 201). In so doing Kenyatta, a Kikuyu himself, often played Kikuyu factions against each other and tried to seek the support of other ethnicities in order to preserve the ruling coalition, overall 'entrench[ing] ethnicity as the dominant basis for political mobilization' (ibid., 215).

In the 1990s, as the idea of democracy spread throughout Africa (Bratton and van de Walle 1997), new ideological movements rose to challenge the Kenyan neopatrimonial state, drawing their membership along class lines. Among them, the Mungiki would soon become one of the most successful private organizations in the country, supported by token donations from tens of thousands of supporters drawn from the marginalized, the urban poor, the young unemployed, and the rural landless. Although consisting primarily of Kikuyu, the Mungiki initially crafted their political identity as a multiethnic movement with national aims, transforming Kikuyu myths and rituals into Kenyan ones (Kagwanja 2003). In essence, the Mungiki were posing a distributive challenge, somewhat imperfectly articulated, but in fundamental contradiction with the distribution of resources and power in the regime.

The automatic response of the Moi government to this challenge was to associate the Mungiki with the 1980s Mwakenya, portraying them as a Kikuyu supremacist project. The rationale was clear: ethnicizing this fledgling opposition as Kikuyu would awake fears by other tribes, weary of the old cautionary tales of Kikuyu imperialism, and would help to reinforce the elite's own patronage networks. The same strategy was deployed in the region of Narok North, where two multiethnic opposition candidates contested the 1992 parliamentary elections. The threatened patron, a minister in the Moi government, launched a campaign of incitement to turn the Maasai against their Kikuyu neighbours. Thanks to the powerful provincial administration accountable to the president, the regime managed to expel an estimated 30,000 Kikuyus from Narok. In the following elections the patron's candidacy was not seriously threatened (Klopp 2001).

These 'ethnic clashes', to use the Kenyan government's term, repeated themselves throughout the country in the 1990s. As a consequence, 'the threat of future massacres has become a routine aspect of Kenyan politics, and 'ethnic clashes' are now part of the elite bargaining process' (ibid., 503). Ethnic violence has become a form of informal repression, a retribalization of the public sphere that reinforces ethnic trust and hinders the rise of civic understandings of citizenship. It is a perfect example of ethnic massacre and expulsion as a form of crisis management, one that left between 1991 and 2001 a total of 4,000 dead and 600,000 displaced (Kagwanja 2003, 26–7, 31–5).

Genocide in Rwanda

Finally, I will review the events that took place in Rwanda between April and July of 1994, which constitute so far the only internationally recognized case of genocide in the African continent. To some it may seem that, as a case, Rwanda has abandoned the realm of broader political science for the narrower field of genocide studies. However, there have been significant efforts by scholars to frame the violence in the political, economic and social history of the Rwandan state and the larger region of the Great Lakes, and upon these studies I myself construct this section. But what I propose here is a re-categorization of Rwanda as the most extreme case of strategic ethnicization and as the only – so far – neopatrimonial genocide.

After more than ten years of research, it is almost beyond any doubt that Rwanda was a case of a threatened elite trying to salvage its position. There have been numerous explanatory hypotheses put forward to explain the *génocidaires*'s intentions, the rationale behind low-level, anonymous perpetrators, or the role of the media in the characterization of all Tutsi as the enemy (Hintjens 1999, 243). But ultimately the roots of the genocide lie within a very small group of people that for two decades had monopolized the state for their own benefit, and that of their regional clients. Known as the *akazu*, this group formed a 'political-military-mercantile network' based in the Northern prefectures of Ruhengeri, Gisenyi and Cyangugu, where most of the government investment was allocated (Reyntjens 1996, 243; Uvin 1999, 270 n. 29). This elite had formed 'a state within a state' from whose patronage fewer and fewer Rwandans benefited over time. Nevertheless, public criticism of the 'Gisenyi boys' by Southern Hutus was often countered with the recurrent claim that differences of class and region were superficial compared with differences in race (Hintjens 1999, 261–2; Mamdani 2001). In other words, whenever the Rwandan neopatrimonial elite was threatened, it exacerbated ethnic divisions (Straus 2006, 198).

The early 1990s introduced a number of major threats to the regime. Economically, the Rwandan state had had to bow to the conditionality of IMF-World Bank structural adjustment programs in order to obtain international funds to weather the economic crisis, resulting in a severe decrease in the general level of income and an intensification of inequality. Politically, 1990 saw the invasion of the Rwandan Popular Front (RPF), composed mainly of Tutsi émigrés and refugees with Ugandan support. The incursion of the RPF in Rwandan soil resulted in the Arusha peace process, which would set an agenda of power-sharing and political liberalization in tune with the wave of democratization that was engulfing sub-Saharan Africa at the time. Therefore the ruling elite faced no less than three major challenges – the rise of a disenfranchised Hutu opposition, the creation of new political parties, and the commitment to share power with a new military player. At stake was the control of the state, 'the most important instrument of accumulation of wealth and reproduction of the ruling class' (Reyntjens 1996, 242). The struggle over this neopatrimonial state would eventually become genocidal.

It is important to stress that the threats to the *akazu* came from both Hutus and Tutsis. Initially, political violence targeted opponents: 'politicians opposed to the presidential majority and/or adhering to the Arusha peace accord, persons active in human rights associations, leaders of civil society, journalists and generally the Tutsi, as a whole considered allies of the RPF' (ibid., 246). Such a pattern would repeat itself in the first days of the genocide. Since 1990 killings of Tutsi and opposition Hutus had been instigated by the ruling Mouvement Révolutionnaire National pour le Développement (MRND) and Hutu supremacists, resulting in thousands of deaths (Lemarchand 1995 and 2005). Hardliners in the regime responded to the twin challenges of the Hutu opposition and the RPF by promoting the image of an RPF-Tutsi connection, expanding the army and the civilian defence forces, training and arming youth militias (like the infamous *Interahamwe*), organizing death lists and death squads, launching a campaign of racist propaganda, and promoting the ideology of 'Hutu Power' (Straus 2006, 25–9).

It is possible to assess the importance of patronage networks at the onset of the genocide. According to the research conducted by Scott Straus, the strongest predictor for the regional distribution of initial ethnic violence is political support for the ruling party – his data shows an earlier onset of killings in areas that were both wealthier and more supportive of the ruling MRND, against other variables that show little or no correlation, such as deprivation, prejudice or incitement (2006, 60–62). These results clearly support the neopatrimonial logic of the genocide in its earliest stages. Later on violence would spread and a host of other social psychological, economic or racist factors would come to the fore. But the onset of violence is strongly correlated with the presence of clients of the patrimonial elite. Indeed, as Lemarchand has written, 'rather than being the result of a genocidal Leviathan orchestrating the killings from above, the carnage is better seen as the work of key 'patrons' or big men, within the army and the government, each trying to make the most of their privileged access to the militias, prefects and burgomasters to mobilize the masses behind the killing machine' (2005, 65).

In light of these findings, it is clear that in Rwanda ethnic ideology was not a causal factor, but a policy tool. And despite the very specific context of a bipolar ethnic situation (reinforced by neighbouring Burundi), or the existence of a strong state and a conformist population, or the onset of the RPF war, what matters for the purposes of this study is precisely that which makes Rwanda similar to other African cases, namely the destabilizing effects of a power crisis and the utmost importance of the control over the state.

Conclusion: Structural Consequences and Implications

In this chapter I have hypothesized and illustrated a causal link between the structural features of neopatrimonial states and the onset of ethnic violence. However, causation can also flow in the opposite direction. Violence, especially violence as a result of strategic ethnicization, may have certain structural consequences for both the legitimacy and the capacity of the state. First and foremost, elite-favoured identity frames are reinforced to the detriment of other frames, such as class or nation, just as patrimonial accountability is reinforced to the detriment of civicness and state legitimacy.

In addition, non-state actors are empowered to the detriment of state authority and capacity, multiplying the risks of conflict and disorder in the future. Lastly, distributive grievances are buried but not solved, and are thus likely to resurface in the future. When they do, the history of failed exercises of voice may tilt challengers toward exit, setting the stage for secessionist movements and civil war.

If my argument is correct, the legacies of neopatrimonialism that I have addressed – unequal power distribution, politicized ethnicity, patron-client networks – combine to produce a volatile mix that is likely to lead to ethnic violence. In terms of prescription, the obvious implication would seem to be that removing one, or several, or all of these elements from the equation would presumably decrease the risk of ethnic violence. Removing ethnic cleavages by relocating populations is not only unfeasible but morally reprehensible – it is precisely what ethnic cleansing aims for. This means that if a state has potentially deployable ethnic cleavages, any attempt at minimizing the prospect of violent confrontation must focus on the other two legacies: an unequal power distribution based on state capture, and patrimonial accountability.

Unfortunately, it is difficult to even begin to understand how to bring about change at such macro-sociological level. Presumably the rise of a middle class would have some positive impact on the rule of law, fostering an economic environment more conducive to business-led growth. This is based on the assumption that, as the state represents less and less of the national economy, with resources flourishing outside of its grasp, it ceases to be perceived as the ultimate prize in power politics. With regards to patrimonial accountability, democracy would seem to be the likely solution, but it is not clear how it affects patterns of representation as vertical redistribution. A true bureaucracy, well trained and based on meritocratic principles, may go a long way towards reducing the impact of patrimonialism. But ultimately this would entail a total shift in the way political legitimacy is construed, which is likely to take time.

I would not want to end on a fatalist note, though. This chapter has characterized the onset of some instances of ethnic violence as a deliberate strategy by endangered elites, and there is indeed little than external actors can do to prevent or hinder such a line of action. However, the spread and contagion of ethnicization is a gradual process, and there may be a role for intervention in the initial moments of confrontation, when the security dilemma still has to set in. International peacekeeping efforts targeted at these early phases of confrontation could in theory prevent violence from escalating into ethnic cleansing or genocide. Whether the international community is able to identify the process before it fully unfolds, and whether it has the political will to intervene, are questions for further debate.

Does all cruelty, as Seneca said, spring from weakness? Perhaps not, but I hope to have shown in this chapter how the heinous episodes of ethnic violence in recent African history can be explored through the lens of threatened neopatrimonial elites, and how there is a certain rationality behind their choice of death over fairness. As I said at the very beginning of the chapter, massacres do not happen spontaneously. There are instigators behind them, and mechanism that account for their success or failure. Understanding these mechanism is fundamental if we are ever to relegate ethnic massacres to history books. The weaknesses of neopatrimonialism may well be beyond our best developmental efforts. The cruelty of threatened elites may well be beyond our moral grasp. But as long as we keep exploring them we can still hope that, eventually, we will learn how to minimize their murderous impact.

Acknowledgements

The slow gestation of the ideas presented in this chapter has benefited greatly from feedback and conversations with friends and colleagues at the University of Pennsylvania and Cornell. In particular, I would like to thank Tom Callaghy, Marton Markovits, Brendan O'Leary, Nicolas van de Walle and Jaimie Bleck for their encouragement, insightful comments, and constructive criticism. To them I owe much of my understanding of Africa and ethnic conflict, and whatever flaws may remain in the chapter are probably the result of not listening to them more carefully.

References

Bates, Robert H. (1983), 'Modernization, Ethnic Competition, and the Rationality of Politics in Contemporary Africa', in Donald Rothchild and Victor Olorunsola (eds) *State versus Ethnic Claims: African Policy Dilemmas* (Boulder, CO: Westview Press).

Berman, Bruce J. (1998), 'Ethnicity, Patronage and the African State: The Politics of Uncivil Nationalism', *African Affairs* 97: 305–41.

Berman, Bruce J. (2004), 'Ethnicity, Bureaucracy and Democracy: The Politics of Trust', in Bruce Berman, Dickson Eyoh and Will Kymlicka (eds), *Ethnicity and Democracy in Africa* (Oxford: James Currey).

Berman, Bruce J. (2006), 'The Ordeal of Modernity in an Age of Terror', *African Studies Review* 49(1): 1–14.

Bratton, Michael and Walle, Nicolas van de (1997), *Democratic Experiments in Africa: Regime Transitions in Comparative Perspective* (Cambridge: Cambridge University Press).

Bourdieu, Pierre (1977), *Outline of a Theory of Practice* (Cambridge: Cambridge University Press).

Brubaker, Rogers (2004), *Ethnicity Without Groups* (Cambridge, MA: Harvard University Press).

Callaghy, Thomas M. (1984) *The State-Society Struggle: Zaire in Comparative Perspective* (New York: Columbia University Press).

Callaghy, Thomas M. (1988), 'The State and the Development of Capitalism in Africa: Theoretical, Historical, and Comparative Reflections', in Donald Rothchild and Naomi Chazan (eds), *The Precarious Balance: State-Society Relations in Africa* (Boulder, CO: Westview Press).

Chabal, Patrick and Daloz, Jean-Pascal (1999), *Africa Works: Disorder as a Political Instrument* (Bloomington, IN: Indiana University Press).

Chazan, Naomi (1982), 'The New Politics of Participation in Tropical Africa', *Comparative Politics* 14: 169–90.

Crisis Group (2004), *Darfur Rising: Sudan's New Crisis* (Nairobi/Brussels: Africa Report No. 76).

Daly, M.W. (2007), *Darfur's Sorrow: A History of Destruction and Genocide* (Cambridge: Cambridge University Press).

Dixon, P.J. (1991), 'Uneasy Lies the Head: Politics, Economics, and the Continuity of Belief among Yoruba of Nigeria', *Comparative Studies in Society and History* 1991: 56 85.

Dunn, John (1986), 'The Politics of Representation and Good Government in Post-colonial Africa', in Patrick Chabal (ed.), *Political Domination in Africa* (Cambridge: Cambridge University Press).

Ekeh, Peter P. (1975), 'Colonialism and the Two Publics in Africa: A Theoretical Statement', *Comparative Studies in Society and History* 17(1): 91–112.

Ekeh, Peter P. (2004), 'Individuals' Basic Security Needs and the Limits of Democracy in Africa', in Bruce Berman, Dickson Eyoh and Will Kymlicka (eds), *Ethnicity and Democracy in Africa* (Oxford: James Currey).

Fatton, Robert (1988), 'Bringing the Ruling Class Back In: Class, State, and Hegemony in Africa', *Comparative Politics* 20(3): 253–64.

Fearon, James D. (1995), 'Rationalist Explanations for War', *International Organization* 49(3): 379–414.

Fearon, James D. and Laitin, David D. (1996), 'Explaining Interethnic Cooperation', *American Political Science Review* 90(4): 715–35.

Hintjens, Helen (1999), 'Explaining the 1994 Genocide in Rwanda', *The Journal of Modern African Studies* 37(2): 241–86.

Hirschman, Albert O. (1970), *Exit, Voice, and Loyalty* (Cambridge, MA: Harvard University Press).

Horowitz, Donald L. (1985), *Ethnic Groups in Conflict* (Berkeley, CA: University of California Press).

HRW (2005a), 'Targeting the Fur: Mass Killings in Darfur', *Briefing Paper*, 21 January.

HRW (2005b), 'Entrenching Impunity: Government Responsibility for International Crimes in Darfur' Vol. 17, No. 17 (A).

Hyden, Goran (1983), *No Shortcuts to Progress: African Development Management in Perspective* (Berkeley/Los Angeles, CA: University of California Press).

ICC (2007), *Situation in Darfur, the Sudan: Prosecutor's Application under Article 58 (7)*, 21 February.

Idris, Amir H. (2005), *Conflict and Politics of Identity in Sudan* (New York: Palgrave Macmillan).

Kagwanja, Peter Mwangi (2003), 'Facing Mount Kenya or Facing Mecca? The Mungiki, Ethnic Violence and the Politics of the Moi Succession in Kenya, 1897–2002', *African Affairs* 102: 25–49.

Kasfir, Nelson (2004), 'Domestic Anarchy, Security Dilemmas, and Violent Predation: Causes of Failure', in Robert. I. Rotberg (ed.), *When States Fail: Causes and Consequences* (Princeton, NJ: Princeton University Press).

Kasfir, Nelson (2005), 'Sudan's Darfur: Is It Genocide?', *Current History* (May): 195–202.

Kaufman, Stuart J. (2006), 'Symbolic Politics or Rational Choice? Testing Theories of Extreme Ethnic Violence', *International Security* 30(4): 45–86.

Klopp, Jacqueline M. (2001), '"Ethnic Clashes" and Winning Elections: The Case of Kenya's Electoral Despotism', *Canadian Journal of African Studies* 35(3): 473–517.

Lemarchand, René (1995), 'Rwanda: the Rationality of Genocide', *Issue: A Journal of Opinion* 23(2): 8–11.

Lemarchand, René (2005), 'Disconnecting the Threads: Rwanda and the Holocaust Reconsidered', in Stefaan Marysse and Filip Reyntjens (eds), *The Political Economy of the Great Lakes Region in Africa* (New York: Palgrave Macmillan).

Laitin, David D. (1986), *Hegemony and Culture: Politics and Religious Change among the Yoruba* (Chicago: University of Chicago Press).

Laitin, David D. (1995), 'Marginality: A Microperspective', *Rationality and Society* 7(1): 31–57.

Lonsdale, John (2004), 'Moral and Political Argument in Kenya', in Bruce Berman, Dickson Eyoh and Will Kymlicka (eds), *Ethnicity and Democracy in Africa* (Oxford: James Currey).

Mamdani, Mahmood (1996), *Citizen and Subject: Contemporary Africa and the Legacy of Late Colonialism* (Princeton, NJ: Princeton University Press).

Mamdani Mahmood (2001), *When Victims Become Killers: Colonialism, Nativism, and the Genocide in Rwanda* (Princeton, NJ: Princeton University Press).

Mann, Michael (2005), *The Dark Side of Democracy: Explaining Ethnic Cleansing* (Cambridge: Cambridge University Press).

Medard, Jean-François (1982), 'The Underdeveloped State in Tropical Africa: Political Clientelism or Neo-patrimonialism?', in Christopher S. Clapham (ed.), *Private Patronage and Public Power: Political Clientelism in the Modern State* (New York: St Martin's Press).

Muigai, Githu (2004), 'Jomo Kenyatta and the Rise of the Ethno-Nationalist State in Kenya', in Bruce Berman, Dickson Eyoh and Will Kymlicka (eds), *Ethnicity and Democracy in Africa* (Oxford: James Currey).

Posen, Barry R. (1993), 'The Security Dilemma and Ethnic Conflict', in Michael E. Brown (ed.), *Ethnic Conflict and International Security* (Princeton, NJ: Princeton University Press).

Posner, Daniel N. (2004), 'Measuring Ethnic Fractionalization in Africa', *American Journal of Political Science* 48(4): 849–63.

Posner, Daniel N. (2005), *Institutions and Ethnic Politics in Africa* (Cambridge: Cambridge University Press).

Prunier, Gérard (2005), *Darfur: The Ambiguous Genocide* (Ithaca, NY: Cornell University Press).

Prunier, Gérard, and Gisselquist, Rachel M. (2003), 'The Sudan: A Successfully Failed State', in Robert. I. Rotberg (ed.), *State Failure and State Weakness in a Time of Terror* (Cambridge, MA and Washington, DC: Brookings Institution Press).

Reyntjens, Filip (1996), 'Rwanda: Genocide and Beyond', *Journal of Refugee Studies* 9(3): 240–51.

Salih, M.A. Mohammed (1989), '"New Wine in Old Bottles": Tribal Militias and the Sudanese State', *Review of African Political Economy* 16(45/46): 168–74.

Schatzberg, Michael G. (2001), *Political Legitimacy in Middle Africa: Father, Family, Food* (Bloomington, IN: Indiana University Press).
Straus, Scott (2006), *The Order of Genocide: Race, Power and War in Rwanda* (Ithaca, NY: Cornell University Press).
Tajfel, Henri (1981), *Human Groups and Social Categories: Studies in Social Psychology* (New York: Cambridge University Press).
United Nations (UN) (2005), *Report of the International Commission of Inquiry on Darfur to the United Nations Secretary General* Geneva, 25 January.
Uvin, Peter (1999), 'Ethnicity and Power in Burundi and Rwanda: Different Paths to Mass Violence', *Comparative Politics* 31(3): 253–71.
Walle, Nicolas van de (2001), *African Economies and the Politics of Permanent Crisis, 1979–1999* (Cambridge: Cambridge University Press).
Weber, Max (1968), *Economy and Society*, ed. Guenther Roth and Claus Wittich (Berkeley, CA: University of California Press).
Widner, Jennifer A. (1992), *The Rise of a Party-State in Kenya* (Berkeley, CA: University of California Press).
Young, Crawford (1994), 'Democratization in Africa: The Contradictions of a Political Imperative', in Jennifer A. Widner (ed.), *Economic Change and Political Liberalisation in Sub-Saharan Africa* (Baltimore, MA and London: Johns Hopkins University Press).
Young, Crawford (2004), 'The End of the Post-Colonial State in Africa? Reflections on Changing African Political Dynamics', *African Affairs* 103: 23–49.
Zeruvable, Eviatar (1997), *Social Mindscapes: An Invitation to Cognitive Sociology* (Cambridge, MA: Harvard University Press).
Zolberg, Aristide (1966), *Creating Political Order: The Party-States in West Africa* (Chicago: Rand McNally and Company).

CHAPTER EIGHT

IRRESOLUTION: THE UN SECURITY COUNCIL ON DARFUR[1]

Marijan Zumbulev

Since 2003, the United Nations Security Council has failed to live up to its responsibility to protect the people of Darfur and to help restore peace and security in Sudan. It has proven powerless to construct a workable matrix of incentives and disincentives to affect the strategic calculations of the warring parties, to steer political talks to a successful conclusion, or to deploy a robust peace force. Its record on Darfur has undermined its relevance and put yet another question mark over its legitimacy.

Few have taken a good lesson out of this experience. Instead, many have rushed into easy explanations of the Council's poor performance, which conveniently deflect responsibility away from national capitals towards New York and, in the end, obscure more than they reveal. Authorities – from government, policy and even cultural circles – have latched onto a facile exegesis that depicts the Council has an overwhelming stumbling block, which a handful of well-intentioned governments have been unable to surmount through no fault of their own. This approach, inspired by either a skin-deep understanding or a deliberate misinterpretation of policy dynamics, is unhelpful and perhaps even dangerous. Instead of mending, it merely perpetuates a flawed strategy that further weakens the Council, the very institution that member-states soon find themselves forced to rely on, once again.

CPA over Darfur: No All-Sudan Strategy

Several strategic mistakes, none of which originated in New York, have hampered the Council's response on Darfur. The first, original sin, was a 2003–2004 international decision to concentrate, at Darfur's expense, on securing a peace agreement to end another Sudanese conflict, between the Khartoum-based Sudanese government and the Southern rebels of the Sudanese People's Liberation Movement/Army (SPLM/SPLA). That war had raged on for over two decades at an estimated cost of two million lives, so the fear that expanding the advanced peace negotiations between 'the North' and 'the South' to include Darfur's complicated dynamics would hurt both was legitimate and understandable. The policy to focus on the track that would soon lead to the signing of a North-South 'Comprehensive Peace Agreement' (CPA) as a first priority was appealing for one more reason. As many of those who were involved in putting together the CPA thought, the agreement contained the seeds for democratic reforms across Sudan, and its effective implementation could, indeed would, help achieve peace in the entire country, including Darfur.

Thus preoccupied, the Security Council received its first briefing on Darfur only on 2 April 2004, nearly a year after the major 25 April 2003 rebel raid on North Darfur's capital of El Fasher, marked by some scholars as the start of the Darfur war. That joint Sudan Liberation Army/Justice and Equality Movement (SLA/JEM) attack on El Fasher's air base and military garrison humiliated Khartoum, and pushed it into revamping its counter-insurgency strategy. In response, Sudan's ruling National Congress Party (NCP) armed and unleashed local, mostly 'Arab' militias commonly called 'Janjaweed' upon millions of Darfur civilians of 'African' tribes.[2] The Janjaweed's scorched earth campaign, supported by Sudanese air power, paid off militarily – but at a tremendous humanitarian cost. By the time of the 2 April briefing to the UNSC, by the then Emergency Relief Coordinator, Norwegian Jan Egeland, thousands of civilians had been killed and many more displaced from their homes.

With its limited attention claimed by the ongoing North-South peace process in Naivasha, Kenya, the Council neglected the alarm bells on several occasions. Attempts to stir it into action on Darfur were initially blocked by internal resistance.[3] After months of international snoozing, the situation in Darfur worsened to an extent the Council could no longer afford to ignore. On 30 July 2004, it adopted Resolution 1556, over Chinese and Pakistani abstentions, demanding that the Government of Sudan (GoS) – de facto another name for the National Congress Party – disarm its proxy, the Janjaweed militias or face possible sanctions. The same text imposed an arms embargo on 'non-governmental entities operating in Darfur'. With neither a mechanism to monitor implementation nor a lot of serious will from critical regional and international actors to make it stick, the embargo was little more than a feel-good gesture.

The summer of 2004 rolled by as conflict parties disregarded the resolution and Darfur continued to burn. Driven by the embarrassment of the Council's impotent silence, as well as by increased public awareness and pressure, the US and some of its European allies pushed for the adoption of a second resolution, UNSCR 1564, on 18 September. The final text of the document merely noted that GoS had ignored the Council and continued to bomb civilians and reiterated the sanctions threat, though directing it this time specifically towards 'Sudan's petroleum sector and the Government of Sudan or individual members of the Government of Sudan'. It also created an international commission of inquiry to report on violations of international humanitarian law and international human rights law, and to determine 'whether or not acts of genocide have occurred, and to identify the perpetrators of such violations with a view to ensuring that those responsible are held accountable'.

Importantly, the resolution came with four abstentions (China, Russia, Pakistan and Algeria), indicating to the National Congress Party in Khartoum that tough follow-through was unlikely. The resolution, the Sudanese Ambassador to the UN told the Council, aimed 'only at pleasing the United States Congress, which believes itself to be the sole conscience of the world'.[5] Sudan's defiance was based on a shrewd, and ultimately correct, analysis of the situation. Khartoum understood that the US government and its allies were keen to score rhetorical points in New York, meant at least in part for public consumption, but were not going to risk full-blown confrontation at a moment when the conclusion of the Naivasha peace process seemed so closely within reach.

Sudan had hit the mark and called the Western bluff. Indeed, it was not until the signing of the Comprehensive Peace Agreement, on 9 January 2005, that the US and UK moved again to up the pressure on Darfur at the Council. Negotiations over what was originally envisaged as one mega-resolution dragged on for weeks and it was only during the final week of March that the Council took action. Three resolutions – whose internal logic was not mutually compatible and which managed to expose divisions within the international community further – were adopted in eight days.

Resolution 1590 established the UN Mission in Sudan (UNMIS) to help with CPA implementation, Resolution 1591 dealt exclusively with Darfur and introduced a sanctions regime, and Resolution 1593 referred the Darfur situation to the International Criminal Court (ICC). Taken together, the three resolutions demonstrated amply – to those who still had any remaining doubt – that there was no coherent international strategy to deal with Sudan and its NCP government. With striking inconsistency, the Council pledged collective allegiance as the 'good cop' in Southern Sudan, while trying to play hardball over Darfur with the same Khartoum interlocutors.

Unlike UNSCR 1590, which was adopted unanimously, the second March resolution, 1591, came into being only after three critical abstentions – two from permanent members China and Russia and another from an African and (and the sole) Arab representative, Algeria. Watered down to avoid a veto, the text nonetheless banned 'offensive military flights' by GoS over Darfur, extended the arms embargo to all parties in Darfur, therefore including GoS, and agreed on individual sanctions. The individual sanctions regime was to target those who violate the embargo, the ban on offensive flights or more generally 'impede the peace process, constitute a threat to stability in Darfur and the region, commit violations of international humanitarian or human rights law or other atrocities'.[5] Such persons were to be banned from international travel and have their assets frozen. A Sanctions Committee of the UNSC was created, as well as a supporting but independent Panel of Experts, to translate the regime into practice and to collect information. The Council threatened additional sanctions in the event of continued non-compliance.

The third resolution, 1593, referred the Darfur situation to the Prosecutor of the International Criminal Court, as recommended by the International Commission of Inquiry established in September of the previous year. That commission found that no genocide had taken place in Darfur but stressed that this conclusion 'should not be taken in any way as detracting from the gravity of the crimes perpetrated in that region. International offences such as the crimes against humanity and war crimes that have been committed in Darfur may be no less serious and heinous than genocide'.[6]

Sanctions: The First Refuge of the Desperate Policy-maker

The 'bad cop' game over Darfur never gained much traction through the UNSC sanctions regime, which turned out to be a hollow shell, an empty threat that merely reconfirmed Khartoum's conviction that it can get away with murder. The sanctions committee created by resolution 1591 did not even meet for the first time until 5 May 2005, and a panel of experts was not appointed until 30 June 2005. Shockingly, the Committee could not agree even on its work guidelines, i.e. did not start working, until 23 March 2006 – 51 weeks after its formal creation. China and Russia led the effort to ensure that these guidelines effectively neutralized any meaningful action by the committee – in the end, decisions were to be made by full consensus. To no surprise, in its three and a half years of existence, the Committee has not agreed to sanction a single individual.

What the Committee has managed to do quite successfully is to delay repeatedly – or even altogether prevent – the publication of reports by the independent panel of experts.[7] The beginning of this sorry record goes back to late January 2006, when the Committee at last released the first final report of the panel of experts, having sat on it for the previous two months. The report detailed massive violations of the arms embargo, including by regional actors such as Chad, Libya and Eritrea, found multiple instances of breaches to the ban on offensive military flights, and identified a list of individuals impeding the peace process in a confidential annex.[8] The annex recommended for sanctions, among others, Salah Gosh, the then-head of the Sudanese National Security Service and the Ministers of Interior and Defense. It also recommended possible consideration of sanctions on the Presidents of Sudan and Chad. The experts had run way ahead of the political pack – nobody was quite ready to countenance turning the screws on heads of state. Even Gosh, whose cooperation on counter-terrorism matters was much valued in Washington, was off the hook. The report and the annex were summarily ignored.[9]

The first – and so far the only – time the Council moved on its targeted sanctions threat occurred on 25 April 2006, three months after the public release of the panel's first report. China, Russia and Qatar had blocked action at the UNSC Committee, forcing Western allies to table a formal UNSC resolution to clear the procedural bottleneck. The same three countries abstained on what became UNSC Resolution 1672, which sanctioned four persons, none of whom was likely to have significant assets in foreign banks or to indulge in extensive foreign travel.[10] The resolution was little more than an exercise in signalling, aimed largely to deflate a bubble of rising expectations among Western constituencies. As a bonus, it was also thought to serve as a form of pressure on recalcitrant rebel factions, at the time engaged in intensive peace negotiations in Abuja, to sign onto what eventually became known as the Darfur Peace Agreement. (The second calculation did not pan out, and only one of the major rebel leaders, Minni Minawi, signed the DPA on 5 May 2006.)

Since April 2006, no serious attempt has been made at the Security Council to alter the calculations of the Sudanese Government, the Darfur rebels, or the regional actors involved in the conflict through sanctions. At no point over the last three and a half years have any of the theoretically available options – better implementation of existing measures, more targeted sanctions, an expanded arms embargo, and specific economic sanctions, to name a few – gained enough traction to be politically achievable. In sum, the sanctions regime has been thoroughly ineffective. That has not prevented the

Council, living in its impervious bubble and driven by fear that facing the sanctions challenge head on will force it to lose even more credibility than it has already expended, to repeatedly renew the regime.[11]

Darfur: Another Ball to Drop

Unfortunately, the compartmentalization of the North-South conflict and Darfur continued well after the January 2005 signing of the CPA. This, second strategic mistake was to focus disproportionately on Darfur and to deprioritize CPA implementation, instead of using that agreement to affect the situation in Darfur positively, as envisioned all along.[12] Darfur monopolized the Sudan discussion for over two years, which were critical for cementing the putative achievements of the CPA. By the time attention partially shifted back to the larger, all-Sudan picture, starting around the middle of 2007, Darfur was in a deeper crisis and the CPA itself was facing possible collapse.[13]

That Darfur emerged worse off, despite all the international engagement, was a sorry, if in retrospect inevitable outcome of two additional and related mistakes. The Darfur track was bungled first because the international community rushed into peace talks without adequate preparation and patience. The negotiations were too heavy on credit-seeking internationals and too light on Darfurians, having largely excluded representatives of political parties, civil society, IDPs, and women's groups. Moreover, the process was entirely divorced from the CPA. For a long while during and after the negotiations of the resulting Darfur Peace Agreement (DPA) it was unclear whether some provisions – particularly those on wealth- and power-sharing in Sudan – could be revisited in order to satisfy all rebel movements without impacting the CPA. The CPA was the sacred cow – already malnourished by that stage – and some hard questions were expeditiously swept under the carpet. The most important part of the negotiation process was conducted under strict deadlines driven less by the main players in Darfur or the situation on the ground and more by the priorities and schedules of foreign actors.[14]

Once the DPA was signed, notably only by the Government of Sudan and one of the three main rebel movements, the international community descended into a collective reverie about its merits and viability. To borrow from John R. Bolton, the boisterous former US Ambassador to the UN, the world wanted a butterfly, so it put lipstick on a caterpillar and declared it a success.[15] As soon as Minni Minawi, one of the SLA faction leaders, put down his signature under the DPA, Council members went full speed ahead, tripping over each other to protect the 'peace agreement' fiction. Calls from sceptical observers doubting the viability of the DPA under such circumstances were haughtily dismissed. At the same time, little was done, at the Security Council or elsewhere, to lure or pressure rebel holdouts to sign on.

The Peacekeeping Mania

The self-imposed, irresponsible delusion of the DPA's imminent success generated an additional mistake – a near-exclusive obsession on getting a UN peacekeeping operation into Darfur, to protect the unworkable peace deal. In a fatal bout of collective amnesia, the Council rapidly unlearned lessons from comparable past experiences, staking its lot – and that of Darfur's civilians – on a peacekeeping force. This obstinate concentration on UN peacekeepers was largely counter-productive. The heavy preoccupation over a peace deployment in a theatre where there was so little peace to keep ironically translated into inadequate international follow-through on the peace agreement itself, thus finishing off the fragile and quite possibly doomed DPA while offering nothing to replace it. The search for the illusory blue helmet panacea exhausted both UN attention and the already depleting international political will. As the UN focused more and more on a peacekeeping operation it could deploy and one Sudan would accept, developments on the ground meant that there was less and less peace to keep.

Widespread international concern notwithstanding, getting an effective UN force into Darfur was not to be. Initial preparation to deploy had begun, more in theory and less in practice, months before the signing of the DPA, driven by expectation that once a peace deal was concluded the UN would be called in to take over from a fledgling African Union force. (That force, the African Union Mission in Sudan or AMIS had been sent into theatre in mid-2004, originally as an observer, but remained under-funded, under-equipped, under-staffed and – many thought – under-appreciated.) The planning process was formally blessed by the UNSC on 3 February 2006, through a Presidential Statement in which the Council asked the Secretary-General to begin contingency preparations for a transition from AMIS to a UN force.

On the heels of the DPA, the Council moved quickly and, on 16 May, unanimously adopted resolution 1679, calling for acceleration of the transition to a UN operation, while urging non-signatories to join the agreement.[16] What was most notable was not in the text – in their explanation of the vote, the Chinese and Russian representatives emphasized that they had supported the resolution on the understanding that *any* UN force would have to be acceptable to the Government of Sudan. Khartoum, which was discernibly hostile to the notion of an effective UN force in Darfur, saw and seized another opportunity – and it refused cooperation on the issue.

As another summer dragged on to an end, the US and the UK, both under heavy pressure at home, decided to push ahead at the Council. In what turned out to be a grave tactical mistake, Washington and London forced the adoption of UNSCR 1706 on 31 August. Among others, the text mandated the existing UN operation in Sudan (UNMIS) to take over AMIS 'no later than 31 December 2006'.[17] The lack of adequate preparation and the impatience of the sponsors came at a deadly price – China, Russia, and Qatar (the only Arab member on the Council) abstained, exposing Council divisions to the world, and most importantly, to the GoS. While both China and Russia professed strong support for the idea of a UN deployment, they made it conditional on a non-negotiable, 'imperative need' for an invitation from Khartoum. The strongest backers of the draft resolution, the US and the EU states on the Council, failed even to get firm African support[18] and thus missed a chance to box the sceptics into a less damaging corner.[19]

Within hours of the vote, the Sudanese Government openly challenged the Council, rejecting the resolution and the idea of a UN force in Darfur. UNSCR 1706 was dead upon arrival.[20] The world community stood exposed, both unwilling and unable to make its way into Darfur over Khartoum's objections. The peacekeeping concept itself was again under existential stress; a Darfur 'peacekeeping' deployment seemed like the policy equivalent of shovelling sand with a pitchfork.

This realization took several weeks to permeate policy circles. Willy-nilly, resolution 1706 was abandoned and tracks changed. After much pressure, an agreement was reached with Khartoum in November 2006. China, having come under increased scrutiny and criticism from activists, played a central role in this episode, sending its UN ambassador Wang to Addis Ababa to seal the deal.[21] That deal was unfortunately more apparent than real: it included a three-phased peacekeeping plan – boosting the AU force first through a 'Light Support Package' to be followed by a 'Heavy Support Package' and, lastly, a hybrid AU-UN operation. The hybrid was to have 'a predominantly African character' and 'troops … as far as possible … sourced from African countries'. The UN agreed to provide 'backstopping and command and control structures'.[22] From a traditional peacekeeping perspective, the experiment was questionable at best and farcical at worst. It was, however, politically expedient, or at least of low cost, for most players involved. The loosely defined framework allowed for the creation of a beast interpreted by each side to its own advantage. All had a vested interest in maintaining the fiction – the Sudanese to play up their 'cooperation', the African Union to save face by not pulling out entirely, the UN to get in under some guise, and the Western powers to placate their publics.

It was a high-stakes game, and one that both the West and the UNSC were rather bad at playing. Engaged in endless rounds of self-applause over securing Sudan's putative concession, the international community again allowed Khartoum to make hay of the situation. Having squeezed the UN into a narrow, one-way tunnel, Sudan continued its masterful delaying tactics. Painfully aware of the need for a minimal level of Sudanese cooperation and of the political near-impossibility of changing course yet again, the Council found itself repeatedly kowtowing to the butchers of Khartoum, merely 'urging' implementation of the two support packages over the next six months.[23]

It was only on 31 July 2007, the last day of the Chinese Presidency of the Security Council for that year, that the Council agreed to establish a UN/AU Hybrid Operation in Darfur (UNAMID), voting unanimously to adopt resolution 1769.[24] UNAMID, projected to be the most expensive peacekeeping operation ever run by the UN and the second largest in the UN's history, was to take over AMIS by 31 December 2007.[25] In theory, the resolution was the pinnacle of a long, arduous journey to send a well-resourced, effective international force to protect the tormented population of Darfur. In practice, the UN was asked to deploy an operation in one of the world's toughest environments[26] relying mostly on second-class troops, often with third-class equipment, over impediments deliberately created by a first-class interlocutor – all while shackled into a politically unavoidable requirement to operate hand-in-glove with the African Union.

Stuck in First Gear

Once exuberance gave way to more sober assessments, few were surprised that very little happened in the ensuring months. In late November 2007, the then-head of UN peacekeeping, Frenchman Jean-Marie Guéhenno found himself forced to complain publicly to the Security Council. Guéhenno recounted how, utterly unembarrassable, Khartoum demanded the right to handpick the countries that could contribute troops to the mission – a dangerous precedent which deprived the mission of critical capabilities and can in the long run fatally undermine UN peacekeeping. It also refused to grant to the UN the right to fly at night, claimed the right to disable its communications equipment, and was not forthcoming on providing land for the troops or facilitating customs clearances. With disarming honesty, Guéhenno told the

Council that peace in Darfur was not possible without a strategic shift by the Government of Sudan. He cautioned that if Sudan does not 'clear the path for the deployment of an effective force, the international community will be confronted with hard choices: do we move ahead with the deployment of a force that will not make a difference, that will not have the capability to defend itself and that carries the risk of humiliation of the Security Council and the United Nations and tragic failure for the people of Darfur?'[27]

Two years after Guéhenno's stark warning, the UNAMID experiment is hardly encouraging. The deployment of the mission has proceeded at a shamefully sluggish pace due to Sudanese obstruction, refusal by timid UN member states to commit ample troops and equipment, the often complicated UN-AU relationship, and immense logistical challenges.[28] Calls for critical assets, especially helicopters, were repeated regularly by the UN and the NGO community – and were repeatedly ignored. Full deployment is still far off – with 18,755 or 72 per cent, deployed by the end of September 2009.[29] Over two years after its authorization – and approximately four years after the Council first spoke of the need for a UN force in Darfur – UNAMID is a far cry from expectations and, to this day, is not capable of implementing critical parts of its already modest mandate meaningfully.

UNAMID's latest mandate renewal, in July 2009, attracted little political and public attention, a testament to the fact that the Security Council, and the international community with it, had entered the last phase of grief over the mission – that of acceptance. Nonetheless, UNAMID has been to a certain extent lucky. Its operational environment changed appreciably since 2006, as Darfur had metastasized into a theatre of lower-level warfare.[30] This allowed the UN and AU underperformers to avoid an outright fiasco; UNAMID muddled along, too ineffective to be relevant and yet viable enough not to cause unbearable embarrassment.

That the UNSC eventually accepted to live with a mediocre mission in Darfur was also the outcome of another dynamic. What was long a truism for many – that the local software of the Darfur conflict (its root causes) was more important than the international hardware (the international force) – slowly caught on, luring political converts eager to make virtue out of necessity. Indeed, most have come to understand that without a peace process to support, UNAMID would inevitably be a grossly inadequate response at best and a dramatic failure at worst.[31]

As the argument that a peacekeeping force could not be a game-changer in an environment where there was no real peace to keep silently prevailed, the UN and the AU found the good sense to replace their respective (and often part-time) Darfur peace mediators with a single, joint envoy. By mid-summer

2008, when former Burkinabe Foreign Minister Bassole was appointed in that role, there was precious little left of the peace process.[32] In particular, rebels remained desperately fragmented, despite efforts to reunify them, both by the international community and, for a while, by Southern Sudan's SPLM. Through Bassole's recruitment, the peace process was about to be given another go when the job, already a poisoned chalice, became even more delicate. On 14 July 2008, barely a fortnight after Bassole's formal appointment, the International Criminal Court indicted Sudanese President Omar Bashir on charges of genocide, crimes against humanity, and war crimes.

The International Criminal Court: The NCP's *Bête Noire*

The UNSC referral of the Darfur situation to the ICC, through the March 2005 resolution 1593, had opened a new, international legal front which was less easily influenced by politics and thus constituted a serious threat to Khartoum. The NCP regime understood this better than most, reacting with clear alarm after the UN referral and taking the unprecedented liberty of publicly criticizing China. (China, unwilling to go out on a limb alone, did not veto the resolution, joining instead the United States, Algeria, and Brazil in abstaining.)[33] As Sudanese anger dissipated, these four abstentions pointed to a second-best strategy – stonewalling the ICC investigation with impunity. The Sudanese government had quickly understood that the Chinese and American abstentions meant the two states with arguably the greatest individual leverage over Khartoum would not spend their political chips inducing Sudanese cooperation with the Court. Over the next three years, the Sudanese regime brushed aside the ICC and its derision of international justice remained unchallenged.

That all changed on 14 July 2008, with Bashir's indictment. The move by the ICC Prosecutor, Luis Moreno Ocampo, took the independent judicial process that the Council had unleashed through the ICC in a direction few of those who had supported Resolution 1593 back in March 2005 would have thought possible, let alone likely. It was the first time the ICC had targeted a sitting head of state, and only the third time such a high-level individual had been indicted by an international tribunal.[34] The Prosecutor's decision was hotly debated in the subsequent months, while the judges of the ICC's Pre-Trial Chamber evaluated the evidence.[35] Arab and African states immediately called for suspension of the ICC proceedings by the UN Security Council, through an invocation of Article 16 of the Rome Statute.[36] Europeans and

Americans insisted they could consider such a step only if the Sudanese regime met a set of political or legal criteria, i.e. if it earned the deferral.

Some analysts argued that the Prosecutor's move created a unique opportunity for the Council to create some momentum around the peace process in Darfur and the more effective implementation of the CPA (see Grono and Hara 2008). As the idea caught on, the Sudanese regime smartly threw some concessional dust in the collective eyes of the international community. It seemingly softened on a few issues, in particular by easing some restrictions on UNAMID's deployment and offering cost-free overtures to engage the Darfur rebel movements in a reinvigorated peace process. Having thus tricked the UNSC into deliberative indecision yet again, it lashed out in early March 2009, when the judges of the ICC Pre-Trial Chamber found sufficient reason to issue an international arrest warrant for the Sudanese president.[37] Within hours, Khartoum expelled 13 international humanitarian agencies from Sudan in putative retaliation, accusing them of violating their humanitarian principles and cooperating with the 'kangaroo court' in the Hague.[38] More strongly than ever, it declared disinterest in the Article 16 issue, claiming it was unwilling to obey 'Western fiat' and did not recognize either the Court or any part of the Statute that established it.

At the time of writing, it is rather premature to pass definitive judgment on the impact of Moreno's indictment and the subsequent arrest warrant. What can be said is that, between the summer of 2008 and late 2009, its net benefit to Darfurians was questionable. For weeks on end, it sucked the air out of the Sudan debate, dominating the infamously limited, short-span international attention to a worrying degree.[39] While it did indirectly facilitate progress on some issues, such as the deployment of UNAMID, it unintentionally displaced others – prominently the Darfur peace process and the reinvigoration of CPA's implementation – to the back burner. Moreover, although the Prosecutor cannot be held responsible for the outrageous NGO expulsion by the Sudanese regime, the fact remains that his strategy enabled the Khartoum government to use its own people as political pawns, and thus may have indirectly caused a deterioration of the humanitarian situation in Darfur.[40] To this day, the real cost or benefit of Ocampo's decision, in terms of suffering in Darfur, remains unknown.[41]

By being the defining Darfur event of the second half of 2008 and at least the first quarter of 2009, the ICC indictment overshadowed the Bassole-run peace process. While international preoccupation with the ICC meant that Bassole had the relative luxury of operating without overly zealous UN or AU supervisors, his course of action had insufficient corrective and little support. Predictably, the indictment also gave a moral and a political boost to the Darfur rebels, further incentivizing their obstructionism at the peace table.

The Use and Abuse of the UNSC

The explanation behind the UN Security Council's abject performance on Sudan is three-fold. First, the Council's potential was undermined by a series of strategic policy mistakes in the international response to Sudan's crises. These mistakes were made in national capitals but have unavoidably limited the room for manoeuvre in New York. Second, the Council was misused by the very (Western) states clamouring for its engagement, its inherent, structural limitations grossly underestimated through repeated bouts of politically-induced wishful thinking. Third, a series of tactical missteps all but doomed the Council's response.

The UNSC was not set up and has never served as *the* unique place where member-states congregate to transcend significant pre-existing differences and hammer together, from start to finish, a collective, coherent international policy. Rather, the Council has operated as an arena where member-states attempt to win some ground but, on practically any issue of importance to the major countries, work within confines imposed by bilateral or multilateral understandings often reached far from the UN building in Manhattan. The Security Council of today, in other words, is a place where tactical decisions are made – but where only rarely, if ever, are overarching geopolitical strategies are crafted.[42]

In the Darfur case, Council failure was *de facto* predetermined by the strategy chosen in certain Western capitals. The idea appeared to be as simple as it was simplistic – use the Council to generate the political will to tackle Darfur, rather than revert to New York once that will had been generated. Its immediate appeal was perhaps obvious in a world at 'war against terror', facing the nightmares of Iraq and Afghanistan, as well as tensions over Kosovo, Iran and North Korea, among others. It saved increasingly precious political capital and the trouble of engaging sceptical but indispensable interlocutors (China, Russia, some Arab and African states) at the highest levels, to make it known that Darfur and Sudan were a real priority. In the end, it laid bare 'the sad reality … that Darfur simply does not matter enough, and Sudan matters too much, for the international community to do more to stop the atrocities' (Grono 2006).

Instead of working persistently at top levels, the US and its like-minded partners merely punted the Darfur issue to New York, and engaged only in occasional bouts of mostly cosmetic advocacy with Beijing and Moscow. That proved sufficient to keep public pressure within inoffensive bounds but did not narrow down strong policy disagreements among key international players. The views of the US and China or the UK and Russia, for example, remained so fundamentally different that they could only be manifested – but never truly bridged – in New York. Having left their bilateral homework to be done at the UN, Washington and London were bound to struggle – and to lose – there.

Acting on instructions from capitals, the US, UK and a handful other delegations were left with no choice but to cajole, trick and bully their way into the little that was actually achievable. That gradually poisoned the atmosphere at the Council, cast a thick layer of doubt regarding Anglo-American intentions, and played a part in inducing a number of critical delays and abstentions. Moves to reconcile largely incompatible positions yielded only watered down statements, as the Council steadily limped towards its own irrelevance. The Euro-American over-reliance on the Council was exploited by the Government of Sudan with some success, as Khartoum went on to paint the Council's actions as illegitimate and the body itself as a façade surreptitiously channelling Western, neo-colonialist interests.

In other words, the strategic battle over the Council's response to Darfur had a largely foregone conclusion precisely because so few diplomatic shots had been fired elsewhere. A botched tactical approach certainly did not help, however. Security Council pressure on the Government of Sudan did not yield a desired response not only due to its limited magnitude but also because it was applied unsystematically, in an ad-hoc fashion, and was often tailored to domestic political winds. Khartoum quickly caught on – sanctions threats and other 'sticks' were more a knee-jerk reaction and less a part of a coherent policy response.[43]

At the end of 2009, the Sudan fundamentals in New York remain the same; identical approaches in the future will likely produce similar results. American and European pressure without Chinese, Russian and African support will amount to little, and it could well backfire. This support cannot be secured exclusively in New York; achieving it requires a more significant investment – concerted and consistent high-level bilateral engagement. Pulling the pressure trigger in New York without such requisite preparation will simply expose, and in the process conceivably widen, differences and, by rupturing the tentative, if minimalist international agreement, will further embolden those in Sudan for whom peace is not a priority.

The Road Ahead

The lessons from the Council's track record on Sudan since 2004 are well worth the study. The situation in both Darfur and Sudan as a whole resembles the lull before a storm. The Darfur peace process is in shambles and UNAMID is incapable of making a lasting, sustainable improvement to the security situation, which has largely leveled but remains poor enough to prevent any return of the refugees and the internally displaced.

In the meantime, the Comprehensive Peace Agreement is extremely fragile, in large part due to years of neglect by the very same international partners who brokered it. Just over a year remains before it is scheduled to culminate in a referendum, which is widely expected to result in a declaration of independence and secession of South Sudan, whether peaceful or violent. Should the CPA unravel, or the NCP and SPLM fail to agree on a soft landing following the referendum, resumption of the North-South armed conflict would be inevitable. That is very likely to drag down Darfur and much of the rest of Sudan back into a full-scale war. Indeed, close observers fear that Sudan could face state collapse on a colossal scale and suck much of the Horn of Africa into a vortex of violence that, in the words of a former high-level UN official, 'would make Somalia look easy'. Its effects could create a tsunami of conflict that hits a lot of Africa and the Middle East.

At this time, it does not appear that disaster in Sudan can be averted without a qualitative shift in international attention, and without a much greater sense of urgency. Neither seems to be on the horizon. As much of the world – and the key parties to the conflicts in Sudan – look to the United States, the White House seems unable or unwilling to pay a more than lip service to the notion of high-level political commitment. That pattern characterized the Bush administration and has remained depressingly similar under Obama.[44]

What has offered some reason for qualified optimism is the gradual American retrieval away from what Kofi Annan's deputy once called 'megaphone diplomacy' on Darfur (see Malloch Brown 2006) to a more measured, calibrated tone and movement towards, again in the words of Mark Malloch Brown, 'a carefully-modulated set of incentives and sanctions which Sudan needs to understand' (*The Independent* 2006). As the US has climbed down from the rarefied rhetorical heights that had deprived its policy of oxygen, creating and sustaining a broader international coalition behind its efforts has become a possibility once again.

The US 'comprehensive' Sudan strategy, launched with much delay and a bit of fanfare on 19 October, has made this possibility yet more realistic. While the strategy offered little policy detail, it is notable for at least four reasons. First, it recognized that the US 'cannot succeed in achieving our policy goals by focusing exclusively on Darfur or CPA implementation – both must be addressed seriously and simultaneously, while also working to resolve and prevent conflict throughout Sudan'. It also acknowledged the US cannot succeed alone, and must 'engage with allies and with those with whom we disagree'. Second, it claimed that Sudanese cooperation on counter-terrorism matters can no longer 'be used as a bargaining chip to evade responsibilities in Darfur or in implementing the CPA'. Third, it explicitly recognized the likelihood of South Sudanese secession. Fourth, it pledged to assess every three months 'at senior levels … a variety of indicators of progress or of deepening crisis' and to include in that assessment 'calibrated steps to bolster support for positive change and to discourage backsliding'.[45]

At five minutes to the Sudanese midnight, Washington appears well aware of some of the critical mistakes of the past five years, which this essay has attempted to outline. Whether enough of the lessons have indeed been learned by Washington's new masters remains to be seen. As so often, their wisdom or folly will be partially tested on familiar grounds – the inevitable United Nations Security Council.

Notes

1 An early version of this chapter, submitted in an anonymous capacity, formed the basis for ENOUGH's eponymous strategy paper, published in July 2008. See http://www.enoughproject.org/publications/irresolution-un-security-council-darfur.

2 The distinction between 'Arab' and 'African' Darfur tribes is as important as it is subtle. For instance, Alex de Waal has argued that, 'The Arab–African dichotomy is historically and anthropologically bogus. But that doesn't make the distinction unreal, as long as the perpetrators subscribe to it'. See http://www.bostonreview.net/BR29.5/dewaal.php and http://conconflicts.ssrc.org/hornofafrica/dewaal/ and http://www.nybooks.com/articles/22771, among others.

3 At the time, the most vocal opponents to discussing Darfur as a stand-alone crisis at the Council were China, Pakistan, Algeria, and Russia.

4 See verbatim record of the proceedings, available at http://www.un.org/Depts/dhl/resguide/scact2004.htm, under 18 September, Sudan.

5 Full text of the resolution available on the UN website: http://www.un.org/News/Press/docs/2005/sc8346.doc.htm.

6 Report of the International Commission of Inquiry on Darfur to the UN Secretary-General, page 4. Report can be downloaded from http://www.un.org/News/dh/sudan/com_inq_darfur.pdf. The Commission was headed by Antonio Cassese,

a prominent Italian law professor and the first President of the International Criminal Tribunal for the former Yugoslavia (ICTY).

7 Only 'final' reports of the Panel have been formally published. All 'interim' reports have never been officially released to the public.

8 http://www.un.org/sc/committees/1591/reports.shtml. The confidential annex has never been publicly released.

9 All subsequent reports of the panel of experts have by and large suffered from the same fate. A few have managed to generate media headlines and in turn political discussions – but have never led to real repercussions for violators. One of the prominent examples is the spring 2007 'interim' Panel report, which was leaked to the *New York Times* (http://www.nytimes.com/2007/04/18/world/africa/18sudan.html). It detailed, among other things, how the Sudanese government continued to fly into Darfur arms and heavy military equipment, in patent violation of the sanctions regime, and how it struggled to disguise its aircraft as chartered by the United Nations. Presented with this evidence, the Council again chose to remain silent.

10 Major General Gaffar Mohamed Elhassan (Commander of the Western Military Region for the Sudanese Air Force); Sheikh Musa Hilal (Paramount Chief of the Jalul Tribe in North Darfur); Adam Yacub Shant (Sudanese Liberation Army Commander); Gabril Abdul Kareem Badri (National Movement for Reform and Development Field Commander).

11 The latest renewal of the Panel's mandate came on 13 October 2009. See http://www.un.org/News/Press/docs/2009/sc9765.doc.htm. Sheepishly, resolution 1891 instructed the Panel to 'assess progress towards reducing violations by all parties'.

12 See, among others, Crisis Group (2006).

13 The UN Secretariat is also at fault here. For too long, it found itself caught up in reactive mode, responding to the Darfur priority de jour, instead of also beating the drum of prevention, alerting all that CPA implementation was dangerously slipping.

14 'In less than a week, government and rebels were compelled to come to a comprehensive agreement'. See de Waal (2006). 'It was a joyless climax: the Sudanese present knew that the wheels had come off, and that the agreement was, like its predecessor, unworkable. But the US and AU had staked all on a huge gamble, and were still determined to make it work against the odds.' 'The Darfur rebels' delegates in Abuja were still struggling to master the 515 paragraphs when they were called on to make a final and binding decision; none of their people in Darfur had even seen a copy.' 'Bit by bit, the DPA became the cover for President Bashir's search for a military solution to the Darfur crisis.'

15 Bolton made this comment during UN General Assembly negotiations over the Human Rights Council in early 2006: 'We want a butterfly. We're not going to put lipstick on a caterpillar and declare it a success.' The US, along with only Israel, the Marshall Islands and Palau, ended up voting against the HRC's creation. Belarus, Iran, and Venezuela abstained, while 170 other states voted in favour.

See http://www.nationalreview.com/comment/schaefer200602020828.asp and here: http://www.un.org/News/Press/docs/2006/ga10449.doc.htm.

16 See text of UNSCR 1679: http://www.un.org/News/Press/docs/2006/sc8721.doc.htm.

17 See text of UNSCR 1706: http://www.un.org/News/Press/docs/2006/sc8821.doc.htm.

18 Many in Africa felt snubbed over what was perceived as underwhelming international support for AMIS, accompanied by recurrent Western criticism of the AU mission's performance.

19 The Republic of Congo did not speak and, unlike the other two states, did not co-sponsor the draft resolution. Tanzania spoke of a 'solution [that] can come only with full cooperation and partnership with … the brother state of the Sudan'. Ghana was the strong voice, noting that it vote reaffirmed 'one of the cardinal principles enshrined in article 4 (h) of the Constitutive Act of the African Union, which recognizes the right of the Union to intervene in a member state in respect of grave circumstances, namely war crimes, genocide, and crimes against humanity'. Its representative – the acting President of the Council – added his reservations 'about inclusion in the draft text of explicit language that implies that the Government of the Sudan can take all the time it wants before allowing the United Nations to deploy in Darfur, or even to refuse to do so, regardless of the cost in human lives'. See text of UNSC Resolution 1706 and verbatim summary of the debate: http://www.un.org/Depts/dhl/resguide/scact2006.htm, under 31 August entry.

20 See, among others, the BBC's coverage of the situation: http://news.bbc.co.uk/2/hi/africa/5304160.stm.

21 For the outcome of the 'High Level Consultation on the Situation in Darfur', see http://www.un.org/apps/sg/offthecuff.asp?nid=950.

22 See Conclusions of the High Level Consultation on the Situation in Darfur, 16 November 2006. http://www.sudantribune.com/spip.php?article18754.

23 Presidential Statement of 19 December 2006 http://www.un.org/News/Press/docs/2006/sc8912.doc.htm; Presidential Statement of 25 May 2007 http://www.un.org/News/Press/docs/2007/sc9027.doc.htm; 16 July 2007 debate following UNSC mission to Africa http://www.un.org/News/Press/docs/2007/sc9079.doc.htm.

24 See resolution 1769: http://www.un.org/News/Press/docs/2007/sc9089.doc.htm.

25 UNPROFOR in Bosnia and Herzegovina had 38,599 military personnel and 803 civilian police in March 1995. (http://www.un.org/Depts/dpko/dpko/co_mission/unprof_p.htm). Initially UNAMID has an approved annual budget of $1.28 billion – which, by 2009 had grown to nearly $1.6 billion – and an authorized strength of 'up to 19,555 military personnel; 6,432 police, including 3,772 police personnel and 19 formed police units comprising up to 140 personnel each; and a significant civilian component'. http://www.un.org/depts/dpko/missions/unamid/facts.html.

26 Parts of West Darfur are over 3,000 km from the nearest port, on the Red Sea.

27 See verbatim record of 5784th meeting of the UNSC, 27 November 2007, link available at http://www.un.org/Depts/dhl/resguide/scact2007.htm. Summary of Guéhenno's remarks can be seen at: http://www.un.org/News/Press/docs/2007/sc9178.doc.htm.

28 While UNAMID did formally take over the African Union mission on 31 December 2007, it remained largely a rehatted AMIS with precious few new troops and police until many months later. As of mid-April 2008, UNAMID had deployed under 40 per cent of its mandated military force, under 43 per cent of its civilian police contingent and, shockingly, only one out of the 19 authorized formed police units. See Report of the Secretary-General on the deployment of UNAMID, 14 April 2008 (http://www.un.org/Docs/sc/sgrep08.htm).

29 See: http://www.un.org/Depts/dpko/dpko/contributors/2009/sept09_4.pdf. UNAMID had 14,638 troops and 169 military observers in theatre, out of 19,555 authorized, as well as 3,941 police out of 6432 authorized (3,772 regular police plus 19 Formed Police Units (FPUs) of 140 persons each).

30 The fighting was no longer only between the many rebel splinters on the one hand, and the Sudanese government and some of its local proxies on the other. According to some researchers, as much as a third of the violent fatalities in Darfur in 2008 were the result of intra-Arab clashes. See http://blogs.ssrc.org/darfur/2009/06/18/understanding-darfurs-arab-militia/ and the report linked therein.

31 Even fully deployed, UNAMID will prove unable to do much more than tinker at the margins of the conflict, struggling to protect about 2.5 million Darfurians now in IDP camps. Its 26,000 troops and police will have to cover an area about ten times larger than what was entrusted to nearly 40,000 blue berets at the height of the Bosnian war in 1995. (BiH territory = 51,129 km^2; Darfur territory = 493,180 km^2) They will have to brave a more challenging terrain and a maddening plethora of fractionalized armed groups, often unaccountable to a central authority – and they will have to face these obstacles unequipped and, most likely, less prepared to take casualties. (UNPROFOR took 167 fatalities, 159 of whom were soldiers. http://www.un.org/Depts/DPKO/Missions/unprof_p.htm).

32 Bassole was formally appointed in June 2008. See: http://www.un.org/News/Press/docs//2008/sga1143.doc.htm.

33 Although the Bush Administration had proudly 'unsigned' the Rome Statute establishing the International Criminal Court, it was in a poor position to veto the resolution. Its attempts to undermine the ICC by arguing in favour of an African-based special tribunal were unsuccessful.

34 Milošević was indicted by the ICTY in May 1999; Charles Taylor was indicted by the Special Court for Sierra Leone on 7 March 2003. Both Milošević and Taylor were brought to court only after they had been forced out of power, i.e. as *former* heads of state.

35 See, among many others, 'Flawed International Justice for Sudan', by Antonio Cassese. http://www.project-syndicate.org/commentary/cassese4. Cassese is currently the President of the Special Tribunal for Lebanon.

36 According to Article 16 of the ICC's Rome Statute, the Council can step in and defer any prosecution for a renewable period of 12 months, through a resolution adopted under Chapter VII of the UN Charter.

37 ICC announcement of the arrest warrant against Bashir can be found here: http://www.icc-cpi.int/NR/exeres/0EF62173-05ED-403A-80C8-F15EE1D25BB3.htm.

38 Notably, the expulsions occurred just days after the appointment of a new Special Envoy on Sudan by the Obama Administration. Ret. Major General J. Scott Gration was appointed on 18 March 2009. Some analysts argued that Khartoum believed it could curry immediate favour with Gration by 'compromising' on a step they should not have made in the first place.

39 For example, the controversy over the ICC indictment spilled over even into the 2008 UNSC debate on UNAMID's renewal. African states, supported by others, demanded that the Council formally acknowledge an African Union request to have the indictment suspended. Out of protest, the United States abstained on the resolution, in a move of little practical significance to the UN operation but of notable symbolic value. As a matter of undeclared policy, the Council tries to adopt all resolutions regarding UN peacekeeping forces by unanimity. See http://www.un.org/News/Press/docs/2008/sc9412.doc.htm.

40 The ICC's move was so controversial that, in political terms, it completely eclipsed Khartoum's expulsion of the 13 humanitarian NGOs. The Security Council, as it was to be expected, remained silent on the expulsions for days after Khartoum's decision. On 26 March, it finally appealed to Sudan 'to reconsider the decision of suspending the activities of some non-governmental organizations in Sudan'. Even that call was shockingly informal, conveyed through a 'press statement' by the UNSC Libyan President. The statement is only available in video from the UN website: http://webcast.un.org/ramgen/ondemand/stakeout/2009/so090326am3.rm – a telling sign perhaps.

41 Following the expulsions, the UN Secretariat agreed to conduct a joint assessment mission with the Sudanese government to estimate their impact. That the UN as a whole succumbed to Khartoum's objection to an independent assessment – not just in the heat of the moment but ever since the expulsions – is both disappointing and baffling.

42 In the absence of significant pre-existing differences among key member-states, the Council is generally capable of playing a major role in defining policy strategies. It has done so in the past, with regard to issues that have had the dubious distinction of being relatively low on the respective priority lists of such member-states, or in those exceptional situations that call for extremely urgent UNSC action and over which major powers essentially agree.

43 This inconsistent application of pressure does not constitute proof that pressure as such does not work versus the Government of Sudan. It only demonstrates

that Khartoum has mastered the ability to exploit the wavering and indecision of the international community.

44 The top three officials in charge of foreign policy in the Obama administration – the President, the Vice President and the Secretary of State – all pledged during the Democratic Presidential primaries that Sudan would be a major foreign policy priority for their teams. In reality, the shortlist of major policy concerns for the current US administration features many of the usual suspects – Iraq, Afghanistan, Iran, Israel/Palestine, and North Korea, among others – but not quite Sudan.

45 Full text of the public version of the US strategy available at http://www.state.gov/r/pa/prs/ps/2009/oct/130672.htm.

References

African Union Peace and Security Council (2004), Communique, 25 May, http://www.africa-union.org/News_Events/Communiqu%C3%A9s/25%20mayCommuniqu%C3%A9%20_10th_.pdf.

Cassesse, Antonio (2008), 'Flawed International Justice for Sudan', http://www.project-syndicate.org/commentary/cassese4.

Grono, Nick (2006), 'Darfur: The International Community's Failure to Protect', *African Affairs*, 30 September, http://www.crisisgroup.org/home/index.cfm?id=4417#_edn30.

Grono, Nick and Hara, Fabienne (2007), 'Sudan: UN Security Council Should Make Government Meet Benchmarks', http://allafrica.com/stories/200807250915.html.

The Independent (2006), 'In Defense of the United Nations', intervies with Mark Malloch Brown, 29 September, http://www.independent.co.uk/news/world/politics/exclusive-interview-in-defence-of-the-united-nations-417986.html.

International Commission of Inquiry on Darfur (2005), Report to the UN Secretary-General Pursuant to Security Council Resolution 1564 of 18 September 2004, http://www.un.org/News/dh/sudan/com_inq_darfur.pdf.

International Crisis Group (2005), 'New Sudan Action Plan', 26 April, http://www.crisisgroup.org/home/index.cfm?id=3391&l=1.

International Crisis Group (2006), Sudan's Comprehensive Peace Agreement: The Long Road Ahead, 31 March, http://www.crisisgroup.org/home/index.cfm?id=4055&l=1.

Kristof, Nicholas (2009), 'What to Do About Darfur', *New York Review of Books* 56(11) 2, July.

Malloch Brown, Mark Malloch (Deputy Secretary-General) (2006) Speech at the 'Power and Superpower' conference by the Century Foundation, 6 June, http://www.tcf.org/list.asp?type=EV&pubid=156.

United States Department of State (2009), 'Sudan: A Critical Moment, A Comprehensive Approach, Office of the Spokesman', 19 October, http://www.state.gov/r/pa/prs/ps/2009/oct/130672.htm.

Waal, Alex de (2004), 'Who are the Darfurians? Arab and African Identities, Violence and External Engagement', http://conconflicts.ssrc.org/hornofafrica/dewaal/.

Waal, Alex de (2006), 'I Will Not Sign', *London Review of Books*, 30 November, http://www.lrb.co.uk/v28/n23/waal01_.html.

CHAPTER NINE

RULE OF LAW, JUDICIAL REFORM AND THE RECONSTRUCTION OF POST-CONFLICT AND FAILING STATES

Muna Ndulo

Introduction

There is general agreement that states weakened due to conflict, such as the Republic of the Congo, or collapsed states, such as Somalia, pose a serious threat to the security of their people and of the international community. Although no universally accepted definition of weak states exists, there is general agreement that such states lack the capacity to perform core functions of statehood effectively. This chapter focuses on one type of weak state – the post-conflict state. It addresses the need for and the challenges to establishing rule of law and a functioning judicial system in post-conflict societies. There is general agreement among development practitioners that the absence of rule of law is a major contributing factor in the crisis of failing states; thus the need to establish rule of law as part of reconstruction efforts is great. The challenges and issues discussed in this chapter apply to all weak states, regardless of whether this weakness resulted from conflict or from state collapse. Post-conflict societies and states are characterized by the lack of rule of law, poor governance, lack of physical security, ethnic conflict, past and present gross human rights violations, impunity of violators and economic devastation and decay. The end of the conflict does not automatically bring peace, security and an end to violence and human rights violations.[1] Such societies, while facing enormous challenges such as addressing past human rights violations, providing justice to previously marginalized groups, and addressing social and economic injustices stemming from structural inequalities that are often the causes of conflict, face the further challenges of articulating a new vision of society, establishing effective governance structures that are responsive to the needs of the people, defining the fundamental principles by which the country will be governed, distributing internal power among the various segments of the population, engaging in effective reconstruction and economic development, and establishing and securing an enduring peace.

The manner in which these processes are handled can play an important role in the consolidation of peace and the establishment of an atmosphere conducive to economic growth and development and the emergence of a legitimate and sustainable state. Many of these issues, if not handled properly, can accentuate existing differences and lead to renewed conflict. At the institutional level, the legacy of conflict shared by all post-conflict societies is the lack of national institutions to deal with past and present human rights violations, massive poverty, violence, displaced populations, monumental underdevelopment, and the challenge of developing a physical infrastructure to support economic development. Institutional infrastructure in place is often at a very basic level, most of it having been damaged during conflict, with key personnel fled, killed or compromised by association with the previous regime – which was most likely complicit in the human rights violations, maladministration and corruption during the conflict.

In response to past human rights violations, a variety of measures has been developed. These include prosecutions at both international and domestic levels, truth commissions, local justice and reconciliation and reparations for victims. All of these options need strong institutions. The most common criticism of prosecutions is that they are driven by vengeance.[2] This criticism can be deflected by creating judicial institutions that are fair and independent, that respect and guarantee due process of law and the presumption of innocence. In the context of post-conflict societies, this will require rebuilding the domestic judicial system and its supporting services. Local prosecutions are preferable to international prosecutions for several reasons: international tribunals can try only a small number of human rights violators and tend to focus on the major perpetrators, leaving middle- and lower-level operatives to domestic courts. Such tribunals are also often perceived by the local population as distant, as in the case of the Rwanda Tribunal, which was located far from the theatre of war and conflict. Partly in response to this, a hybrid local tribunal composed of international and local judges was established in Sierra Leone. Local tribunals have an enduring positive effect on the local justice systems and on articulation of norms. The use of local tribunals can help in the development of a culture of justice and accountability and ensures that norms established during the prosecution of past human rights violations will not vanish when the tribunal or specific trials are over.[3] Additionally, the court system is strengthened and legitimized and is trained for the long-term role of protecting the constitution and human rights and ensuring the rule of law.

Establishing the rule of law, reforming judicial institutions and other oversight institutions should, therefore, be a core task in post-conflict societies.[4] As observed earlier, post-conflict societies need judicial reform to provide mechanisms for addressing both past and current human rights violations, for advancing the rule of law and constitutional governance, and for the settlement of disputes. Once established, these mechanisms play a critical role in preventing future abuses. They also contribute to transitional justice in that they enable the courts to provide criminal accountability for past abuses.[5] In addition, through case law, they help to document the historical record of abuses and conflict. This brings us to a discussion of what needs to be done to modernize the law and judicial institutions in post-conflict societies so that they can play the role we prescribe for them above. First, there is a need to adapt the law and to develop legal, administrative and political institutions in light of the special needs and conditions of post-conflict societies. No major social change occurs or is put into effect in a society which is not reflected in some kind of change in its laws.[6] Law is the instrument through which goals are promoted, implemented and reviewed. The kinds of laws that are written and the way they are interpreted by the judiciary will determine the type of reconstruction and development that takes place in a post-conflict society. It is widely acknowledged that in order to implement developmental or political reforms, a society must make use of the legal order to transform and bring about the necessary institutional change. Seidman and Seidman (2006, 29–30) have identified three reasons why law is the instrument of choice in the reform process: 1) governments use rules to communicate their prescriptions to public employees; 2) positive law's *autra vires* rule holds that a public official may not so much as lift an official finger unless authorized by law; and 3) at its core, the rule of law prescribes a government not of men and women, but of laws.

The principle of legality needs to be extended beyond the prosecution of past human rights violations to the discharge of services and the regulation of economic processes. It is essential to the reconstruction and development process in post-conflict societies that legal systems furnish general organizational constructs that make efficient administration of government and efficient public or private entrepreneurial activities possible. The law can further contribute to development and reform by conferring impersonality, legitimacy and to some extent, stability on the political and social structure of the nation state. The strengthening of the state is an important indirect contribution of the legal order to the development process because the state provides at once: 1) a national market; 2) a centralized source of general decision making and long range planning; and 3) a more impersonal and less restrictive centre of social gravity than the primary group, which might in fact exacerbate conflict and state collapse. A formal system is indispensable to the growth and workings of a modern economy not only as a source of tools for reaching certain economic objectives but as a framework for economic life. However, reform and institutional building in post-conflict societies must be well designed and developed in consultation with the people among whom reforms will be implemented in order to reflect their particular circumstances and to give citizens a sense of ownership of the reforms. For a reform to have any hope of success, it must be context driven.

The option of prosecution in dealing with past human rights violations requires the courts to play a significant role both in the prosecutions and in establishing the rule of law. In all post-conflict countries the establishment of the rule of law has been accepted as essential for the promotion of reconstruction and long-term stability. Development and peace-building actors now engage in extensive rule of law projects, based on the belief that promoting rule of law will contribute to good governance, conflict resolution, protection of human rights, and economic development (IMF 1997; Economic Commission for Africa 2005, 2; World Bank 1994; Messick 1999, 117).[7] Nwabueze (1993, 189) has observed that the one institution above all others essential to the preservation of the rule of law has always been and still is an honest, able, learned, and independent judiciary. The courts are forums through which individuals can seek individual and collective justice and guarantee the sustenance of democracy.

The concern for good governance and the rule of law in post-conflict countries is particularly significant because of the way in which their absence can negatively impact the development process and contribute to the eruption of conflicts and accelerate state collapse. This chapter attempts to examine judicial reform and the rule of law in post-conflict societies and their relevance to good governance and the establishment of a state that is sustainable, stable and capable of exercising the range of state responsibilities that should be exercised by a state. It focuses specifically on the kinds of issues that need to be addressed in judicial reform and on the challenges of promoting rule of law in post-conflict societies.

The Judiciary, Prosecutions and the Rule of Law

Although the rule of law and judicial reform have been recognized as central to domestic and international efforts to promote good governance and sustainable peace and development (UNDP 2008; Ndulo 2003, pp. 315, 328), they remain subject to divergent criticisms from scholars and policy makers. There are those who argue that it is wrong to prioritize the rule of law and judicial reform in the midst of the many challenges that face post-conflict societies. Others argue that most rule of law projects seek to intervene too early in the rebuilding process and that often the aims and time frame proposed are unrealistic. The short answer to these criticisms is that rule of law projects do not seek to be the panacea to reconstruction of post-conflict societies; rather they seek to lay the framework within which the rebuilding efforts and protection of human rights can be promoted and secured.

The rule of law connotes the use of state power to establish through legislation the economic and social system agreed upon by the people through constitutionally sanctioned representative institutions or other acceptable surrogates. Typically, the division and regulation of state power is established through the national constitution, and as such is a charter of government (Pyle 1999, 215). The constitution is a body of fundamental principles by which a society organizes a government for itself, defines and limits its powers, and regulates the relations between its organs *inter se* and with the citizen (Nagle 2002, 510). It is crucial that the framework be responsive to the needs of the people. Resource distribution, which is often at the center of conflicts, is a function of political power that in modern states is shared through a framework provided for in a country's constitution. As Pheroze Nowrojee observed after Kenya was threatened with state collapse and almost joined the ranks of failing states in 2008,

> the small battles about the constitution are only derivatives of a fierce competition between various communities in Kenya over the resources provided both by mother nature and [by] human production. It is the struggle for livelihoods that is manifested in battles for power and representation. The most fundamental law of the land, the constitution, needs to provide a consensual framework within which conflicts, competition and struggles for livelihoods will be managed. (Nowrojee 2006)

The rule of law – through the prior existence of basic laws governing various areas of official operations – implies the assurance of some sort of predictability in the conduct of state officials as they perform their state duties (Ndulo 2003, 339). It demands precise definition of the roles and status of such public officials by law (Ocran 1984, 303). It commends the creation of control devices to ensure that public officials abide by these norms, and that if they do not, their actions will be held invalid by courts of law (ibid., 305). It embraces procedural guarantees necessary to assure fairness in adjudication of disputes and the application of sanctions. When a general rule is being applied, it demands equal treatment before the law for all persons and in all cases where that particular rule applies. Unifying all the elements of the juridical quest for legitimacy are the demands for legal barriers to arbitrary government actions (defined as actions taken without legal authority) and the demand for procedural safeguards, especially during trials for individuals alleged to be in conflict with the law' (ibid., 302).

The key aims of the rule of law, then, are to limit state power, thereby checking its arbitrary, oppressive and despotic tendencies, and to ensure the equal treatment and protection of all citizens irrespective of race, ethnicity, class, status, religion, place of origin, or political persuasion. These aims imply a legal framework that legitimizes state actions, that is procedurally fair and enforced impartially (particularly in regard to laws of human rights, public security and safety) (Peerenboom 2002, pp. 471, 472). Authority is legitimate if there is an established legal and institutional framework, and if decisions are taken in accordance with accepted institutional criteria, processes, and procedures (Hung 2004, 111). The idea of a constitutional democratic government, or constitutionalism, connotes a government defined, regulated, and limited by a constitution (Nwabueze 1993). Constitutional democracy is founded upon the notion of checks and balances, namely that different institutions – the legislature, the judiciary, and the executive – while operating independently of each other, simultaneously act to check each other's operations and balance each other's powers (Henkin 1992, 885). All three institutions are duty-bound to uphold the rule of law (ibid.).

A government operating under a written constitution has no power other than that granted to it by the constitution, either expressly or by necessary implication (Nwabueze 1993, 36). It has been pointed out that the mark of good governance is above all else its effectiveness in nurturing and promoting the best qualities in its people – the habits of obedience to government as the constituted authority, its laws and its interposition in the settlement of disputes and the redress of grievances; the habits of integrity, probity, fairness, self-restraint, and discipline in the conduct of social relations and public affairs; the spirit of enterprise, hard work, self-reliance and inventiveness in the pursuits and activities of life; and the quality of public-spiritedness and patriotism in matters affecting the interests of the community (ibid.). Good governance fosters qualities such as initiative and inventiveness in its people and tends to further improve their overall intellectual and moral qualities. The success of a country depends in part upon such qualities, especially in terms of protecting human rights and maintaining and promoting economic development and the well-being of society

Judicial reform and the rule of law must therefore: 1) regulate and limit the powers of government and provide mechanisms to ensure the efficacy of such limitations; 2) provide measures that ensure accountability of political leaders on the basis of openness, probity and honesty; 3) ensure that past human rights violations are punished and that there is no impunity; 4) ensure that the human rights of the people are fully protected; 5) ensure that disputes, including those concerning the constitutionality of legislation and government acts, are adjudicated impartially by regular, ordinary courts independent of the protagonists; 6) ensure that ordinary laws applied in the execution of governance and adjudication of disputes are made in conformity with the provisions of the constitution and in accordance with the procedure for law-making prescribed therein, and that such procedures conform to internationally accepted human rights norms; 7) formulate clear and transparent processes by which political leaders and government officials are held accountable for their actions to the people; 8) ensure that the safety of citizens is guaranteed, and that contracts are fairly enforced, both between the public and private operators and between private operators and the state; 9) ensure that public agencies are responsive to the needs of the public and promote social and economic development for the benefit of all citizens in an equitable manner; and 10) promote accountability through provision of information (Paul 1993). Judicial reform is particularly important because the effectiveness of constitutionalism as an element of the rule of law depends on how the limitations imposed on the government by the constitution are interpreted and enforced by the courts (ibid., 32).

Judicial Reform in Post-conflict States

Promoting rule of law and good governance in post-conflict situations will require, *inter alia*, 1) building the capacity of state institutions to address the root causes of conflict, and 2) building institutions for delivery of services such as health, education, justice and dispute settlement as well as police and correctional services to maintain law and order. In sum, the rule of law and good governance entails first and foremost a government that lives up to its responsibilities by ensuring the effective delivery of public goods and services, the maintenance of law and order, and the administration of justice (World Bank various years). It also involves the creation of an efficient and dynamic market – which secures economic growth and prosperity, as well as a vibrant civil society – which facilitates interaction between the state and economic and social actors within the state. The indices for institutional effectiveness, among others, include the following: 1) respect for the rule of law by all the actors in the political process; 2) independence and capacity of the judiciary;

3) mechanisms for self-regulation and external oversight of the activities of the executive and legislative organs; 4) transparency, accountability of oversight bodies, and mechanisms for the active participation of civil society and the private sector in decision making; 5) the degree of involvement of decentralized structures in decision making; 6) gender representation in all spheres of decision making; 7) effective delivery mechanisms servicing the poor; and 8) independence of the legislatures in drafting and enacting relevant legislation (Armstrong 1994, 281; World Bank 2001, 30 and 1989, 61).

Reforming judicial institutions is a core task in United Nations peacekeeping missions. The United Nations sees a direct connection between justice and peace. This is reflected in the Charter, which states that the founding states were determined to 'establish conditions under which justice and respect for obligations arising from treaties and other sources of international law can be maintained' (United Nations Charter, Preamble). Implementing of rights involves a wide range of actions, from drafting legislation to training judges and lawyers and modernizing court systems, police forces and prisons. The aim is to develop respect for human rights among a nation's population and to buttress the upholding of these rights.[8] Due process is almost invariably a casualty during conflict and therefore needs to be re-established. Although there may be disagreements about methods, the goal is quite clear. It is to transform institutions that perpetuated or were complicit in conflict and the violation of human rights into institutions that support peace, promote development and protect human rights. It is also to create institutions that promote accountability for past and current human rights violations.

The United Nations missions in the Democratic Republic of the Congo (DRC), Liberia and Sierra Leone provide useful examples of UN efforts at reconstructing judiciaries in post-conflict states. Notwithstanding the different mandates, different security situations, and different justice sectors, there are cross-cutting issues affecting the United Nations missions' support of the judiciary in the DRC, Liberia and Sierra Leone. In the first place, the three missions operate in contexts where internecine civil wars have combined to disrupt justice sectors already weakened by decades of mismanagement and corruption. In each of these countries the situation upon UN entry was characterized by the absence of a capable state and by lack of transparency, accountability, or the ability to enforce law, respect human rights, or share resources effectively and fairly amongst the peoples that comprised those states. Quite apart from the fact that all three countries have United Nations Charter Chapter VII mandates, the fundamental tasks the missions have been mandated to carry out are essentially the same as well. Although the exact wording of the respective mandates is different, the missions operate in functionally similar ways. Effectively, the three missions all 1) monitor the judiciary, 2) advise the government on legal matters and matters that intimately concern the judiciary, 3) train judicial officers and auxiliaries, the police and correctional officers in legal matters and human rights, 4) engage in reform of substantive law to align it with human rights norms, and 5) construct physical infrastructure related to the administration of justice.

A third similarity the three UN missions share concerns the causes of the civil wars that conspired to erode even further the alarming state of the judiciary in each country. The DRC, Liberia and Sierra Leone are resource-rich countries and the civil wars that afflicted their communities were to a greater or lesser extent resource-based (UNDP 2005a and 2005b). Consequently the humanitarian situation in these countries is depressingly bleak. There is sufficient empirical evidence to prove that civil wars emerging in resource-rich environments tend to result in higher levels of indiscriminate violence and, consequently, in higher levels of human rights violations and disruption of institutions (Weinstein 2007).

The United Nations in DRC, Liberia and Sierra Leone has the daunting task of transforming judiciaries plagued by profound and serious institutional ills into functioning, effective and independent courts. The ills include lack of access to justice, lack of physical resources, corruption, ill-trained judges, a culture of impunity, long delays and irregular execution of judgments. In several of the rural areas people rarely have access to any type of justice, formal or otherwise. Courts are far apart and villagers have to travel long distances to access courts, and there are not enough of them. The length of trials, often caused by frequent adjournments, discourages litigants from using the court system. As a result of corruption and widespread incompetence, the judicial sector suffers from a legitimacy crisis. Similarly, the Liberian judiciary suffers from corruption, impunity and lack of public confidence (see http://unmil.org/1content.asp?ccat=ljss&zdoc=1).

In 2003 the United Nations Mission to Liberia (UNMIL) established the Legal and Judicial System Support Division to fulfil its mandate to assist the Liberian government in developing a strategy for consolidating a national legal framework, including judicial institutions. Pursuant to this resolution the United Nations has engaged in capacity building by, among other things, training higher level judges and court officials, as well as government officials, in legal matters. They have also supported the government on record keeping. The Sierra Leone mandate is to consolidate peace, foster reconciliation, and nurture a culture and environment conducive to economic development (see http://www.uniosil.org/). The activities of the mission include helping the government of Sierra Leone to build the capacity of state institutions to address the root causes of the conflict, establishing a human rights commission, and strengthening the rule of law – which entails developing the independence and capacity of the justice system and that of the police and correctional services. The Sierra Leone judicial reform project includes the establishment of a special court to try those bearing the greatest responsibility for the gross human rights violations during the Sierra Leone conflict.

Elements of an Independent Judiciary

This section will examine factors that are crucial to the development of an effective judiciary, such as independence of the courts and appointment procedures of judges. The maintenance of an independent and accountable judiciary is fundamental to ensuring accountability for human rights violations, the rule of law, constitutionalism and the protection of human rights and the constitution. In democratic states, courts are charged with the task of reviewing government acts for compliance with the bill of rights and the constitution and with providing a forum to ensure government accountability. Only an independent judiciary can effectively review government acts, ensure the rule of law and guarantee observance of human rights; thus review of governmental acts by an independent body is an essential mechanism of good democratic governance.

Judicial Independence

Judicial independence is recognized in many international and regional human rights instruments[9] as constituting one of the cornerstones of the rule of law and good governance.[10] It involves two principles: 1) that judicial power must exist separate from and independent of executive and legislative power, and 2) that judicial power must repose in the judiciary as a separate organ of government, composed of persons different from, and independent of those who compose the executive and legislative branches. Whilst discussion of the independence of the judiciary in the rule of law discourse often centres on protecting and promoting the rights of judges in the higher courts, it must be recognized that magistrates and customary law justices require comparable protection, not least because it is they who deal with the vast majority of cases, both criminal and civil, and it is in them that much of the public confidence in the legal system resides.

The main pillars of judicial independence are institutional and financial autonomy. These encompass the need for an appropriate appointment procedure, security of tenure, satisfactory conditions of service which the executive cannot adversely affect, and the provision of adequate financial resources and appropriate terms and conditions for all those involved in the administration of justice. Yet independence comes at a price. Judges and magistrates must recognize that they are duty-bound to provide society with the highest possible standards of service and commitment and that a failure to maintain these standards is rightly a matter of public concern. As Stephens has observed: 'What ultimately protects the independence of the judiciary is a community consensus that such independence is a quality worth protecting.'[11] Similarly, the Chief Justice of the Indian Supreme Court observed: 'Wise judges never forget that the best way to sustain the dignity and status of their offices is to deserve respect from the public at large by the quality of their judgments, the fearlessness, fairness and objectivity of their approach, and by the restraint, dignity and decorum which they observe in their judicial conduct.'[12] The courts should play a dynamic role in post-conflict societies. They should build a relationship of trust with the population, which in coming out of conflict often views the courts as alien, oppressive, irrelevant institutions whose doors have always been kept closed from ordinary people.

Judicial Appointment and Tenure

Although some have argued that judicial independence requires the removal of all political considerations from the appointment process (Roberts-Wray 1966, 478), this is not necessarily appropriate. In times of political and economic transformation such as is common in post-conflict societies, the judiciary must be sympathetic to the country's needs, and its membership should reflect broadly the country's gender, ethnic and racial composition (Georges 1967, 38). Upholding the judicial oath of office to administer justice *to all persons* represents a considerable challenge for judges who are inevitably the product of their social conditioning, education, gender and ethnicity. If they are to discharge fully their judicial oaths and to enjoy the broad confidence of the people, they must be drawn from a wide array of backgrounds to ensure a better understanding of the experiences of those with whom they will be dealing. In many constitutions the President appoints judges after consultation with the Judicial Service Commission. This body is typically set up under the constitution. It varies in composition from country to country. To perform its task competently, it should be composed of men and women who posses legal knowledge and are of high integrity. Whatever approach is adopted, it is essential that candidates for judicial appointment be professionally competent persons of proven integrity who enjoy the confidence of both governors and governed alike. Security of tenure is a key element of judicial independence; judges on permanent appointment who are not at the mercy of a possible executive order abolishing their tenure are free to make independent judgements;[13] conversely, lack of tenure breeds insecurity and can only lead to judgments that simply comply with the wishes of the ruling government of the day.

Lower Courts and Customary Law Courts

As pointed out earlier, in most post-conflict countries, lower courts and customary law court justices are often the 'forgotten' persons in discussions on judicial reform. This is most unfortunate, for they play a crucial role in the judicial system given that they hear the vast majority of both civil and criminal cases. Lower and customary law courts are also the places where the most impoverished, powerless, and defenceless in society often go. If they have no confidence in lower and customary law court justices and officials, perceiving them as dispersing a lower form of justice, this has a significant detrimental effect on society and the development of the rule of law. Not only does it impact adversely on the administration of justice, but it also carries with it significant social and economic consequences, including potential resort to self-help and informal ways of meting out justice, which can rekindle conflict (Harchard and Ndulo 1994, 94).

Yet in many post-conflict countries, the lower and customary law courts face serious difficulties. First, they often face substantial obstacles to operation, including serious structural limitations such as inadequate office space and lack of the most basic materials such as paper and desks.[14] These obstacles, combined with isolation from a supportive legal community, can lead to poor morale and performance. Here the only real solution is for states to provide lower and customary law courts with facilities and support comparable to that given to the higher courts. Secondly, lower and customary law court justices often experience poor conditions of service and a general lack of human rights training. Addressing such issues will inevitably take time, but the goal must be to ensure that lower and customary court justices enjoy, as far as possible, comparable training and conditions of service as judges in the higher courts.[15] Finally, there remain serious problems relating to court staff. Corruption, incompetence, inefficiency and lack of a 'service' ethos for court users must be addressed. As with justices themselves, the first challenge is to provide appropriate training and conditions of service for such staff, and the second is putting in place a transparent system of appointing court staff.

Accountability and the Status of the Judiciary

Judicial independence and judicial accountability are closely related. These must be upheld in the context of respect for the judiciary as such respect is an integral part of the rule of law. A society must support and protect the judiciary, for judges remain an easy target for those wishing to make partisan political capital. In return, society should expect judges to accept fair and temperate criticism of judgments and to maintain appropriate standards of ethical behaviour. To help retain the sensitive balance between independence and accountability, post-conflict states must be encouraged to develop judicial ethics codes that apply to adjudicating complaints by members of the public against members of the judiciary. Such codes of ethics are an extremely desirable means of establishing and containing the parameters for public expectations and criticisms of judicial conduct.

Ideally, such a code should deal with both the exercise of judicial duties and extra-judicial activities and, in particular, require judges to disclose their assets (this is essential to guard against potential corruption and conflict of interest). Rules that may seem straightforward and obvious to lawyers have little meaning unless they provide the public with a clear statement of what to expect from their judges. It is extremely useful, for example, to know that judges who cause undue delay in the hearing of cases, have conflict of interest issues, or serve in a politically sensitive capacity are justifiably open to public criticism and official censure. The effectiveness of such codes largely depends upon their wide public dissemination.[16]

To maintain public confidence it is necessary to develop an effective method of upholding judicial accountability as well as offering appropriate protection for judges against unfounded criticism. Legitimate criticism of judges arising from the discharge of their duties, even if somewhat emphatic and unhappily expressed, is permissible as an exercise in freedom of expression.[17] However, unjustified and unreasonable attacks undermine the judiciary's constitutional role.[18] This is why public support for the judiciary – particularly from the government – is essential.[19] Furthermore, in fulfilment of their commitment to uphold the rule of law and protect human rights, it is the duty of legal professional bodies such as law societies and bar associations to speak out in defence of judicial independence. A transparent and independent removal procedure is also essential, but removal of judges should not be left in the hands of the executive. Executive power in this area provides a potential weapon through which to intimidate judges and thus helps to create or maintain a pliant judiciary. In effect, executive power to remove undermines the separation of powers and the independence of the judiciary.

Another matter which impacts the independence of the judiciary is funding. Sufficient funding to enable the judiciary to perform its functions to the highest standards should be provided. Appropriate salaries, supporting staff, resources and equipment are essential to the proper functioning of the judiciary. As a matter of principle, judicial salaries and benefits should be set in a transparent manner. The salaries and benefits should be secured by law. The administration of monies allocated to the judiciary should be under the control of the judiciary. Financial autonomy is fundamental. Without it, the executive can seriously impact judicial independence by either limiting the judiciary's access its own funds (allocated by parliament) or by assuming control of the services and staff upon which the judiciary depends.

The Need for a Representative Judiciary

As stated earlier, judges must be drawn from an array of backgrounds that reflects the populace they represent if they are to be perceived as fair and legitimate.[20] In Africa, where ethnicity is a major problem, the judiciary should reflect the country's ethnic diversity if it is to gain legitimacy in all communities. Most African states comprise multi-ethnic societies with low levels of ethnic integration. If not managed properly, ethnic diversity can be a source of instability and conflict. The need to maintain gender balance within the judiciary is also imperative.[21] Encouraging equality requires states to identify and tackle the factors that inhibit the entry of women onto the bench; for example, requiring women to go on circuit or be posted away from their home areas is an inhibitory factor to be avoided. The 'fast-tracking' of appropriate candidates is also necessary, although this should not be done at the expense of rigorous qualification requirements, for the principle that judicial appointments are made on merit is inviolable. Arguably, the appropriate approach to redressing imbalances is for all levels of the judiciary to have, as an objective, a selection system based on 'merit with bias', i.e., that where two candidates are of equal merit the bias should be to appoint a woman or member of an under-represented minority.

Oversight Bodies, Accountability and Rule of Law in Post-conflict and Failing States

Judicial reform and rule of law projects should include the establishment of credible and functional oversight bodies responsible for promoting the rule of law and complementing the work of the courts. Effective and efficient courts require an institutional environment that fosters cooperation among the active institutions. During conflicts, institutions such as the civil service, the police and correction services decay. They become abusive and dysfunctional. Thus in post-conflict society, these bodies must be transformed into fair, efficient institutions. To do this requires a network of complementary norms and mechanisms, including: 1) state adherence to human rights treaties; 2) effective and accessible state institutions where individuals can obtain redress for human rights breaches; and 3) an active human rights NGO community. Some, though not all, of these (such as oversight bodies) may be promoted through specific institutional and capacity-building efforts. These agencies are typically charged with promoting the rule of law, respect for human rights and a culture of human rights, and justice in the civil service and other government institutions. Additionally, they are charged with monitoring and assessing the observance of human rights, and with taking measures to secure appropriate redress where human rights have been violated (Human Rights Watch 2001, 11). They are charged with the elimination of corruption, abuses of authority and of public office; and the promotion of fair, efficient and good governance. They provide a viable, inexpensive forum for the investigation and resolution of human rights complaints and have the potential to lighten the caseload burden of regular courts (ibid.). The effectiveness of these institutions will depend on their independence from other branches of government, their capacity (in terms of human and material resources), the integrity of the officials running them, the transparency of their decisions, and the timeliness of their work in resolving complaints (Paul 1999, 132). These institutions include human rights commissions, anti-corruption commissions and ombudsmen (Reif 2000, 67). The creation of these institutions should be accompanied by the stimulation of citizens' collective awareness of specific human rights and the strengthening of local and national civil society organizations' capacity to seek redress. This is especially important as a major obstacle to citizens' ability to use these institutions is ignorance – of the existence of formal texts and rules and of the institutions established to protect them. Additionally, lack of access may be an obstacle either because of expense or because of the sparse availability of these institutions.

Access to Courts and Other Oversight Institutions

Access to the judiciary and other watchdog and oversight institutions remains a key element of the concept of rule of law as generally understood, albeit one that is often elusive in post-conflict states. The majority of people in post-conflict countries can neither assert nor defend their legal rights in criminal or civil matters. While effective operation of the rule of law depends to a large extent on the effectiveness and independence of a judiciary and oversight bodies that have the capacity and normative independence to grant citizen access to the courts and to adjudicate disputes between citizens and between citizens and the state, access to justice in post-conflict societies is notoriously hampered by lack of available courts and delays in trials. The legal system is perceived by many as not protecting the rights of all citizens equally and effectively. The poor and marginalized groups in society generally receive little protection, and the general perception is that corruption and economic status play a major role in one's ability to access justice. These difficulties tend to undermine public confidence in the ability of the courts and oversight institutions to act as a check on the executive or to provide a forum for the protection of human rights and the advancement of the rule of law. Corruption completely undermines the legitimacy of the judiciary. It leads people to regard courts as inappropriate forums for the resolution of disputes and protection of human rights.

The accessibility factor requires that courts and other agencies charged with the promotion and protection of human rights be available to the population that the institutions are designed to protect (Human Rights Watch 2001). Access to justice means that justice should be affordable to all, and those who cannot afford it should be provided for through legal aid. The challenge for national institutions is to develop mechanisms to facilitate accessibility; there are several useful strategies that may be employed to this end. One is to carry out regular nationwide tours to help create greater awareness of the existence of the relevant institutions and to foster positive links with local officials. Similarly, holding advertising campaigns and encouraging media coverage of oversight body activities provides a higher public profile for them.

A more structured approach is to decentralize the offices of these bodies. The cost of establishing regional and district centres is far outweighed by the benefits achieved in making justice accessible to ordinary people by bringing it closer to where they live. In any event, when services are not decentralized the costs are simply shifted to the poor, as they have to bear the cost of the travel which becomes necessary to access services.

Yet another mechanism for improving accessibility could be to adopt a generous approach to the matter of who has standing to bring cases. While it would at the same time be necessary to ensure that courts were not overwhelmed by hopeless cases, third parties could be permitted to lodge complaints on behalf of complainants who because of their particular circumstances were unable to do so. This could involve allowing NGOs to bring complaints on behalf of people who for one reason or another are not able to access the system on their own. This focuses on the nature of the complaint and is particularly useful protection for the more vulnerable members of society who may find it difficult, if not impossible, to lodge complaints.

For such cases, an investigation should not depend upon receipt of a complaint. An ombudsman or a human rights commission, rather than waiting for complaints to be brought forward, must go out to unearth corruption, maladministration and violation of human rights, whether the public complains or not. This is particularly important in poor states where many people remain susceptible to governmental abuse of power but do not complain either through ignorance of their rights or because of unfamiliarity with government systems or fear of reprisal. In addition, states should be encouraged to develop legal aid schemes to promote legal assistance for those who cannot afford private legal services.

Conclusion

The rule of law can only operate where there is clear commitment by leaders to operate within the law in both public and private interests. Parliament and the executive and its agencies must obey court rulings. Where the rule of law applies, no one is above the constitution – not the president, not the parliament, not the executive; and every governmental act, law, or policy must conform to the constitution (Ocran 1984, 302). Legal accountability for past human rights violations, improvements in respect for human rights, and the consolidation of rule of law in post-conflict countries all depend on the strengthening of institutions that underpin democracy, good governance and the rule of law. Such institutions include the courts, the police, correctional services, and oversight institutions. There is a critical need to strengthen the human and institutional capacity of these institutions and to improve their operational effectiveness. There must be real and effective access to the courts, human rights commissions, and other oversight institutions. These are the challenges that must be met if good governance and the rule of law are to take root in post-conflict countries. It must be realized that these goals take time to achieve. They require patience on the part of stakeholders and the international community and a realization that the parties concerned are in it for the long haul. Weeks, months and years can pass without a positive outcome being achieved, and programmes and incentives can fail. Creating civic and political institutions, building an effective judicial system, and shaping government and legislation that will rule a society are not tasks that can be achieved overnight. This point is particularly important for donors – who often channel their support in the form of time-bound projects without a strategic framework or long-term commitment to institution building – to understand. It is often said that donors approach institution building as a short-term, time-bound, project-based enterprise, even while acknowledging that institution building is a long-term, homegrown, multidimensional process (Rice and Patrick 2008). Further, the processes to succeed must have legitimacy in the eyes of the parties involved. Legitimacy is a characteristic that must permeate the entire process of building institutions and promoting the rule of law. In the end this effort cannot succeed unless the economic conditions in post-conflict countries improve and develop to a level where the countries have the capacity to sustain the institutions necessary for prosecution of past human rights violations, entrenchment of good governance, protection of human rights, and establishing the rule of law. Finally, the success of rule of law projects and judicial reform is inextricably linked to the eradication of poverty, for poverty itself undermines the capacity of institutions charged with promoting of the rule of law.

Notes

1 Louise Arbor observed: 'Countries emerging from conflict often suffer weak or non-existent rule of law, inadequate law enforcement, insufficient capacity in the administration of justice, and increased instances of human rights violations' (Office of the UNHCR 2008).
2 Also Office of the UNHCR 2006a.
3 When establishing the Special Court for Sierra Leone (SCSL), the United Nations Security Council recognized the need to adopt a model that could leave a strong 'legacy' in Sierra Leone, including improved professional standards. Indeed the Security Council referred specifically to the 'pressing need for international cooperation to assist in strengthening the judicial system of Sierra Leone' (UN Doc. S/RES/1315 (14 August 2000)).
4 See generally the report of the Secretary-General on the rule of law and transitional justice in conflict and post-conflict societies (S/2004/616).

5 As a UNHCR report observes, 'a reformed police service, for example, can professionally investigate the abuses committed during the conflict or the authoritarian regime; a reformed prosecutor's office can effectively issue indictments; and a reformed court can impartially render judgment about those past abuses' (Office of the UNHCR 2006b).

6 We are conscious of the fact that the term 'law' is not precise. We take a wide view of the term, along the lines of Friedman, who looks at law as an aspect of culture that goes beyond 'law's' structure and substantive dimensions. In this broader definition, 'law' embraces attitudes and values affecting behaviour related to law and its institutions. Thus viewed, law becomes a cause as well as a result of social change and development. See discussion of Friedman's views in Dayal (1984, 95).

7 Messick observes that the recognition that good governance is essential for economic growth has sparked renewed interest. Since 1994 the World Bank, The Inter American Development Bank (IDB) and the Asian Development Bank have either approved or initiated more than 500 million in loans for judicial reform projects in 26 countries.

8 As the Office of the United Nations High Commission for Human Rights rightly observes: ' a better rationale for prosecutions of massive human rights violations is to convey to citizens a disapproval of violations and support for certain democratic values. Strong expression of formal disapproval by State institutions committed to human rights and democratic values can help to persuade citizens as well as institutions of the centrality of those values' (Office of the UNHCR 2006).

9 'Everyone is entitled to a fair and public hearing by an independent tribunal …' (article 10, Universal Declaration of Human Rights, UN GAOR, 3rd Sess. UN) Doc. A/810pmbl); '… everyone shall be entitled to a fair and public hearing by a competent, independent and impartial tribunal established by law' (article 14.1, International Covenant on Civil and Political Rights). See also Article 7(1) African Charter on Human and People's Rights.

10 Its significance has also led to the development of the *United Nations Basic Principles on the Independence of the Judiciary,* which are designed to 'secure and promote' judicial independence (para. 1). Basic Principles on the Independence of the Judiciary, adopted by the Seventh United Nations Congress on the Prevention of Crime and the Treatment of Offenders held at Milan from 26 August to 6 September, 1985 and endorsed by General assembly resolutions 40/32 of 29 November 1985 and 40/146 of 13 December 1985. See also the similar views of the International Commission of Jurists, *States of Emergency: their Impact on Human Rights* International Commission of Jurists 1983, 434–7 and Nyerere 1968. 109–14.

11 Noted by Cartwright 1998, 39. The issue of judicial accountability is discussed below.

12 *Narmada Bachao Andolan v. Union of India and others* (1999) 8SCC 308.

13 Compare Kenya, where the Constitution of Kenya (Amendment) Act 1988 repealed the security of tenure provisions in the 1962 Constitution. This blatant

attempt to make judges serve at the whim of the President provoked considerable internal and external criticism and led to a 1990 constitutional amendment that substantially resorted to the pre-1988 position: see Constitution of Kenya (Amendment) Act 1990. See also Kuria and Vaquez 1991.

14 These extend to such basic items as run-down buildings, no lockable cupboards to store records and evidence securely, lack of reference materials and inadequate security for personnel buildings.

15 Local courts also function in all the African states. Given their wide-ranging jurisdiction over family law, succession and the like, their work impacts directly on the majority of the people and particularly those in the rural areas. In practice their structure and operation varies considerably and a discussion on the courts is therefore beyond the scope of this chapter.

16 For example, ensuring that a copy of the code is readily available in all the major languages to all litigants.

17 Ogilvie Thompson C.J. in *S. v. van Niekerk* 1972 (3) SA 711 (A) at 720.

18 There are two modes of conduct that fall within the scope of criminal contempt. One is contempt in the face of the court. The other is conduct calculated to bring a court, a judge or the administration of justice through the courts generally into contempt. It is sufficient 'if it is a scurrilous attack on the judiciary as a whole, calculated to undermine the authority of the courts and endanger public confidence, thereby obstructing and interfering with the administration of justice. See *Chokolingo v. A-G of Trinidad and Tobago* [1981] 1 All ER 244 (PC) at 248 per Gubbay C.J. *In re Chinamasa* [2001] 3 LRC 373 at p. 384.

19 Regrettably, in many countries the politicization of the post has effectively removed the Attorney-General from playing any meaningful supportive role for the judiciary. See generally Goredema (1997), in which he argues that the politicization of the post of Attorney-General means that the incumbent cannot perform his/her functions in an independent manner, with the result that the institution is 'emasculated'.

20 See, for example, para. 7 of the Bloemfontein Statement of 1993: '... it is fundamental to a country's judiciary to enjoy the broad confidence of the people it serves: to the extent possible, a judiciary should be broad-based and therefore not appear (rightly or wrongly) beholden to the interest of any particular section of society'.

21 One of the Principles enshrined in the *Latimer House Guidelines* states: 'It is recognized that redress of gender imbalance is essential to accomplish full and equal rights in society and to achieve true human rights. Merit and the capacity to perform public office regardless of disability should be the criteria of eligibility for appointment.' The *UN Basic Principles on the Independence of the Judiciary* state that in the selection of judges there shall be no discrimination against a person on grounds of sex (para. 10).

References

Armstrong, Patricia (1994), 'Human Rights and Multilateral Development Banks: Governance Concerns in Decision Making', *American Society of International Law Proceedings* 88(277), 280–81.

Cartwright,S. (1998), 'The Judiciary: Qualifications, Training and Gender Balance', in J. Hatchard and P. Slinn (eds), *Parliamentary Supremacy and Judicial Independence: A Commonwealth Approach* (London: Cavendish).

Dayal, Shiv (1984), 'Dynamics of Social Change and Development: Legal Education and Developing Countries', in Muna Ndulo (ed.) *Law in Zambia* (Nairobi: East African Publishing House).

Economic Commission for Africa (2005), 'Good Governance in Africa', Report, Addis Ababa.

Georges,P.T. (1967), 'The Court in the Tanzania One-Party System', in A. Sawyer (ed.), *East African Law and Social Change* (Nairobi: East Africa Publishing House).

Goredema, Charles (1997), 'The Attorney-General in Zimbabwe and South Africa: Whose Weapon – Whose Shield', *Stellenbosch Law Review* 8(45).

Hatchard, J. and Ndulo, M. (1994), *Readings in Criminal Law and Criminology* (Lusaka: Multimedia).

Henkin, Louis (1992), 'Commentary on International Law: Constitutionalism, Democracy and Foreign Affairs', *Indiana Law Journal* 67(Fall).

Human Rights Watch (2001), *Protectors or Pretenders? Government Human Rights Commissions in Africa* (New York: Human Rights Watch).

Hung, Veron Mei-Ying (2004), 'China's WTO Commitment on Independent Judicial Review: Impact on Legal and Political Reform', *American Journal of International Law* 52(Winter).

International Commission of Jurists (1983), *States of Emergency: Their Impact on Human Rights* (Geneva: International Commission of Jurists).

International Monetary Fund (1997), 'Good Governance, The IMF Role', Report , Washington DC.

Kuria, G.K. and Vaquez, A.M. (1991), 'Judges and Human Rights: The Kenyan Experience' *Journal of African Law* 35, 145–6.

Messick, Richard E. (1999), 'Judicial Reform and Economic Development: A Survey of the Issues', *World Bank Research Observer* 14(1) (February).

Nagle, John Copeland (2002), 'Choosing the Judges Who Choose the President', *Capital University Law Review* 30.

Ndulo, Muna (2003), 'The Democratization Process and Structural Adjustment in Africa', *Indiana Journal of Global Legal Studies* (Winter).

Nowrojee, Pheroze (2006), 'The November 2005 Referendum and Kenyan Politics Today: Directions in Constitutional Reform', Africa Research and Resource, Forum (ARRF).

Nwabueze, B.O. (1993), *Ideas and Fact in Constitution Making, The Morohundiya Lectures, Faculty of Law, University of Ibadan* (Ibadan: Spectrum Books).

Nyerere, J. (1968), *Freedom and Socialism* (Oxford: Oxford University Press).

Ocran, Tawia (1984), 'The Rule of Law as the Quest for Legitimacy, in Muna Ndulo (ed.) *Law in Zambia* (Nairobi: East African Publishing House).

Office of United Nations High Commission for Human Rights (2006a), *Rule-of-Law Tools for Post-Conflict States: Prosecution Initiatives* (New York and Geneva: UNHCR).

Office of the United Nations High Commission for Human Rights (2006b), *Rule-of-Law Tools for Post-Conflict States: Vetting an Operational Framework* (New York and Geneva: UNHCR).

Office of the United Nations High Commissioner for Human Rights (2008), *Rule-of-Law Tools for Post-conflict States: Reparations Programs* (New York and Geneva: UNHCR).

Paul, James C.N. (1993), 'Developing Constitutional Orders in Sub-Saharan Africa: An Unofficial Report', *Third World Legal Studies*, 1–34.

Paul, James C.N. (1999), 'Human Rights and the Legal Structure of Security Forces in Constitutional Orders: The Case of Ethiopia', *Third World Legal Studies*

Peerenboom, Randall (2002), 'Let One Hundred Flowers Bloom, One Hundred Schools Contend: Debating Rule of Law in China', *Michigan Journal International Law* 23(Spring).

Pyle, Jeffrey J. (1999), 'Race, Equality and the Rule of Law: Critical Race Theory's Attack on the Promise of Liberalism', *Boston College Law Review* 215(May).

Reif, Linda C. (2000), 'Building Democratic Institutions: The Role of National Human Rights Institutions in Good Governance and Human Rights Protection', *Harvard Human Rights Journal* 13, 1–69.

Rice, Susan E. and Patrick, Stewart (2008), 'The "Weak States" Gap', Brookings Institution, Washington, DC, http://www.brookings.edu/opinions/2008/0307_weak_states_rice.aspx.

Roberts-Wray, Kenneth Owen (1966), *Commonwealth and Colonial Law* (London: Stevens).

Seidman, Ann and Seidman, Robert (2006), 'The Deadlock of Law and Development', in Muna Ndulo (ed.), *Democratic Reform in Africa: Its*

Impact on Governance and Poverty Alleviation (Athens, OH: James Currey and Ohio University Press).
United Nations Development Program (2005a), *Human Development Report* (New York: UNDP).
United Nations Development Program (2005b), International Cooperation at a Crossroads: Aid, Trade and Security in an Unequal World (New York: UNDP).
United Nations Development Program (2008), *Strengthening the Rule of Law in Conflict/Post-conflict Situations: A Global Program for Justice and Security 2008–2011* (New York: UNDP).
United Nations Mission in Liberia, Legal and Judicial System Support Division, http://unmil.org/1content.asp?ccat=ljss&zdoc=1.
Weinstein, Jeremy M. (2007), *Inside Rebellion: The Politics of Insurgent Violence* (Cambridge; Cambridge University Press).
World Bank (various years), *Governance and Development* (Washington DC: World Bank).
World Bank (1994), *Good Governance: The World Bank's Experience* (Washington DC: World Bank).
World Bank (1989). *Sub-Saharan Africa: From Crisis to Sustainable Growth* (Washington DC: World Bank).
World Bank (2001), *Governance and Development* (Washington DC: World Bank).

List of Contributors

Sarah Cohen Wood is an Associate and Conflict Specialist with Governance and Institutional Development, ARD, Inc. She previously served at USAID as the Strategic Planning and Learning Coordinator for the Office of Foreign Disaster Assistance in the Bureau for Democracy, Conflict and Humanitarian Assistance. She has also worked as the USAID liaison for the State Department Offices for the Coordinator for Reconstruction and Stabilization (S/CRS). Ms Wood has worked in several countries in Africa and specializes in the role of civil society in post-conflict and transitioning environments. For three years she managed the NGO Sector Strengthening Program, designed to enhance the institutional capacities of local NGOs and civil society organizations in fragile and post-conflict countries. Ms Wood is a specialist in Monitoring and Evaluation and designed the first local workshop for local and international NGO and USAID Mission staff on Conflict Sensitive Monitoring, focusing on the Mano River Union. She recently worked for the Office for Foreign Disaster Assistance in Darfur, Sudan and was stationed in both North and South Darfur.

Margaret Grieco holds her doctorate from the University of Oxford. She is the first Full Professor of Transport and Society, a post which she holds at Edinburgh Napier University, Scotland. She has previously been Professor of Sociology at the University of Ghana, Lagon, staff member in the Africa Region of the World Bank and Visiting Full Professor at the Institute for African Development, Cornell University. She is currently Academic Associate at the IAD. She has published extensively on migration patterns and upon gender, transport and information communication technology most particularly with respect to Africa.

James Hentz is Professor and Chair of the Department of International Studies and Political Science at the Virginia Military Institute, where he has spent the last 10 years. He taught at Marist Brothers' High School in American Samoa from 1979–1981, and he taught secondary school at Saint Charles Lwanga Seminary in Zambia from 1987–1989. In 2003, he was a visiting Fulbright Scholar at the Miklós Zrínyi National Defense University in Hungary. He was a visiting scholar at Rand Afrikaans University in Johannesburg, South Africa in 1993–1994, during which time he witnessed the transition to democracy in South Africa. Dr Hentz's scholarship focuses on

African politics and security. He is the co-editor of *New and Critical Security and Regionalism: Beyond the Nation State* (2003), editor of *Obligation of Empire: US Grand Strategy for a New Century* (2004), and author of *South Africa and the Logic of Regional Cooperation* (2005). He is editor of the forthcoming journal, *African Security*, which will be published by Taylor and Francis/Routledge. He is on the editorial board of *Academic and Applied Research in Military Science: An International Journal of Security, Strategic, Defense Studies and Military Technology* (Hungary) and *Scientia Militaria: South African Journal of Military Studies* (South Africa).

Marcel Kitissou is part of the Doctoral Faculty in Public Policy and Social Issues at Union Institute and University; and he is a Senior Visiting Research Scholar at the Center for Global Studies, George Mason University as well as a Visiting Fellow, Institute for African Development, Cornell University. Dr Kitissou began teaching at the University of Benin, where he directed the Institut Superieur de Presse (du Conseil) de l'Entente (ISPE). He also served as Associate Director of the Ecole Nationale d'Administration (ENA) of Togo. Professor Kitissou taught history and political science from 1994 to 2001 at the State University of New York at Oswego, where he also directed the Peace Education and Conflict Ethos (PEACE) Institute. Kitissou was also Visiting Fellow with the Peace Studies Program of Cornell University from 1999–2001 and is currently Visiting Fellow with the Institute for African Development of the same institution. His research focus is on African studies, defence policy, sociology of politics and collective action, public administration and international relations. He served as Executive Director of the Africa Faith and Justice Network (a Washington, DC-based research and advocacy NGO) from August 2001 to February 2005. He is currently Faculty Director of the Global Humanitarian Action Program and of the Summer Institute in International Development at George Mason University (USA).

Muna Ndulo (LLB University of Zambia; LLM Harvard University; D.Phil. Oxford) is Professor of Law and Director of the Institute for African Development at Cornell University. He is also Honorary Professor of Law at the University of Cape Town, South Africa and a former Professor of Law and Dean of the Law at University of Zambia. He has extensive international and UN experience, having served as Legal Officer in the International Law Branch of the United Nations Commission on International Trade Law; as Legal Adviser and Political Advisor to the United Nations Observer Mission in South Africa; the United Nations Assistance Mission to east Timor, the United Nations Mission to Kosovo; and United Nations Mission to Afghanistan.

He has published extensively and his major interests include governance, economic development, and human rights.

Cameron G. Thies is Associate Professor and Obermann Center Scholar at the University of Iowa. His specialty is international political economy. Professor Thies's work focuses on two principal themes: the role of conflict on the development of the modern state and agricultural trade policy. He has recently written an article on the effect of political geography on the state building efforts of sub-Saharan Africa, and he is the author of numerous other articles on state building including 'The Political Economy of State Building in Sub-Saharan Africa' (2007) and 'The Political Economy of Agricultural Protection' (2007), both published in the *Journal of Politics*.

John Weiss is Associate Professor of History at Cornell University. He is in the process of establishing the Service Learning Component of a course on International Humanitarianism. He has conducted workshops on 'Organizing Ghostbusting: Research on the Construction of Public Memory in Bosnia', Tuzla, Bosnia, March 2002 and 'After the Vichy Syndrome: Methodological and Thematic Problems in the Study of the Construction of Public Memory', Workshop on the Legacy of the French Resistance held at Cornell in November 2000.

Pablo Yanguas is a PhD Student in the Department of Government at Cornell University. Mr Yanguas's research focuses on state building in Sub-Saharan Africa, with a particular emphasis on the interactions between state capacity, identity politics and economic development.

Dunia Zongwe is an LLM candidate and a research assistant at the Law School, Cornell University and a fellow of the Institute for African Development. He studies international business law and is writing his thesis on the relationship between human rights and the exploitation of mineral resources in the Democratic Republic of the Congo. Recently, he has been doing legal work on Congolese law for Oxford University Press (International Law in Domestic Courts) and New York University (Globalex). In the autumn of 2007 he worked as a student intern at Ithaca City Court in Ithaca, New York. Mr Dunia has participated in human rights advocacy campaigns on specific events occurring in Somaliland, South Africa, Sudan and Zimbabwe; and in several international moot court competitions in Cameroon, the United States and South Africa. In 2004, he was granted a two-term British exchange student scholarship to study the legal systems of Asia and Africa at the School of Oriental and African Studies (SOAS) in London.

Marijan Zumbulev is the UN Advocacy Director in New York. He has worked with Crisis Group Belgrade (summer 2003) researching the state of the post-Milošević Serbian economy, and he joined Crisis Group New York in June 2004. He holds an MPA from the Woodrow Wilson School at Princeton University and an MA in Nationalism Studies from Central European University.

Index